BRUTAL

BRUTAL

Manhood and the Exploitation of Animals

BRIAN LUKE

UNIVERSITY OF ILLINOIS PRESS

Urbana and Chicago

Frontispiece: Bronia Galuzzo for the Fund for Animals, 1996.

Library of Congress Cataloging-in-Publication Data
Luke, Brian, 1962–
Brutal : manhood and the exploitation of animals /
Brian Luke.
p.   cm.
Includes bibliographical references and index.
ISBN 978-0-252-03176-2 (cloth : alk. paper)
ISBN 978-0-252-07424-0 (pbk. : alk. paper)
1. Animal welfare. 2. Human-animal relationships.
I. Title.
HV4703.L85   2007
179'.3—dc22   2007005141

Dedicated to Doug, Dave, and Gary

Contents

Acknowledgments

This analysis of manhood and animal exploitation could not have been imagined and articulated without the work of the feminist theorists of animal liberation, especially that of Carol Adams, Josephine Donovan, Marti Kheel, and the late Andrée Collard. I also acknowledge the fundamental contributions of the analytic philosophers of animal rights, particularly Tom Regan and Peter Singer. As it has for so many animal advocates, Singer's *Animal Liberation* changed my awareness forever.

I offer special thanks to David Nibert, Paul Benson, Kelly Besecke, and, especially, Jennifer Whiting, my philosophy dissertation director at the University of Pittsburgh, and Liz Dulany and Jennifer Clark, my editors at the University of Illinois Press.

Portions of this book have appeared previously in these articles: "Justice, Caring, and Animal Liberation," "Taming Ourselves or Going Feral?" "Solidarity Across Diversity," "Animal Experimentation as Blood Sacrifice," "A Critical Analysis of Hunters' Ethics," "Violent Love," and "Animal Sacrifice" (see the bibliography for full citations). I am grateful to the editors and publishers of these articles. I also thank Rosalind Solomon, Howard Davies, and the Fund for Animals for providing the photographs that appear in this book.

The members of my family inspire me with their compassion and respect for all beings and support me regardless of where my thoughts lead—my parents, Robert Luke and Susan Luke, my brothers and their partners, Doug Luke, Susan Englund, David Luke, Stephanie LaBella, Gary Luke, and Liza Burke, and my sons, Alex Luke and Adam Luke.

I am deeply appreciative of groups such as Mobilization for Animals, People/Animals Network, the Fund for Animals, the Humane Society of the United States, People for the Ethical Treatment of Animals, Friends of Animals, and all the other organizations working against the exploitation of animals. The theoretical analysis developed here and my criticisms of specific tactics are respectfully offered in the spirit of comradeship towards the achievement of our common cause.

BRUTAL

Gender and the Exploitation of Animals

Picture hunting, trapping, vivisection, slaughter, and animal sacrifice. Imagine them in concrete detail, even attaching faces and names to those who are killing animals. Now picture a demonstration against one of these institutions, again putting names and faces on the protestors. What do you see?

Most likely you saw men killing and women protesting. Try reversing the genders. Imagine that over 90 percent of hunters are women, that women invented animal experimentation and continue to be the primary vivisectors, that those who drive cattle to slaughter are not "cowboys" but "cowgirls," that the priestly class of animal sacrificers was comprised exclusively of women. Imagine also an animal rights movement so overwhelmingly male that its protests are dismissed as the excesses of manly emotion. The dissonance of such a scenario is a measure of how deeply intertwined animal exploitation and certain gendered norms are in our consciousness.

What is it about men, women, and animal exploitation? This book offers some new answers to that question. Other treatments of the subject often focus on women, asking why women support animal liberation more often than do men. Framing the question in this manner suggests that there is something puzzling about opposition to animal exploitation, as if we need to point out something special about women to account for it. I find animal exploitation more of an enigma than animal liberation, the latter being an expectable consequence of humanity's deep and recurring sympathies for animals. For me the question is not so much why women oppose animal exploitation as why men support it.

Before addressing the central issue of gender, I first consider the nature and moral legitimacy of our treatment of nonhuman animals.

Animal Exploitation

Years ago, when I was first becoming involved with issues of animal exploitation, I toured an animal research facility at the University of Pittsburgh. The tour director was the veterinarian charged with tending the animals when they were not being subjected to experimental surgeries. We were not shown any actual experiments but were led through various holding facilities, room after room of cages holding monkeys, mice, and dogs. At one point our guide gestured toward a chain-link enclosure in which half a dozen beagle puppies tumbled over each other on a bare concrete floor. He said, "Beautiful, aren't they? At least this way they have a purpose."

The primary way we relate to nonhuman animals in this society is in terms of their purpose—that is, their purpose for us. How are they useful? Are they of any use to us at all? Do they block or disturb our plans in some way? We do not answer these questions personally, on a case-by-case basis, but categorically. We decide for a species, a breed, a strain, a sex, or a population of nonhuman animals "what they are for," and we construct institutions to carry out those uses (see table 1). In farming, ranching, market hunting, trapping, and commercial angling animals function both to furnish humans with food and clothing and as commodities exchanged to facilitate the capitalist accumulation of wealth (thus, those animals are living stock or "livestock"). Some of these animal products are expensive enough that their purchase is useful for making conspicuous displays of one's elite status. In recreational hunting and angling, animals are classified as moving targets for those who enjoy killing or capturing others against their will. Scientists declare that various sorts of animals are useful for determining product toxicity, studying basic physiology, testing pharmaceutical and surgical therapies, developing surgical skills, measuring environmental impact, or for passing anatomical knowledge to students. We enjoy staring at certain animals, so they are put on display in zoos and aquaria. Other animals fit nicely into our homes, providing us with amusement, affection, light service work (such as guard duty or "pest" destruction), or emotional value as the recipients of our nurturance. "Pet" animals may also be collected as symbols of elite status or put on display competitively (for example, at cat and dog shows). Many animals can be made to work for us, providing labor power or transportation, assisting the disabled, entertaining us through performances in circuses,

Table 1. Categories of Animal Use

Animal Defined As	Associated Institutions
Stock	Farming, ranching
Sustenance	Farming, ranching, trapping, market hunting
Sport	Recreational hunting
Status symbol	Couture, exotic foods and pets
Specimen	Vivisection, dissection
Slave	Entertainment, gambling, general labor, etc.
Spectacle	Zoos, aquaria
Showpiece	Breeding industry
Succor	Pet industry
Sacrificial offering	Patriarchal religion
Snag	Land development, pest extermination, etc.
Scourge	Pest extermination

rodeos, bullfighting rings, theme parks, and motion pictures, and serving as the objects of speculative wagering at the racetrack, cock pit, and dog pit. And numerous religions have declared the ritual slaughter of animals to be a useful or required means of appeasing the divine.

Apart from all these specific ways animals are deemed to serve our purposes, we also determine that some animals are merely obstacles blocking our progress or interfering with us in some way. These animals are designated "pests" or "vermin," and we try to wipe them out. In some cases we destroy them, not deliberately but as an expected yet unintended consequence of our continuous development and expansion. Road kills are examples of this, as are all the animals killed in the process of clearing and/or cultivating land.

The term "exploitation" is applied to the process of using one's skills, other people, animals, or nature for the fulfillment of one's purposes. Though the "exploitation" label can be intended neutrally, that is, without any implication of disapproval, when applied to people and animals it may also communicate a negative moral assessment. To exploit another is, first, to harm another for one's own benefit, and, second, to extract this benefit by the application of force, deception, or some other unjust process. It is the second part of this definition that carries the moral weight—without some injustice in the process, the use one makes of another is not exploitative in the negative sense.

Most of the ways humans use animals do involve harming them, usually in serious ways, including the imposition of injury, pain, and death. Whether these institutions are exploitative in the evaluative sense depends on whether the process can be morally justified. In each of the institutions of animal use the animals are forced to participate. Indeed, the basic feature of institutionalized human/animal relations is domination. Humans decide what we want from other animals and we take it. Using force to harm another for one's own benefit is a paradigmatic example of exploitation. To avoid this conclusion in a particular case requires special pleading: Why is it that in *this* case forcibly taking what we want from another at the expense of their injury, suffering, or death is morally acceptable?

There is no dearth of attempts to legitimate our domination of animals. The standard defenses of animal use fall into three general categories: those that refer to human rationality, those that claim divine sanction, and those that describe exploitation as natural (see table 2). While the rationalistic arguments have been analyzed extensively by philosophers of animal rights, the naturalistic arguments have received much less attention. The first section of this book assesses the naturalistic arguments in detail.

NATURALISTIC ARGUMENTS

In chapter 1 I discuss the idea that there is a natural empathic barrier between species. According to this view, those who work against the institutions of animal exploitation are aberrant, their sympathies for others crossing the

Table 2. Justifications of Animal Exploitation

I. Rationalistic arguments
 A. Human superiority
  Human lives are intrinsically more valuable than animal lives
 B. Reciprocation
  We only have moral duties to those who can reciprocate
 C. Replacement
  Some animals would not exist if we did not exploit them
II. Theistic arguments
 A. Human sanctity
  We were created in God's image
 B. Sacrifice
  God requires us to make blood offerings
 C. Creation
  God created animals for our use
III. Naturalistic arguments
 A. Human chauvinism
  Our contempt for other species is natural
 B. Predatory instinct
  Men are hunters by nature
 C. Competition
  It is natural for species to exploit each other

boundary of what is normal and natural. The animal defender, so profligate with her affections, should thus not be taken as a model for others.

This pathologizing of sympathetic connection to animals is not directly rebutted by the prominent philosophers of animal rights. Instead, they tacitly concur with the devaluation of emotion and direct their effort toward portraying animal rights as the most reasonable position from a purely unemotional point of view. Yet the disparaging of human sympathies for animals remains a conveniently quick means for dismissing opposition, thereby begging evaluation on its own terms. In chapter 1 I challenge the postulation of a natural empathic species boundary by outlining the range and depth of human sympathetic connection with other animals. Affection for animals and the disinclination to harm them permeate human life. The feelings that form the basis for opposing animal exploitation are not restricted to a minority of emotionally abnormal individuals. Rather, they are shared by humans in general, including those who actively participate in and defend the exploitation of animals.

Complementing the picture of a sympathetic barrier between humans and other animals is the image of a natural competition between species. Animal exploiters commonly justify their actions by portraying life as a struggle in which only those who are willing and able to aggress against others can live and thrive. According to this perspective, people have survived to this point because humanity, particularly male humanity, has developed a predatory nature.

I argue in chapter 2 that this defense cannot withstand scrutiny. Men's psychology and physiology are not those of a natural predator but of something rather more ambiguous. We have the capacity to destroy other animals, but we tend to feel uneasy about it. We can live on animal-based foods, but in modern society we do better overall the more we reduce the amount of animal fat in our diets. In general we are very capable of thriving without making use of large-scale industries of animal exploitation such as hunting, animal farming, and animal experimentation. The reality is that the human exploitation of animals is freely chosen, not a necessity imposed by our inherent nature.

Ecological arguments offered in defense of men's hunting are also weak. Apologists for men's hunting claim that the extermination of original predators such as wolves leads to ecological unbalance that can be remedied by human hunting. Other writers have challenged this claim, maintaining that men's hunting does not resemble that of truly natural predators. I reiterate this point and also criticize a different part of the argument, questioning whether men's hunting would be a good thing even if it completely mimicked natural predation. The presumption that truly natural predation is inherently good is shared by both defenders and opponents of animal exploitation. Yet this proposition, a crucial plank in the defense of men's hunting, is difficult to maintain, as I show in chapter 2.

These criticisms of the naturalistic arguments have relevance not only to the moral assessment of animal exploitation but also to the determination of appropriate long-term strategies for the animal liberation movement. If we are by nature unsympathetic toward nonhuman animals, then considerations of abstract principles of justice may be more relevant to encouraging animal advocacy than appeals to compassion for oppressed animals. Also, if the exploitation of animals derives from aggressive tendencies or innate callousness inherent to man, then the abolition of these institutions may require the deployment of mechanisms of social control designed to check our "beasts within." These and other issues regarding the ethics and politics of animal liberation are discussed in detail in chapters 6 and 7.

RATIONALISTIC ARGUMENTS

The rationalistic arguments for animal exploitation are the main focus of philosophical work on animal rights.[1] A brief overview of the arguments and their difficulties is presented here. The human superiority argument maintains that humans possess some trait or collection of traits that other animals lack, and that these traits make us superior to nonhumans in a way that justifies our exploitation of them. Generally these traits are related to our mental or rational capacities. We are described as uniquely political, tool-making, religious, moral, cultural, historical, emotional, empathetic, conscious, self-aware, linguistic, artistic, rational, noninstinctive, or immortal, and these traits, or some combination thereof, are claimed to underlie the greater intrinsic significance of human life.

The first difficulty for this argument lies in showing that the favored superiority-conferring trait is actually sufficient to justify the exploitation of beings lacking that trait. We may be unique in some way that is morally irrelevant. Consider, by analogy, the arguments we would hear if cheetahs ruled the earth. Imagine that the vast preponderance of the earth's resources were designated for creating space for cheetahs to occupy and for making their lives safe, secure, and fulfilling. Cheetahs not being technologically capable of directly exercising this dominance themselves, humans do it for them. We use our technological and social sophistication for projects such as modifying ecosystems to better suit cheetah populations, destroying indigenous species and moving other species in, and so on. We build factory farms to produce cheetah food and amusement parks where cheetahs can go to run and chase other animals. Every species of plant and animal is evaluated and treated according to its usefulness in making cheetahs happier, healthier, and more numerous. This includes human animals, since human life and development are also subordinated to the overarching end of furthering cheetah well-being.

Now imagine that some person growing up in this cheetah-centric world asks the obvious question: "Why are my needs and the needs of every other creature on this planet subordinated to the desires of cheetahs?" Her parents give the standard answer: "Because cheetahs are the fastest land animal on earth. They are unique and special, possessing the greatest intrinsic worth because of their tremendous foot speed. No one can run as they do."

If this child is like most people, she won't puzzle over this answer too long but will accept it (it being repeated, after all, by every person in authority) and go on to do her duty in helping to maintain cheetah dominance. But if she has a particularly inquisitive or rebellious nature she might not let it rest. She might go on to say, "So what? So what if cheetahs are the fastest?" A difficult question to answer.

From our point of view back here in the human-centered world, cheetah foot speed is morally irrelevant. It makes them faster, not inherently superior. Being different is not the same as being better. When our rational capacities are promoted as "that which separates us from the beasts," the intention is to indicate our superiority over other animals. But the significant possibility is that uniquely human traits are just as morally irrelevant as foot speed, that they may make us different from other species but do not give us greater inherent worth.

The suspicion that our rationality is promoted self-servingly, to excuse our exploitative practices rather than because they actually confer superiority of the requisite sort, is buttressed by the fact that the mark of distinction keeps shifting as our knowledge of animals progresses. The criterion for human uniqueness is perennially unstable. Specific definitions of what separates us from the animals are promulgated, but when counterexamples are found the definition is adjusted. To cite just one instance of this, humans used to be characterized as the tool-using animal. As examples of tool use among nonhumans multiplied, we became the tool-*making* animal. Now ethologists have published accounts of tool making among nonhumans, so we have become "the only animal that uses tools to make other tools."[2] When animals that use tools to make other tools are found, we will find something else unique about our technology (perhaps we're the only animal that uses tools to make tool-making tools). A similar dynamic transpires for all the other parameters used to distinguish us from nonhumans, as we find examples of art, morality, politics, culture, language, and so on among other animals.

The human superiority argument is circular. Traits distinguishing us from other species are made salient after the fact, in justification of morally dubious practices to which we are already committed. We do not exploit animals because we are superior to them, we claim superiority in order to excuse the exploitation. This conclusion is reinforced by a hypocrisy inherent in our application of the superiority criterion. We protect humans from the sorts of exploitation to which other animals are subject and claim that this differential treatment is justified by virtue of our possession of certain rational capacities. Yet whatever rational capacity we focus on is actually absent in many humans, because they are too young or are mentally disabled in some way. Since we argue that these humans still have a right to be protected, we are evidently not applying our own stated criterion consistently, leaving the suspicion that what is going on is not ethics but domination, the bare exercise of power over nonhuman others.

This critique of the human superiority argument is called the argument from marginal cases, and it has a prominent place in philosophical treatments of animal rights.[3] Though the marginal-cases argument poses a significant ethical challenge to the status quo, I have argued elsewhere that with a sufficiently determined callousness its animal rights conclusion can be avoided without inconsistency—for example, by allowing the so-called marginal humans to be subject to exploitation.[4] This shows that the moral rejection of exploitation is not based on considerations of logical consistency alone; animal liberation requires sympathetic responsiveness as well.

The other two rationalistic arguments for animal exploitation, the replacement argument and the argument from reciprocity, are subject to the same challenges from our sympathies and considerations of consistency as is the human superiority argument. The replacement argument maintains that though killing another sentient being is prima facie wrong, institutions such as animal farming can be justified by reference to the fact that farmed animals would not even exist without our intention to breed them and market their body parts. The slaughtered animals die prematurely, but they are "replaced" by the next generation of livestock, so at least they all get a short life out of it. The argument from reciprocity maintains that the only creatures that can have rights are those that are able to respect the rights of others. Since most nonhuman animals cannot do this—they are not moral agents—they have no rights demanding our respect.

There are many problems with these two arguments, but I will merely point out here that as with the human superiority argument, a consistent application of these principles would actually undermine the ethical treatment of humans. There are many humans, such as infants and some mentally disabled people, who are not capable of recognizing and respecting the rights of others. So a requirement of reciprocity would render them subject to exploitation. And as Evelyn Pluhar points out, the "replaceability argument applies to any individual with a welfare, including human beings."[5] If we brought a series of children into the world solely for the purpose of selling them into slavery, would our originating intention make their exploitation morally acceptable? Presumably children possess some trait or set of traits that renders their exploitation unacceptable, regardless of the intentions of those who brought them into existence. But a general ethical commitment to protect those with such traits would run into the same difficulty with marginal cases that the human superiority argument faced: Either some people lack those traits, thus rendering their exploitation acceptable, or the traits are so broad (for example, sentience or subjectivity) that all people and most animals are protected, rendering the argument useless as a defense of animal exploitation. It is through reasoning of this sort that philosophers such as Tom Regan and Peter Singer argue that an individual's possession of sentience or subjectivity is sufficient for moral considerability.

THEISTIC ARGUMENTS

The human superiority argument and the replacement argument are secular arguments with theistic counterparts. The creation argument, which states that our exploitation of animals is permissible because that is why God created them, corresponds to the replacement argument. Each looks to the original intent, human or divine, in bringing a species, breed, or individual into existence to determine how those animals may be treated. As such, the creation argument faces the same difficulty as its secular counterpart, namely, the fact that once in existence, sentient beings have their own welfare interests that run counter to their creators' exploitative intentions. Why should the creators' desires trump the animals' own? The creation argument faces an additional difficulty: determining divine intent regarding animal existence. We know why animal farmers breed cattle, but why God created the various nonhuman species is rather more opaque and subject to theological dispute.[6]

The human sanctity argument is the theistic counterpart to the human superiority argument. According to both arguments, humans possess traits that other animals lack (either by virtue of the processes of natural evolution or, in the theistic case, by virtue of being the only animal created in God's image), and these differences render it acceptable to exploit animals but not people. Whether the human sanctity argument is susceptible to the problem of marginal cases depends on how one understands the notion of being created in God's image. If this means that we possess some rationalistic capacity, such as self-awareness, morality, language, or the like, then the marginal cases argument does apply, since there are humans lacking those capacities. If, on the other hand, the divine aspect of humanity is independent of the rational capacities possessed by normal adult humans, then the human sanctity argument escapes the problem of marginal cases but faces a new difficulty: showing that the presence of this divine aspect is necessary for warranting protection from exploitation. Suppose, for example, that the divine aspect is possession of an immortal soul that can survive separation from one's physical body. It is difficult to see why possession of such a soul would be necessary for moral considerability, since even supposing that nonhumans lack souls, they are still conscious and able to experience pleasure and pain. Moreover, it would seem that killing a mortal animal might actually be more morally problematic, not less, than killing a human with an immortal soul since only in the nonhuman case would killing entail the permanent cessation of conscious existence, as Andrew Linzey argues in *Christianity and the Rights of Animals*: "If, for an animal, this life is all that he can have, the moral gravity of any premature termination is thereby increased rather than lessened."[7]

The remaining theistic argument, based on the divine imperative to offer blood sacrifices, is still directly operative in the killing of millions of animals every year—for example, in the ritual sacrifices accompanying the Muslim Hajj. It also indirectly supports the killings of animals in hunting, vivisection, and meat production through the retention of a relatively desacralized ideology of sacrifice in modern Western society. My analysis of the structure and ideology of patriarchal blood sacrifice, including its application to the modern practice of animal experimentation, is presented in chapters 4 and 5 and summarized later in this introduction.

A moral justification of some sort is necessary for us to remain complicit in this society's routine subjugation of animals. In the absence of a workable defense, the confinements, the shooting and trapping, the experimentation, the buying and selling of body parts, the slaughter, and all the harms imposed to further human purposes are revealed as nothing more than the powerful taking what they can get so long as they can get away with it. The rejection of animal exploitation as morally indefensible is called "animal rights" or "animal liberation." These terms refer to a moral position but also to a political movement that seeks to abolish the major institutions of animal exploitation. The animal liberation movement focuses its attention primarily on the large-scale institutions of animal farming, hunting/trapping, and animal experimentation but also regularly protests the abuses of animals in circuses and rodeos and at times challenges angling, the confinement of animals in zoos, aquaria, and pet shops, and the killing of homeless pets at "shelters." The unifying theme in all these campaigns is the conviction that we should stop harming animals unnecessarily, even if this means abolishing entrenched institutions.

Though concern for animal well-being and a general disinclination against harming animals are common and normal facets of human life, relatively few members of modern society take these sympathies to their logical, abolitionist conclusion. Animal liberation is still a minority position. One of the pressing questions for anyone concerned with the politics of animal exploitation is how to account for this. Why do so many actively perpetrate or tacitly comply with animal exploitation? Conversely, what brings a relatively small number to renounce animal exploitation and seek its abolition?

Gender and the Treatment of Animals

Any complete understanding of why some people exploit animals while others seek to liberate them will undoubtedly be complex and include many factors. But there is an obvious starting point. A cursory glance at the memberships of groups that exploit animals and groups that oppose such exploitation reveals striking gender differentiation.

Throughout its history, a large majority of activists in the animal protection movement has been female. Moreover, women have most often been the founders and leaders of animal protection organizations.[8] This pattern continues to the present. A survey taken at the 1990 March on Washington for the Animals found females comprising 80 percent of the activists. A follow-up study done at the 1996 march got similar results, finding 76 percent female representation.[9] These results are consistent with other studies. Reviews of sociological literature on the animal rights movement find that all studies show a preponderance of female activists, ranging from 68 to 80 percent across surveys.[10] This coheres with my personal experience, during which it has not been at all uncommon to find myself the only man present at a meeting of animal activists.

Within animal exploitation itself the gender differentiation is even more apparent. Throughout the twentieth century well over 90 percent of North American hunters have been male.[11] "Man the Hunter" is a longstanding and highly entrenched image, and this affects our perception of other institutions of animal exploitation, such as meat production. Though the animals whose body parts are sold in supermarkets today were generally not killed by hunters, the archetype of the manly hunter colors our perception of whose work it is to kill animals. Such associations, along with the continuing stereotype of the macho cowboy driving livestock to slaughter, support a deep cultural linkage between meat and manhood, with one result being that vegetarian women outnumber vegetarian men nearly three to one in the United States.[12] Our other major industry of deliberate animal killing, vivisection, is also highly male dominated both in practice and in imagery. Female vivisectors were unheard of and unthinkable when the practice was institutionalized in the late nineteenth century. Today, of course, females do vivisect, but they are still a small enough minority to be considered aberrant by both researchers and animal activists. In such an environment, women who pursue a career in vivisection may feel they have something to prove—that they can put aside "girlish weakness" and kill animals with the best of men—and animal activists respond to them with an extra measure of repugnance, as if a male vivisector's callousness is unfortunate but expected, whereas a female's is both lamentable and deviant.[13]

Given the obviously gender-differentiated nature of both animal exploitation and animal liberation, it is remarkable that activists do not generally proceed as if gender were an important factor in the struggle. Most protests and writings by animal liberationists do not even mention gender. High-profile animal rights conferences do acknowledge the issue, in that Carol Adams (author of *The Sexual Politics of Meat*) is frequently invited to speak. But this exposure has not led to any appreciable change in movement protest strategy, organizational structure, or rhetorical stance. The standard abolitionist characterization of vivisection, for example, is that it is a cruel and outdated research methodology that continues to be perpetrated because of institutional inertia and the careerism of its practitioners ("habit and money," as Amy Achor puts it).[14] Though this analysis may be correct so far as it goes, it makes no mention of the salient fact that throughout the history of vivisection, its practitioners have been largely male and its opponents largely female. Sociological studies frequently report statistical correlations between gender and animal issues but rarely attempt to analyze animal rights or animal exploitation in terms of gender.[15] Indeed, sociologists at times go out of their way to reject such framing, as when Lyle Munro insists that "strictly speaking, animal rights issues are gender neutral," immediately subsequent to having quantified the predominance of women within animal protection movements.[16]

The main exception to the gender-blind approach to animal liberation is in the opposition to hunting. Antihunting activists and writers do mention sport hunting's strong association with the mystique of manhood. It may be that the gendered associations of hunting are so overt that activists cannot help but acknowledge them. Also, whereas the vivisection industry typically projects a gender-neutral image (they are just people doing things to help other people), the practitioners of hunting are deliberately and self-consciously gender specific—hunting is a way for the guys to get away from their wives, an arena for initiating sons into manhood, a haven of male exclusivity. Though some hunting advocates have lately been moderating their masculinist rhetoric, this is only a very recent anomaly in an institution that has historically been proudly and openly of men, by men, and for men.

One hint as to why, apart from some antihunting rhetoric, animal activists generally avoid focusing on gendered aspects of animal exploitation is suggested by Rachel Einwohner's study of animal rights campaigns.[17] In following various campaigns conducted by an animal rights group based in Seattle, Einwohner found that the predominance of women activists was remarked upon by the targets of some campaigns but not by others. Hunters surveyed by Einwohner described animal rights activists as women, whereas circus patrons did not, despite the fact that both groups encountered the very same activists. Einwohner theorizes that since hunters already see themselves in gender-specific ways, they describe and evaluate their critics in gender-specific ways as well. On the other hand, circus patrons generally understand themselves in gender-neutral ways (families doing something fun for the kids) and tend correspondingly to view activists in nongendered ways.

Significantly, Einwohner also found activists achieving greater success in their campaign against circuses than in their campaign against hunting. Attendance at the targeted circuses dropped noticeably during the years of the campaign, while hunting practices were largely unaffected by activist efforts. In fact, while not a single hunter changed his point of view regarding the sport after hearing the activists' position, the reaction of circus goers was mixed, some dismissing activists as extremists, others listening carefully to the activists' concerns and reevaluating their own position. Notably, hunters' universal dismissal of activist concerns was couched in gendered stereotypes: Activists were seen as overly emotional, uninformed women, whereas hunting was characterized as rational ecological management derived from the scientific principles applied by objective men.

Activists are very sensitive to this particular dynamic, understanding that gender prejudice is frequently used as a basis for dismissing the claims of female activists. In sexist society men's views carry more weight than do women's. It is understandable, then, that activists may not want to call attention to their own predominantly female membership by highlighting male predominance within the vivisection and meat industries. With respect to hunting, though, there is no way to avoid the gender issue, since hunters bring it up first.

While the reluctance of animal activists to foreground gender is understandable, it is not necessarily the best decision in the long run. Pursuing a gender-neutral approach carries its own risks, not the least of which being the perpetuation of an incomplete understanding of animal exploitation that can hinder possibilities for progress. There is a gendered pattern to the progress of the animal rights movement to date. Two of the most dramatic successes have been in fur sales and in the use of animals to test cosmetics for toxicity. Both have shown marked declines at least partially due to activist efforts; both industries market products strongly associated with women. This raises the question of whether the success here, which contrasts with the much more modest or nonexistent animal rights success in industries lacking such strong female connotations, is in some way linked to the gendered aspect.

This question becomes even more pointed when one examines the status of products similar to fur and cosmetics but for their gendered associations. Consider fur versus leather. The U.S. fur industry has declined dramatically since the mid-1980s; since then the number of wild animals trapped for their fur has dropped from seventeen million to three million and the number of caged mink facilities has declined by more than 50 percent.[18] U.S. retail fur sales fell 45 percent between 1986 and 1991 before flattening, and fur trade globally has been in similar straits.[19] During the same time period, world production of bovine skins and hides increased by 2.4 percent and sheepskin and lambskin production increased by 5.3 percent, continuing the same steady growth of the previous decades.[20]

Consider also animal testing on women's and men's personal care and beauty products. Table 3 includes two lists: a dozen major brands and manufacturers found in men's sections of the local drug store (cologne, men's shaving products, etc.) and a dozen major brands and manufacturers found in women's sections (perfume, cosmetics, etc.). When these products are checked

Table 3. Companies that Do and Do Not Test on Animals

Men's Brands	Women's Brands
Brut	Clairol
Calvin Klein	Elizabeth Arden
English Leather	Helene Curtis
Gillette	Kotex
Grecian Formula	L'Oreal
Old Spice	**Avon**
Pierre Cardin	**Chanel**
Ralph Lauren	**Estee Lauder**
Schick	**Liz Claiborne**
Stetson	**Mary Kay**
Trojan	**Merle Norman**
Norelco	**Revlon**

Note: Highlighted companies have publicly renounced animal testing.
Source: PETA's "Companies that Do/Don't Test on Animals," April 2005,
    www.caringconsumer.com.

against their company's policies regarding animal testing, a striking result is found: Seven of the twelve women's product lines have publicly renounced animal testing, while only one of the men's companies has done so.

How might we understand such markedly different changes in animal use industries? The primary strategy employed by the animal rights movement involves three steps: (1) publicly revealing the harms caused to animals by a particular industry, (2) showing that those harms are unnecessary, and (3) calling for the cessation of those harms through the abolition or reform of the industry. This might be called a sympathy-based framework in that the expectation that people will be moved toward abolition through a revelation of gratuitous harm is grounded in an assumption of human sympathies toward animal well-being. Although this assumption of human sympathy for animals is well founded, as I show in chapters 1 and 6, it should be noted that the inclination to act on such sympathies is conditioned by our gender identities. In particular, feminine gender roles typically include an expectation of responsiveness to the needs of others, while masculine gender roles often include an expectation of a willingness to override or disregard our sympathies for others.

This gender differentiation can affect how our sympathies for animals are treated. As a society, we expect women to respond to the suffering of animals; we see that as a "natural" part of womanhood. Men, on the other hand, are expected to subsume whatever feelings they might have against the infliction of harm on animals to the grand project of Man's Taming of Nature. Such cultural understandings of male and female "nature" can affect the willingness of an individual to join an animal rights campaign. Although for females such activism can be taken as an extension of conventional femininity, for the male the same activism raises doubts concerning his masculinity.

Such observations partially explain both the preponderance of women in animal liberation and the gendered pattern in animal liberation's most notable successes. Just as the choice of whether to join the animal rights movement can be influenced by how participation enhances or undermines our gender identities, so also our purchasing decisions are affected by their gendered associations. While it is feminine to buy only "cruelty-free" cosmetics, in that such a decision exemplifies a woman's caring responsiveness to the suffering of others, it is masculine to continue buying and consuming animal products even after being informed of how the animals are harmed because this demonstrates a man's ability to override his sympathetic hesitations.

Before completely reducing the gender-differentiated results of animal rights campaigns to this process, however, we should note the following. Both men *and* women continue to buy the products of the "manly" exploitation of animals in vivisection and meat production. Conversely, women and men together are making decisions leading to the cessation of cosmetics testing on animals and the restructuring of the fur industry. In understanding how the animal liberation movement has differed in its impact on "men's" and "women's" forms of exploitation, it is useful to think of gender not merely in terms of individuals making decisions to protect their own identities but also in terms of men and women working together to construct masculinity and femininity as such. In essentialist terms, masculinity and femininity are seen as natural, whereas in normative terms, masculinity and femininity are seen as good things worthy of every preservationist effort. While not cohering together well (if gender roles are natural, why do we need to work so hard to preserve them?), the essentialist and the normative perspectives are somehow maintained simultaneously in this society. Both perspectives motivate men and women to support institutions that are in congruence with gender stereotypes and to oppose institutions that are in tension with the same images.

When a woman in this society buys a steak, she is purchasing a product that is imaged as the result of a man killing an animal. If she then cooks the steak for her traditionally structured family, she is facilitating a man's consumption of this product of male violence. There is relatively little gender tension in their joint construction and affirmation of masculinity. The tension that exists lies in her supposedly natural responsiveness to suffering going unheeded via the financial support she cedes to the slaughter industry. This tension is mitigated by the deference to manhood traditionally expected of the female. Though femininity is threatened by her complicity in violence against animals, it is ultimately salvaged by understanding her actions as prototypically feminine submission to the imperatives of manhood.

Within the patriarchal household there is no room for male opposition to meat, and there is very little room for female opposition (she might choose personal vegetarianism, but this is quite different from publicly insisting on abolishing the meat industry). The situation is rather different with respect to cosmetics testing and fur. While it is tacitly understood that men are ranching or trapping the fur-bearing animals, and that men are running the laboratories that test products on animals' bodies, it is not generally understood that this violence is being done for the sake of male consumption. While meat is taken to be for men, fur and cosmetics are represented as being for women. Notwithstanding the fact that traditionally men have purchased fur for women to wear as a symbol of the man's wealth and status (and even today, in this postfeminist age, men continue to be the primary consumer purchasers of fur),[21] fur is seen as a woman's product. Likewise, the fact that beauty standards are constructed in large part by a mass media owned and managed predominantly by men does not stop us from seeing cosmetics testing on animals as driven by putative female desires for elaborate self-beautification. Fur and cosmetics have both been used to help implement a particular construction of gender roles, one in which women are held to be naturally and ceaselessly engaged in decorating and adorning their bodies to attract the attention of men.

In this context, revelation of the harms done to animals via cosmetics testing and fur production has a very different effect than revelation of the harms done to animals in other industries. The former, we think, causes harm to animals for which *women* are ultimately responsible. While we find the thought of any animal suffering unpleasant, it is animal suffering attributed to women that we find intolerable. We can live with the thought of men injuring animals—indeed, we support such processes—because this coheres with our image of masculinity. But females causing animal abuse through their "demands" for certain products conjures frightening gender confusion, the prospect of women forgetting their nurturing side and becoming aggressive like men. Thus we see not only individual women refraining from buying cosmetics tested on animals but also the men running the cosmetics companies deferring to the animal rights position. Cosmetics companies publicly boast of renouncing animal testing in order to boost their image and market share, while the producers of men's fragrances and personal care products proceed as if they have never heard of the animal rights movement. Indeed, the male counterpart to women's "cruelty-free cosmetics" is not "cruelty-free cologne" but the reverse, an affirmation of animal exploitation: English Leather, Chaps, Stetson, Stetson Untamed, Polo, Safari, and so on, all deploying textual and visual images of men's dominance over animals in order to enhance the product's perceived masculine sexiness.

The vehemence with which women's wearing of fur has been attacked by animal activists suggests that we see something especially heinous there, something even more intolerable than gratuitous cruelty as such. We have not seen men in leather jackets being accosted, verbally harangued, and physically assaulted. "Fur Free Friday" is a well established day of action, but when will we mark "Sans Suede Saturday"? Animal activists, defending themselves against charges of sexism in their choice of target and tactic, often claim that fur is simply more vulnerable than other exploitative industries: The product is more obviously inessential, the harm caused to the animal is more grotesque, and the public support for this issue is more widespread. The last claim begs the question of whether public support for this issue is stronger because of the gendered associations of fur. That the first two claims are not supportable becomes clear once one considers the horrendous abuses meted to animals in factory farms and research laboratories, and the salubrity and ready availability of non-animal-based systems of nutrition and healing. Trapping, ranching, testing on animals—these are not inherently more pernicious than other forms of animal exploitation. But since their products are thought to result from women's demands, we are able to approach a societal consensus that they represent unacceptable levels of cruelty to animals. Killing animals for sport, for science, for a steak dinner, or a leather jacket—that is not excessive violence, that is men's violence. This society is certainly willing to intervene against women becoming manly through an overly direct connection to animal abuse, but it will not stop men from being men.

Nor has the animal rights movement yet asked it to. Animal activists continue the nongendered critique of exploitation, acting as if we live in a world in which some people (of irrelevant sex) exploit animals for other people (of indeterminate sex) while a small minority of people (of unmentionable sex) mount an opposition. This gender-blind framing accurately portrays only a small fraction of the human domination of other animals. The major institutions of animal exploitation—meat production, vivisection, sport hunting, sacrifice—are not cases of humans versus animals but of men versus animals. In this book I refer to these institutions as "men's exploitation of animals," not as a regression to an invalid universal use of "men" to mean human, but to accurately reflect the fact that male humans are the primary perpetrators of these abuses and women the primary human opponents.

Clarifying that the issue is not so much human dominance as it is human male dominance is a starting point in the development of our understanding of the root reasons for animal exploitation. The question now is why men exploit animals.

Man Against the Animals

Not only is membership in the organizations devoted to animal liberation and animal exploitation gender-divided, as discussed above, but so are expressions of support for liberation versus exploitation. Stephen Kellert, who has studied the attitudes and practices of Americans regarding animals and nature, summarizes the pattern:

> Women consistently express greater humanistic and moralistic sentiments toward nature—particularly strong affection and emotional attachment to individual animals, especially pets. Women also reveal greater moralistic concerns than men, illustrated by less support for practices presumably involving substantial harm and suffering inflicted on animals including hunting, trapping, and various wildlife "harvesting" activities. Women are also much more likely to join groups opposed to the consumptive use of animals, whereas men account for most of the members of hunting and fishing organizations. Men express far greater support than women for the practical exploitation and domination of animals and nature.[22]

All other studies of attitudes toward animal use find similar results.[23] Moreover, the gender divide over support for animal exploitation holds cross-culturally and across age groups.[24] Some men do support animal rights, of course, often when some number of the other demographic factors statistically associated with such support are present, such as having grown up in an urban area or as being young, liberal, less educated, less masculine, or more supportive of feminism. Women's greater tendency to oppose animal exploitation, on the other hand, persists even in the absence of such factors.[25]

Thus gender consistently emerges as the most significant factor underlying attitudes toward animal exploitation. Various explanations have been offered for this, perhaps the most common being that women's orientation toward nurturance and compassion naturally leads them to support animal protection more often than men.[26] Theorists who suggest such explanations do not generally assume that women's differential nurturance is innate but accept that it may be primarily or even entirely due to socialization. Even apart from actual gender differences in degree of nurturant responsiveness, a societal expectation that women should be more oriented toward caring might explain the gendered patterns in animal rights and animal exploitation.

This "Woman the Nurturer" explanation focuses on sex role expectations and character differences between men and women. A second class of explanations focuses on women's social position. Charles Peek and others surveyed the evidence of a strong connection between having companion animals and participating in animal rights activism. They write that identity with companion animals (pets) is "likely greater among women than men due to women's structural location within the household" and speculate that "such identity could increase women's concern for animals and forge a link between gender and animal rights support."[27]

Feminist animal advocates have identified another relevant element of women's structural location. In patriarchal society women are oppressed in ways that are often remarkably similar to the abuses applied to exploited animals.[28] The perception of a common oppression might give women an enhanced capacity to empathize with exploited animals, leading to support for animal liberation.[29] According to Rheya Linden, president of Animal Liberation Victoria, this "link is very easy to make for women because women have known what it is to live in patriarchies."[30] On the other hand, consciousness of a common female/animal subjugation can have the opposite effect. Some women turn against animal liberation as they seek to change their own targeted status by becoming animal exploiters themselves. Thus we see Mary Zeiss Stange advocating women's hunting on the grounds that "Woman the Hunter is a necessarily disruptive figure," destabilizing the patriarchal trope that only men are naturally inclined toward killing.[31]

While structural and character-based explanations of the gender differences regarding animal exploitation are both part of the story, they do not furnish a complete account. As Stange's case indicates, there are different ways for women to respond to their structural position and not all of them lead to animal liberation. Character-based explanations are also incomplete. Arguing that women are more likely to support animal liberation than men because they are trained to take a more relationship-oriented, caring perspective simply raises the question of why we socialize the genders in this particular way. It is possible that men's association with animal exploitation is itself a major contributor to our gender stereotypes, including in particular the stereotypes of feminine caring and masculine callousness. In other words, the order of explanation might be wrong. Do men support animal exploitation more often than women because we are less caring, or are men less caring than women because we exploit animals? If the latter, then we need to figure out why men exploit animals before we can fully understand our current standards of gendered behavior.

Moreover, there is empirical evidence that character differences cannot fully explain the gender split in support for animal liberation. Statistical analysis of survey results indicates that gender remains a significant factor in determining one's attitude toward animal liberation *independently* of one's orientation toward caring.[32] Within a group of men and women, all of whom are equally caring, the men are still more likely than the women to support animal exploitation.

The explanations summarized above focus on women as opponents of animal exploitation. This book addresses the converse, men as exploiters and as supporters of exploitation. In exploring this side of the issue I go beyond relating animal exploitation to norms of masculinity. It is important to see the congruence between the mystique of manhood and the things men do to animals in hunting, vivisection, and meat production. This is a crucial part of our understanding of animal exploitation, and I contribute to the literature on that topic with chapter 3. That chapter addresses the sexuality of men's hunting, extending work by writers such as Marti Kheel and Andrée Collard showing how men's attacks on wild animals intersect with an eros of male dominance.[33] But we must also determine why our society eroticizes male dominance and, more generally, why we construct norms of gendered behavior that facilitate men's continued exploitation of animals.

To answer this I look at gender in terms of class interests, not just in terms of roles or structural location. If the exploitation of animals serves men's interests in some way it does not serve women's interests, then the gender-differentiated levels of support for the exploitation are explicable. Moreover, this would explain why the differentiation persists across categories of age, nationality, political persuasion, and nurturant tendencies. A basic thesis of this book is that humans are generally inclined against harming animals. Women are more likely to act on this sympathy and support animal liberation because the institutions of animal exploitation do not serve their interests in the way that they serve men's. This hypothesis does not contradict, but rather supplements, explanations relating to socialization and structural position.

The interest pertinent here is our desire for respect, specifically the respect that accrues to those whose labor is deemed socially valuable. The ability to generate and maintain life, both human and nonhuman, is highly valued across cultures. Women have an overt capacity to generate and maintain life through gestation and suckling. Lacking these capacities, men seek other ways to demonstrate generativity. Social institutions that position men as life generators enhance men's overall social status and thus serve men's interests. Such institutions do not serve women's interests and, indeed, may even operate contrary to their interests if they devalue or disempower women while elevating men. The purpose of chapters 4 and 5 is to show in detail how two intertwined institutions of animal exploitation—sacrifice and vivisection—function to buttress men's social status by positioning men as the primary generators of human life.

I take sacrifice as the model of men's exploitation of animals. The sacrifice of animals has been a nearly universal feature of men's religious life. Meat production and consumption developed as correlates of religious sacrifice, and only recently has the meat industry come to be somewhat desacralized. Men's hunting of animals, typically distinguished from ritual sacrifice by anthropologists, in fact exhibits many sacrificial aspects.[34] And vivisection, I argue in chapter 5, is not merely similar to religious sacrifice; in fact, the two are structurally and functionally indistinguishable, leading to my conclusion that vivisection is modern Western society's particular version of animal sacrifice.

So sacrifice is an apt starting point for the attempt to understand men's exploitation of animals. I build on the work of the late Nancy Jay. In her 1992 book *Throughout Your Generations Forever,* Jay showed that across cultures animal sacrifice functions to establish paternity. Men become fathers, generators of life, through the ritual killing of an animal. While Jay showed *that* sacrifice establishes paternity, she did not develop an account of *how* it does so. She also excluded modern Western sacrificial rituals, such as vivisection, from her analysis. In chapters 4 and 5 I explain how sacrificial institutions are able to effectively position men as the primary generators of human life. Hunters, vivisectors, and other ritual sacrificers tell us that the work they do is crucial for the maintenance of human (and sometimes animal) well-being. Without their products—meat, modern medicine, and divine appeasement— humans would not exist, or so we are assured. In believing these assurances we cast men as the primary generators of human life, in that these forms of animal exploitation are structured as paradigms of manly work.

This analysis explains men's differential support for the major institutions of animal exploitation, but it does not imply that the support is inevitable. Even if the desire for respect is timeless and the ability to generate and maintain life is a source of respect in all cultures, there are ample opportunities for male generativity that do not involve the domination of others. The construction of a manhood based on domination proceeds from an historically contingent presumption, namely, that male identity must develop in opposition to female identity. If women generate life directly and positively, and men cannot be like women, then it follows that men's way of generating life must be indirect and negative, proceeding via the controlled destruction of others. In this dichotomous view, human society is maintained through a polarized division of labor: Women create life while men cause death. Once we discard the sexist insistence that male and female modes of being cannot overlap, it becomes obvious that men need not sacrifice animals in order to contribute to human society. The inherently female activities of gestation and suckling are essential to reproducing human life, but they are not sufficient; there are many other activities necessary for maintaining human society that men and women may perform equally.

Activities such as planting, gathering, teaching, building, cooking, cleaning, and so on are essential to human life and obvious potential sources of esteem. Insofar as they are nonviolent activities lacking any elements of domination, however, they fail to strongly enhance one's status as a man. Within our present sexist society this matters, and this stands as a barrier to the willingness of men to consider dismantling animal exploitation. In this sense the struggle for animal liberation is also a struggle against a manhood defined by sexism.

PART ONE

Justifying Men's Exploitation of Animals

Once upon a time a wolf was lapping at a spring on a hillside. When looking up, what should he see but a lamb just beginning to drink a little lower down. "There's my supper," thought he, "if only I can find some excuse to seize it." Then he called out to the lamb, "How dare you muddy the water from which I am drinking?"

"Nay, master, nay," said the lamb, "if the water be muddy up there I cannot be the cause of it, for it runs down from you to me."

"Well then," said the wolf, "why did you call me bad names this time last year?"

"Oh, that cannot be," said the lamb, "I am only six months old."

"I don't care," snarled the wolf, "if it was not you it was your father!"

And with that he rushed upon the poor little lamb and ate her all up. But before she died she gasped out, "Any excuse will serve a tyrant."[1]

1

The Species Boundary

Must one suppose oneself mad because one has the
sentiment of universal pity in one's heart?

—Victor Hugo, *The Alps and Pyrenees*

In 1988 the *Utne Reader* published Rosalind Solomon's photograph of a Peruvian woman, Catalin Valentin, breast-feeding a lamb.[1] This photograph provoked an extreme response from the readership. Some saw an image of peace, nurturance, and harmony between species. Others found the picture shocking, even grotesque, a gross and indecent violation of a natural boundary between species. One woman saw perversion: "The photo mimics the innocent gesture of the mother/child images of our traditions yet it presents the perverted usage of a woman's body to feed the appetites of an animal." Others felt it was an "exquisitely tender photo," a "beautiful image—lyrical, erotic, peaceful" and "nothing short of 'real-world' holy."[2] Those who were offended by the photo tended to construe it sexually, as "a form of bestiality" and as "a little eroticism" slipped in to spice up the magazine. One woman even associated it with sexual violence between people:

> I have represented people who have been convicted of doing significant damage to the rectum of their three-year-old daughter. I sat through a trial last week where the defendant put a broken light bulb in the vagina of a woman at some time roughly contemporaneous with murdering her. I look at autopsy photographs for a living. Get the picture? I'm used to disgusting.
>
> The photo on your endpaper so repulsed me I had to tear it out before I could read the rest of the magazine.[3]

Readers who were shocked saw an unforgivable transgression of species boundaries. According to this point of view there are certain things we are only supposed to do with members of our own species, particularly sexual intercourse and suckling. These two activities are linked in that both are part of the process of producing the next generation.

Biologists define species membership in terms of the possibility of producing fertile offspring. One might use this scientific definition of species membership to ground a claim that certain activities between members of different species are unnatural. Extending care toward members of other species might be deemed unnatural when that caring exceeds certain bounds—such as caring attempts to end the exploitation of other species. A typical argument of this sort is found in Richard Hummel's book on hunting. He writes that "individual animals do not have rights comparable to human rights. Humans are at the top of the food chain and it is a principle of nature that no level in the chain has moral obligations to any other level."[4] Such references to our place in the food chain, though common, are inherently weak because they invalidly slide from *is* to *ought*. To say that we are "at the top of the food chain" means nothing more than that while humans are able to exploit nearly every other species on the planet, rarely are we ourselves exploited by other species. This statement of what is the case, that we exploit other animals, says nothing in itself about whether we ought to continue acting in such a manner. The central question of whether we have moral obligations to members of other species is assumed, not supported. We should take care to distinguish empirical and ethical statements, especially when assessing arguments from nature, since the term "natural" can be used either way, or sometimes both ways at once.

Activities deemed naturally to occur only between conspecifics do in fact happen between members of different species. Sexual activities occur between members of different species. Suckling between members of different species also occurs. Moreover, this suckling is also very often effective in that the young do take nourishment; not only do millions of young humans gain some nourishment from the cow's milk they are fed, but there are also numerous cases of women suckling nonhuman animals in order to feed them and help them to grow.[5] This activity is, therefore, not unnatural in the sense that it never happens or is ineffective, only in that it is not the usual way young mammals get nourished. But this observation is not a moral judgment. It is an empirical generality very different in character from the shocked outrage evoked by Catalin Valentin's suckling of a lamb. Those comments indicate moral evaluation, not the judgment that nursing between species *cannot* happen but that it *should not* happen. They are supposing that is unnatural in this morally loaded sense.

One *Utne* reader suggests that our reaction to the image of a woman suckling a lamb is determined by our attitudes toward nonhuman animals: "As long as we regard other animals as essentially different from ourselves and less deserving of respect, we will continue to be troubled by Catalin and her lamb." This comment raises the possibility that our sense of what is natural between species depends on our prior attitudes toward animals. The attitude that animals are essentially different from and beneath us, as I suggested in the introduction, is typically engendered by a commitment to the systematic exploitation of animals. How we construct the "natural" boundaries between species may also be driven more by our relation to the institutions of animal use than by the realities of what happens in nature and what works.

Is there a natural division between species, one that carries moral implications for how we should treat members of other species and members of our own? Is it natural for people to care only for other humans while exploiting nonhuman animals as game, livestock, and research material? These are the questions addressed in this chapter and the next.

According to naturalistic arguments, it is acceptable for people to exploit animals because this is natural. These arguments complement the rationalistic arguments summarized in the introduction. When developed consistently, rationalistic arguments lead to a devaluation of nonrational humans. They imply that nonrational humans should be exploited as animals currently are or that they may be protected but that this protection is supererogatory, that is, it goes beyond what they actually deserve by inherent right. To avoid this diminishment of the moral status of nonrational humans, proponents of animal exploitation must bring in considerations other than those employed by the rationalistic human superiority argument. They must say that it is somehow appropriate to give special treatment—protection from exploitation—to all humans irrespective of the great range of capacities we possess. Being human must carry moral weight in and of itself. One way to develop this position is to claim that species membership itself carries moral significance, that one naturally should give greater weight to the interests of members of one's own species, even to the extent of harming others for the sake of one's conspecifics.

The argument from nature is not a single line of reasoning but a class of related arguments. I distinguish three primary forms of this argument: (1) exploitation between species is natural, (2) humans (particularly men) are predatory by nature, and (3) humans naturally protect members of our own species but to extend such consideration to nonhumans is unnatural. The third argument is discussed here; the first and second arguments are discussed in the next chapter. The general position developed in this chapter is that regardless of the relative degree to which we are inclined to protect humans versus other animals, we show such a consistent inclination to sympathize with the plights of nonhuman animals that it becomes impossible to maintain that the extension of moral consideration to nonhuman animals is contrary to human nature.

Species Solidarity

Recall one woman's reaction to the photo of Catalin Valentin suckling a lamb: It is a perversion for a woman's body to be used to feed an animal. There is something natural and appropriate, it is suggested, for humans to use our bodies and minds to care for each other, but not to care for members of other species. There is a certain natural solidarity between members of the same species, such that it is not only appropriate for us to direct our resources toward other humans but also appropriate and natural for us to prefer humans in cases of conflict between species, even to the extent of harming nonhuman animals to benefit people. Animal exploiters often defend themselves by implying that their critics have misplaced their affections from their proper object—other people—and unnaturally transferred them to animals. Over the course of many antihunting demonstrations, for example, I noticed that hunters and their defenders consistently call protesters "dykes" and "fags." The reflexive use of these epithets perplexed me until at one protest I heard a hunter condescendingly advise female activists that "someday, when they had children" they would understand. The assumption evidently is that people with children do not misdirect their energy toward animal issues (and isn't it obvious that lesbians and gays do not have children).[6] This attitude toward animal advocacy dates to the onset of the animal rights movement. Consider, for instance, the dismissal of the antivivisection movement by nineteenth-century physiologist Elie de Cyon: "Is it necessary to repeat that women—or rather, old maids, form the most numerous contingent of this group? Let my adversaries contradict me, if they can show among the leaders of the agitation one girl, rich, beautiful, and loved, or some young wife who has found in her home the full satisfactions of her affections."[7] A proper woman directs her affections only to her husband and her children.

The resumption of animal rights activism in the latter part of the twentieth century engendered disbelief and amusement more than dispassionate refutation. The first official demonstration of People for the Ethical Treatment of Animals (PETA), for example, garnered headlines because people found it incredible that anyone could care about the conditions under which chickens had their throats cut. Those who think chicken welfare is worth agitating for were widely seen as lunatics.[8]

One may claim that we should direct our resources to humans first, and that we should further human interests even if that means harming nonhuman animals in the process. But can this claim be supported by reference to some natural species solidarity between humans? I argue in the following that there is no natural speciesism among humans. People are not normally indifferent or hostile to the well-being of animals. In fact, in many circumstances we go out of our way to care for nonhuman animals. And this caring is not unhealthy for us but contributes to human flourishing.

One of the most indelible impressions I have from my childhood is of my father rescuing a frozen seagull from our front yard. I grew up in Wisconsin, on the shore of Lake Michigan. One extremely cold winter morning as he was leaving for work, my father spotted a seagull standing stiffly at the end of the driveway. The bird was alive but frozen solid. He brought the gull into the house where my mother and father placed him on a towel on the bathroom floor to give him a chance to revive. For my parents this was normal, natural behavior. If a creature is in need, you try to help. My memory of this childhood event has always been accompanied by the assumption that the gull survived and was released. It was only recently, in the course of writing this book, that I asked my parents about the frozen gull and was told that in fact the bird did not survive.

Years later I was part of another memorable animal rescue effort. Picking up my four-year-old son from his preschool in Dayton, Ohio, I saw a rabbit sitting on the grass median between the sidewalk and the street. He did not move away even as my car approached. I thought this was peculiar and that maybe he was injured. As I slowly walked up to the rabbit, he began hobbling away, dragging himself into the street at my approach. I then saw blood around his hindquarters. I knew he was likely to be hit by a car, so I kept walking toward him until he had gotten himself out of the road. I went into the school building and discussed the situation with the teachers and clerical staff in the school office. They had no concrete suggestions, other than one of the secretaries, who said we should wring his neck to "put him out of his misery." I pointed out that he was not obviously dying but may just have a leg injury from which he could recover if not left vulnerable to predators.

I got my son Adam from his class and explained the situation to him. I asked him what he thought we should do. He responded without hesitation:

"Take him to the hospital to be fixed." This course of action had somehow escaped all the adults in the school office. Adam and I wrapped the injured rabbit in a towel and drove to the veterinary clinic. The receptionist there told us that by law they were not allowed to treat wild animals, but she gave me directions to the one wildlife rehabilitation center in the region, about twenty miles outside of Dayton. We drove to the center. The rabbit was still alive when we got there. The worker examined the rabbit and said that he had a broken leg but no evident internal damage, so he did have a chance of recovering. He explained to me that the center received about fifteen hundred animals a year, all injured or orphaned wild animals people brought in with hopes they could be helped.

The next day at Adam's preschool, two of the adults made a point of addressing me about the rabbit. The secretary who had casually suggested that we wring the rabbit's neck came to me and apologized for the suggestion, saying that she grew up on a farm and that was just the way they were with animals. Another woman approached me nearly in tears. She thanked me for what we had done the previous day and told me how moved she had been to see that.

It is a commonplace that animal rights activists are primarily from the city and, as such, do not see animals and our relations to them the way that farmers and hunters do. The implication is usually disparaging, that urban animal activists have a deficient understanding of how the world really works. Those who grow up on farms know that we must injure and kill animals at times. We can provide care for them as well, but only within the limits of what is useful and profitable for us. We cannot afford to be too sentimental about the lives of domesticated or wild animals. The kind of sympathetic concerns that drive animal rescue and protection efforts are anomalous. According to this point of view such sympathies arise only from the recent unnatural separation of large numbers of people from direct acquaintance with the natural cycles of interspecies exploitation. This interpretation is not accepted by animal rights advocates, such as sociologist David Nibert, who accept the connection between increasing urbanization and the rise in empathy for animals but see the latter as an adventitious benefit of demographic change:

> Forced to give up family farms, millions saw their day-to-day economic dependence on the direct exploitation of other animals diminish as they moved to urban areas and took up blue- and white-collar jobs, some of which provided for a reasonable level of economic comfort. Possibilities for empathy

for oppressed others grew, so long as the oppression was not directly related to one's own economic aspirations or other self-interested pursuits. Consequently, the capacity for many humans to be moved by the suffering of others has increased.[9]

I learned something about caring for animals from being around my parents, seeing how they treated nonhuman animals with respect and concern and how they did so without fanfare. For them it was normal and unremarkable behavior. My parents are not farmers, and I've never known them to hunt or fish. I acknowledge that my family relations and my nonfarming, nonhunting background have conditioned my ability to be responsive to the needs of nonhuman animals, as they have for my sons. But it does not follow from this that my sympathies—or anyone else's—for nonhumans are unnatural or anomalous.

All of our dispositions are conditioned by our environment. This is just as true of farmers and hunters as it is of urban animal rights activists. Just as our capacity for sympathetic responsiveness to animals can be enhanced by growing up away from farms, so can this responsiveness be constricted by the experience of growing up on a farm. In general, those who commit themselves to the exploitation of animals find ways to limit their emotional connection to the beings they hurt.[10] One study found that North American farmers have reduced empathy for the animals they use but heightened empathy in response to a description of a rhinoceros killed by poachers.[11] With respect to our sympathetic concern, we are a flexible species, capable of being callous and unfeeling when we believe the situation calls for it. But this is quite different from saying that we are naturally unconcerned about the well-being of members of other species. The evidence suggests the contrary, that sympathetic responsiveness to animals is a regular feature of human life.

In the following I summarize some of the indicators of our deep disposition to care for animals. In doing so I do not dwell on the question of degree, on whether we tend to care for animals as much as we do for people. The issue of degree is often brought into discussions of animal rights through the lifeboat scenario: If you were in a lifeboat with insufficient provisions, who would you save, your daughter or your dog? I find this question misleading and ultimately irrelevant. In general, animals are not exploited in order to save people. Certainly sport hunting and animal farming in the industrialized West are not necessary for human survival. Even with respect to animal experimentation, where the lifeboat scenario is most often employed, there are serious questions about how necessary the research really is for human well-being.[12]

Even if some animal experimentation has provided otherwise unachievable human benefits, the lifeboat scenario is not a valid way of defending the practice. The scenario is intended to reveal that in a crisis situation we protect humans at the expense of nonhumans. But by designating that the human in question is one's daughter, the scenario is loaded against the acknowledgment of our dispositions to protect animals. Suppose we revise the question: If you were in a lifeboat with insufficient provisions, who would you save, your beloved pet dog or a human you have never met before? Not all of us would prefer to save the human stranger. If the strongly inculcated social mandate that we *should* prefer saving the human were removed, it may be that most people would fight to save their companion animal at the expense of the unfamiliar human. The fact that Westerners grow up in an adamantly anthropocentric (human-centered) culture invalidates the use of the scenario to show any natural speciesism among humans. Our willingness to entertain or to express certain preferences has already been circumscribed by ubiquitous presentations of the human superiority argument.

Moreover, suppose the question were phrased as follows: In the lifeboat situation, who would you sacrifice, yourself or your child? Most of us would sacrifice ourselves to save our child. But the implicit logic of the original lifeboat argument was that if we would sacrifice a dog to save a human, then it is okay to institutionalize this by experimentally sacrificing dogs for human therapies. If this logic works, then it would follow from the modified scenario that we should institutionalize the experimental sacrifice of adults to find therapies for our children.

Our disposition to sacrifice ourselves for our children in a crisis, though, does not lead to the conclusion that we should begin vivisecting adult humans. We care very much about the protection of our children, but we also care about the well-being of adults. The reasonable result of this is we insist on institutions that provide for children without exploiting adult humans. Similarly, if we care about the well-being of animals, even if we do not care for their well-being quite so much as we care for the well-being of ourselves or our children, the reasonable approach is to find institutions that provide for human interests without exploiting nonhuman animals. For this reason I focus in the following on the primary question of whether there is a natural human tendency to care about the well-being of animals, not so much on the less relevant question regarding the degree of this caring.

Crossing the Boundary

This section considers four areas of human life that manifest our disposition to care about animal well-being: human attitudes toward the treatment of animals, animal rescue, pet keeping, and moral qualms regarding the harming of animals.

ATTITUDES TOWARD ANIMALS

Stephen Kellert's empirical research is significant here. Kellert distinguished nine basic attitudes toward animals and nature and developed surveys to measure the presence of these attitudes in modern North Americans. His studies indicate the strength of each attitude in an individual as well as the prevalence of each attitude across individuals. For our purposes the most relevant attitudes are these five:

> "Humanistic"—feelings of strong affection and attachment to individual animals, typically pets.
> "Moralistic"—concern for the ethically appropriate human treatment of animals, with strong opposition to exploitation of and cruelty toward animals.
> "Dominionistic"—interest in the mastery and control of animals.
> "Utilitarian"—imputing significance to animals based on their usefulness to people.
> "Negativistic"—active avoidance of animals due to dislike or fear.[13]

Kellert measured the presence of each of these and four other attitudes in his sample of Americans. The highest one could score for the presence of a given attitude is 1, and the lowest is 0. The highest average scores for Americans were in the humanistic and moralistic categories, while the average score in the dominionistic category was the second lowest.

The average score on the utilitarian scale was higher than on the dominionistic but lower than on the humanistic and moralistic. In other words, Americans on average are more oriented toward expressing affection for animals and avoiding causing them harm than they are toward using animals and establishing control over them. Kellert found that approximately 35 percent of Americans are strongly oriented toward affection and attachment toward individual animals, while 20 percent strongly express a utilitarian view and only 3 percent are primarily interested in mastery and control of animals.[14]

Thus Kellert's research indicates that affection for individuals is the prevailing attitude of Americans toward animals. Moreover, his results on the humanistic scale may be misleadingly low. With emotional attachment to animals construed as unmanly or childish, people in our society (particularly men) may refuse to admit the feelings they have for animals, as author Tom Rose's example indicates: "Just moments before I unexpectedly found myself on the way to cover the story [of three trapped gray whales], I was ridiculing my friend Carolyn Gusoff for her unrepentant emotional desire to see the whales freed at any cost. Of course, I wanted them freed as much as anyone, but was too embarrassed to admit it."[15]

Although the anonymity of the survey may have allowed some of the embarrassed to be honest about their strong affections for animals, others may have internalized the depreciation of these affections to the extent that they cannot acknowledge the presence of such feelings even to themselves. Thirteen percent of Kellert's respondents agreed that "love is an emotion which people should feel only for other people, not for animals." Regardless of their actual feelings for animals, these 13 percent are not likely to admit the following: "I have owned pets that were as dear to me as another person" (yet 66 percent did agree with this latter statement).[16] The responses to these two statements (among others) are used by Kellert to estimate the proportion of people oriented toward the humanistic attitude, even though the statements do not directly address the respondent's affections for animals: The first addresses what the respondent thinks about loving animals, and the second only addresses the respondent's affection for animals relative to his or her affection for humans.

Thus 35 percent should be taken only as a lower bound on the proportion of Americans strongly oriented toward affection for individual animals. Even this is a strikingly sizable minority, given the prevalence of institutions that motivate a curtailment of our attachments to animals. We should expect a society like ours but without these institutions to include an even higher proportion of people taking the humanistic attitude. In particular, the existence of animal farming greatly influences attitudes toward animals, among farmers themselves but also among the public in general. Kellert's research revealed "a pronounced lack of sympathy for most cruelty and animal protection concerns among farmers." With "a somewhat emotionally detached view of animals," farmers scored lower than any other demographic group on the humanistic scale and highest on the utilitarian scale. And farmers scored second highest on the dominionistic scale, after males. The latter, gendered association is explicated in part 2 of this book.

Kellert found that 20 percent of Americans are strongly oriented toward the moralistic attitude, which is the opposition to inflicting pain, harm, or suffering on animals. He mentions that "the moralistic attitude is often associated with feelings of strong affection for animals."[17] This is supported by the high statistical correlation between the humanistic attitude and the moralistic attitude. The only attitude correlated more highly with the moralistic is the naturalistic, which is the attitude characterized as "a strong interest in and affection for the outdoors and wildlife.[18] While hunters often express strong interest in and affection for wildlife, they form only one small part of the group expressing a naturalistic attitude, and they do not account for the association between the naturalistic and the moralistic attitudes. Hunters and trappers actually score lower on the moralistic scale than any other animal activity group apart from livestock producers. Hunters, trappers, and anglers also score below the general population on the humanistic scale, as do livestock producers and birdwatchers.[19]

So even though concern and affection for animals are often devalued in our society, and even though certain animal use groups have an interest in promoting an instrumental view of animals' value, affection for animals and concern about their abuse by humans are still more common attitudes in this society than the desire to dominate or exploit animals. This, together with the correlation between animal farming and the utilitarian and dominionistic attitudes mentioned above, support my contention that contrary to any characterization of human concern for nonhuman animals as unnatural, sympathetic responsiveness toward animals is a common human tendency that may nonetheless be lost, restricted, or overridden in special circumstances.

The circumstance most relevant to the curtailment of our attachments to animals is a commitment to exploitation. We are able to cut off our feelings for others when we feel that their domination, abuse, or exploitation is necessary. This moral and psychological flexibility is one of our natural capacities. But to determine our natural relations with nonhumans, we also need to know how we respond to them when we do not believe that their exploitation is necessary. In these circumstances our dispositions are toward caring and protection.

ANIMAL RESCUE

Our responsiveness to whales is relevant here, because industrialized North America no longer maintains an industry devoted to their exploitation. Whales are one group of animals that we believe we do not need to hurt. The attitude now is one of great concern and mobilization for whales when they are threatened. For instance, in 1988 three California gray whales became trapped off the coast of Point Barrow, Alaska. The ice holes through which the whales were surfacing to breathe were in the process of freezing over, which would have resulted in the whales drowning. A rescue attempt was mounted, ultimately costing $5.8 million and directly involving all the following: local subsistence whalers, professional biologists, environmental activists, 150 journalists, the oil industry, the U.S. National Guard, and the U.S. and Soviet federal governments.[20] If we ask why the rescue was pursued at such great lengths, a cynical answer in terms of the self-interest of the participants would be to some extent correct. But to leave it at that would give only a superficial and distorted understanding of the final cause of the rescue. The participation of these groups in the whales' rescue served their interests only by virtue of a deep and widespread concern for the whales' well-being among people generally. The media cannot play to emotions people do not have: Whale rescues boost ratings because people care about whales, especially whales who have become individualized through their special circumstances.

Our interest in rescuing whales was behind the financial success of the hit movie *Free Willy*. This film, which grossed over $323 million, tells the story of a young boy rescuing a whale from a seaquarium owner who planned to kill him for the insurance money. The real-life whale who played Willy in the film, Keiko, was captured as a calf near Iceland by a commercial hunter. After several years in a Canadian sea park, Keiko was sold to a seaquarium in Mexico City, where he was confined in an oval pool measuring ninety feet by forty-three feet by twenty feet (Keiko himself is twenty-one feet long). Like many captive whales, Keiko's confinement was causing him to die a slow death. The pool was small, too warm, and its filtration system could not handle the mass of excrement a whale releases. He was underweight, lethargic, and suffering from a skin disease. Blood seeped from ragged abrasions on his chin. A marine mammal scientist who examined him determined that he could die any day.[21]

The irony of the star of a motion picture about freeing whales languishing in captivity was evident. Magazines such as *Life* and *People* published numerous stories about Keiko's plight. The publicity ultimately led to the formation of the Free Willy Keiko Foundation, funded by grade school bake sales and the donations of corporations and individual millionaires. The foundation built Keiko a seven-million-dollar facility in Oregon, to which he was airlifted in 1996 and there nursed back to health. But the ultimate goal was to set Keiko free in his home waters off of Iceland. In 1998 Keiko was airlifted once again, this time to a one-million-dollar floating sea pen constructed in the harbor of Heimaey, Iceland. Keiko was taught how to catch live fish and gradually weaned from his dependence on humans. In the summer of

2002 he was released from his netted pen. Staff monitored his progress as he swam one thousand miles across the North Atlantic to the coast of Norway, arriving in excellent physical condition after having fed himself for close to sixty days. On December 12, 2003, Keiko died of acute pneumonia while in the company of staff who had been caring for him in the Taknes fjord of Norway.[22] The entire cost to free him exceeded twelve million dollars.[23]

Stories of whale rescue show the lengths we will go to help animals when we are not already committed to their exploitation. Although Americans hardly remember the commercial exploitation of whales, in Iceland commercial whaling continued until it was internationally banned in 1986. Thus the people of Heimaey had a mixed reaction to Keiko's arrival. The Icelandic children, who have never seen whales killed for subsistence or profit, welcomed Keiko with banners and shouts of "Velkominn, Keiko!" while the adults who grew up with whaling were less enthralled, saying of the expensive rescue, "It's too much."[24]

KEEPING PETS

We tend to assist wild animals who are injured or orphaned. Sometimes we return these animals to the wild, sometimes we do not. If we keep them long enough we call them our pets. Responding to the depth of people's interests in animals, multi-billion-dollar industries have developed around the breeding, sale, and maintenance of pet animals. The practice of pet keeping, in its cross-cultural prevalence and its frequently avid pursuit, demonstrates the strength and depth of human interest in and affection for nonhuman animals.

As noted above, two out of three Americans surveyed by Kellert claim at some time to have had a pet as dear to them as a person. At any given time, about half of all Americans have pets, and more than 84 percent have had a pet at some point in their lives.[25] The proportion of pet owners in Europe is the same, about one-half.[26] The prevalence of pet keeping is replicated transnationally: One recent study reports 68 percent of Costa Rican households and 64 percent of Australian households having at least one pet.[27] The variety of species kept as pets is extensive. Dogs and cats are most common in rich countries, but all of the following are also kept as pets in substantial numbers: horses; various species of birds, fish, amphibians, and reptiles; insects; and many small mammals, such as rabbits, gerbils, hamsters, mice, rats, and raccoons.[28] In Costa Rica, in addition to the many domesticated species kept as pets, numerous households also keep wild animals such as parrots, fish, turtles, tortoises, iguanas, agouti, deer, toucans, spider monkeys, howler monkeys, squirrels, and various spiders and insects.[29]

Many theories of pet keeping devalue the practice in some way. This is unsurprising given the tension between the merciless exploitation of farm and laboratory animals on the one hand and the tremendous efforts exerted to nurture and protect pet animals on the other hand. Thus pets are understood as gratuitous status symbols by one writer and as outlets for the desire to dominate nature by another.[30] Other theories, while less directly condemnatory of pet keeping, still negate or minimize the role of affection for pet animals. One psychoanalytic account, for example, considers attitudes toward animals to "stem from an unconscious displacement from a human object toward whom they cannot be expressed." The author claims that though many pet owners "may become dimly or even clearly aware of the erotic element involved" in their relations with their animal companions, few "become aware except through psychoanalysis of the fact that the animal represents a sister, mother, father, or other relative."[31] Here animals are considered place-holders for humans—they are never significant enough in human life to generate responsiveness on their own terms. And many theorists attempt to reveal hidden economic or ecological benefits of keeping members of a certain species as pets, as if this is necessarily a better explanation for the practice than the pet keepers' own professed affection for their companion animals.[32]

It is certainly true that pets are sometimes kept as status symbols, or to be dominated, or for some economic benefit. But no explanation that omits human affection for animals can completely account for the practice. In fact, the evidence suggests that affection and companionship are by far the most important elements motivating pet keeping in our society.

Victoria Voith describes a number of cases in which people put up with extreme inconvenience rather than give up a pet.[33] One man's dog had chewed up the house, costing him three thousand dollars. Conflicts with a neighbor over their dog led one family to move rather than part with their pet. In another case, a woman's dog would occasionally bite her on the back or arm while she slept. In one family, a pet Doberman had bitten the two-year-old child on the face. For various reasons, there was no way to rule out the possibility of this happening again in uncontrolled circumstances. The family tried unsuccessfully to find another home for the dog, and finally, rather than kill the Doberman, they took the burdensome precaution of supervising the dog and child whenever they were together.

When asked why they kept these animals, the owners responded that they loved the dog, that the dog was part of the family, that they were attached to the dog, and so on. Given the costs and risks involved in keeping their pets, no other explanation seems tenable. Voith concludes that the many people who state that they feel toward their pet as though he or she were their child should be taken at their word: Just as parents generally do not "euthanize" inconvenient children, many people keep their pets long after they have in some obvious sense become a liability.

Surveys of pet owners consistently reveal the centrality of feelings of companionship and affection to the human/pet relationship. The words people most frequently use to describe relations with their pets are "love," "affection," "companionship," "trust," "loyalty," "need," and "care."[34] In one survey pet owners ranked companionship, love and affection, and pleasure, respectively, as the top three "advantages" of owning a pet,[35] and in another study, 87 percent of respondents considered their pet a member of their family and 96 percent of those who had ever had a pet who died or was permanently lost described the loss as a time of sadness, grieving, and crying.[36]

The interactions between humans and their pets are revealing. Aaron Katcher observes that

> people behave toward pet animals with some of the social acts that are usually reserved for fellow humans with whom they have a close and friendly relationship. To explore the nature of this close relationship, we looked at people touching and talking to animals. We observed that the gestures used to touch animals are ones which would be signs of intimacy if directed toward other human beings. Interestingly, we found that men use gestures of intimacy with animals with the same frequency as women, . . . whereas studies of touching between adults in the United States indicate that in public situations women almost always use more intimate touches than men.[37]

Sharon Smith's study of interactions between humans and their pet dogs affirms our commonsense understanding of the attachment:

> Despite belonging to different evolutionary orders, these dogs and people cooperated in coordinating their interactions so that the interaction continued at least momentarily. They responded to each other behaviorally in a variety of ways. Yet it appeared that at any given moment their behavior was not random. They appeared to interact for the purpose of interacting; no material outcomes were apparent, such as access to a limited resource like food. In this way the interactions of these people and their dogs resembled those of members of the same species.[38]

The practice of keeping animals as companions is by no means unique to modern Western culture but is extremely common across cultures. As is the case here, pet keeping in other cultures generally involves nurturance and protection based on emotional attachment.

The antiquity of the human-companion animal bond is indicated in the following passage:

> In 1978, at a late Palaeolithic site in northern Israel, a unique human burial was discovered. The tomb contained two skeletons: that of an elderly human of unknown sex, and, next to it, the remains of a five-month-old domestic dog. The two had been buried together roughly 12,000 years ago. The most striking thing about these remains was the fact that whoever presided over the original burial had carefully arranged the dead person's left hand so that it rested, in a timeless and eloquent gesture of attachment, on the puppy's shoulder.[39]

Historical research indicates that the practice of keeping dogs as pets is not a modern innovation but "a constant component in the annals of Western civilization."[40]

James Serpell surveys the pet-keeping practices of non-Western cultures in his book *In the Company of Animals*. Three features of this survey stand out: the large number of non-Western cultures, in many different geographical regions, that have avidly pursued pet keeping, the tremendous number of different species humans have nurtured and protected, and the great depth of attachment shown by these people for their companion animals.

Pet keeping is widespread among the indigenous peoples of North and South America. Serpell states that "for the Indians of South America animal taming and pet-keeping were practically minor industries."[41] Europeans exploring the New World found each of the following being tamed, nurtured, and protected by natives: raccoons, moose, bisons, wolves, bears, monkeys, opossum, labba, acouri, deer, pigs, dogs, cats, sloths, rodents, tapir, peccaries, ocelots, margays, and, in one case, a jaguar. Native South Americans also make pets of an enormous variety of large and small birds. And Serpell cites cases of pet keeping among the following peoples outside the Western Hemisphere: Australian aborigines, stone-age Andaman Islanders, Semang Negritos of Malaysia, the Puana Dyaks of Borneo, and native Fijians, Samoans, and Hawaiians.

Serpell cites many reports of the strong attachments between tribal people and their animal companions:

> Sir John Richardson ... wrote that "the red races are fond of pets and treat them kindly; and in purchasing them there is always the unwillingness of the women and children to overcome, rather than any dispute about price."
>
> A later visitor also mentions that the inhabitants of St Domingo (Jamaica) were so fond of their little dogs that they carried them on their shoulders wherever they went and "nourished them in their bosoms."

"I told the Indians that they could train their cormorants to bring them fish if they fastened rings round their necks. In conception, rather than in execution, this project amused them very much; it is clear that they thought of the birds always as guests, never as servants." Fleming went on to say that the Indians "were very fond of all these creatures, and treated them well."

In general, the Barasana [Indians of eastern Colombia] look after their pets extremely well. Women will suckle puppies and hand feed other young mammals, even masticating plant foods such as manioc and banana for their tame parrots and macaws. One individual was also observed to spend hours catching small fish to feed a pet kingfisher. . . . According to Stephen Hugh-Jones who has studied the Barasana for several years, pet-keeping is not motivated by economic or practical considerations. These people simply enjoy the business of looking after and nurturing their pets. The animals are a continual source of discussion and entertainment, and are regarded as an integral part of the community.

According to the anthropologist Luomala, affection for selected pets was part of a marked Polynesian trait, "men, women and children, of all social ranks, fondled, pampered and talked to their pets, named them, and grieved when death or other circumstances separated them."[42]

Compare this citation by Simoons and Baldwin:

Ehrenreich and Cook . . . emphasized the [Brazilian] Indians' delight with animals, their sense of oneness and equality with the animal world, their amazing skills at taming wild, often shy creatures, and their warm treatment of animals as members of the family, with captive wild mammals frequently being breast-fed by humans or, occasionally, by domestic dogs. This fond treatment was based, both writers insist, not on concern with the animals' economic products, but simply on a desire to have animals nearby for pleasure and entertainment.[43]

I conclude that pet keeping in non-Western tribal cultures differs little from that of modern Western civilization. In both cases the practice is widespread and characterized by strong affection for pets, great efforts to keep pets, and views of pets as family and community members.

MORAL QUALMS

We are inclined to be affectionate with animals. When we are confronted with animals that are hurt, our tendency is to want to help them. This leads to conflict and stress when we also feel committed to one or more of the institutions of animal exploitation, such as farming, vivisection, or hunting.

Our reactions to these institutions are not neutral. I have shown videotapes of animal slaughter to my environmental ethics classes for years, and the students consistently react with shock and horror. Periodically students will tell me that watching those videotapes was one of the most moving and memorable experiences of their college life. They want to do something about the violence, something to stop it or at least to halt their complicity in the abuse. This is evident in the comments I frequently receive about a change in their eating habits, usually something along the lines of "I didn't eat meat for three weeks after I saw that videotape."

The animal liberationist reaction to this distress is to seek the abolition of the institutions that inflict the abuse. Those who cannot bring themselves to countenance abolition find ways to live with the violence. A common strategy is to remove it from our consciousness as much as possible. We see this approach especially in the ways that adults talk to children about animals. Adults typically avoid revealing to children how animals are hurt by institutions such as animal farming.

Children's books consistently withhold the information that farm animals are protected so that they may later be sold to slaughter, and parents and teachers cooperate in this deception. Children are kept in ignorance of the source of the meat they are fed. Several years ago I accompanied my son's kindergarten class on a field trip to Aullwood Audubon Center and Farm, a part nature preserve, part working farm set up to give educational programs to children. A young woman giving the presentation to our class explained that they kept goats, sheep, pigs, chickens, rabbits, and cows at the farm. She asked the class, "Why do we keep these animals here?" Some of the children answered, "Because we like them?" This wasn't the answer the instructor was looking for, so she repeated the question. Other children answered, "To take care of them?" The instructor said, "No" and repeated the question yet again. One child said, "Because they are our friends?" At this point the instructor gave up asking and just told us: "We keep them here because we eat them." It was remarkable to me that out of a class of thirty, not one child had volunteered this answer. Most of them had been eating meat for years yet they had never been told its source.

Or perhaps they had been told but the information had not sunk in. The connection is difficult to accept given the conflicting images: animals as cherished friends, animals killed and chopped up for their flesh. My mother's sister told me that when she was first told where meat comes from, she refused to believe it. As adults we delay telling young children about this reality. We may say to ourselves that they cannot understand or that we should not tell them something that might disturb them at such a young age. For example, an animal rights group tried to buy time to show an advertisement about chicken farming prior to screenings of the feature film *Chicken Run*, a movie in which anthropomorphized farm animals attempt to escape before being slaughtered. The advertisement was rejected on the grounds that scenes depicting chickens stuffed into cages with no room to move "will cause unacceptable distress to young children."[44] This indicates adult sensibilities as much as it reflects what children can actually handle. When adults find bloodshed disturbing, we presume that children will as well, though this is not always the case. Once, when my sons and I were walking along the bank of the Miami River in Dayton, Ohio, we watched as a man pulled a large fish out of the water onto the dock. He took the fish off the hook and put him on his string, pushing a thick pin with a line attached through the fish's mouth and out through his gill. Red blood gushed from the fish. Even though I had seen this process before, the blood nauseated me and I wanted to move on. My children were not so repulsed; they were fascinated and wanted to stay and continue watching.

The animal stories told to children reflect our values as adults. We portray animals as protected friends because that is the way we prefer to see them. On the rare occasions when slaughter is revealed in a children's story, it is most often portrayed as a dire threat from which the animal is saved. For instance, in *Charlotte's Web* the pig is rescued from slaughter by an enterprising spider, and in the movie *Babe* the title character escapes slaughter by virtue of his remarkable herding abilities. This is the world that we would prefer, one in which no animal actually gets slaughtered, so this is the artificial world we construct in the stories we tell children.[45]

Bambi is one of the few children's films about man's predation in which an animal protagonist is not saved, Bambi's mother being killed off-screen by a hunter. Hunters despise this film because they presume it is responsible for a large measure of antihunting sentiment.[46] They know the emotional impact of thinking about hunting from the point of view of the prey. Disney's *Bambi* is exceptional; we generally refrain from telling such stories so we do not have to think about how we harm animals. When finally told the truth about animal exploitation, young people usually accept it quietly enough, but they do sometimes rebel, thus creating a nuisance for the parent who hunts or eats meat: "My son's first moral action . . . occurred at age four. At that time, he joined the pacifist and vegetarian movement, and refused to eat meat, because as he said, 'it's bad to kill animals.' In spite of lengthy Hawk argumentation by his parents about the difference between justified and unjustified killing, he remained a vegetarian for six months."[47] It is easier to avoid such conflicts by not raising the issue of how we get meat from animals.

Silence is not an option available to farmers, who must eventually tell their children where the animals go when they are trucked away. The emotional conflict is more serious for farmers than for consumers of meat since farmers actually feed and protect the individual animals that are ultimately to be slaughtered. On smaller family farms people still have face-to-face contact with their stock. Coming to know the distinctive individuality of the animals, emotional attachments arise that militate against the violent culmination of the husbandry. Farmers are thus very aware of the need to help their children learn to curtail potentially disruptive sympathies. One of the ways they do this is by giving strong support and encouragement to children as they first experience the process of selling into slaughter an animal they have personally tended.

I witnessed an example of this process when a local fairground was hosting the annual county fair. One of the fair activities was a 4–H auction, a public auction at which farmers' children sell a farm animal they have personally tended. The initiates take turns parading their goat, pig, or steer in front of an audience while an emcee makes encouraging comments over the loudspeaker system. When a boy enters the ring, the announcer comments appreciatively on the appearance and behavior of his animal, and when a girl enters, the announcer comments appreciatively on the appearance and behavior of the girl and of her animal. The weight of the animal is announced, and the audience bids on how much they are willing to pay for the animal per pound. The audience is filled with farmers who understand that this is a training exercise for the youth; they do not buy the animals to make a profit. Once they have made a purchase they immediately resell the animal at market price to the butcher parked outside the arena. The market price is often below the purchase price, but the farmers good-naturedly accept this small loss as part of the cost of encouraging the young farmers-to-be.

Before the auction the animals are kept in stalls where they can be examined by judges and the public. This is also a chance to meet and talk with the novice farmers. The year that I went to the 4–H auction, a local animal rights group of which I was a member was planning to purchase an animal. Rather than sell the animal to slaughter, as is the norm, the group had arranged to place the animal in a nearby sanctuary. News of this plan circulated among the 4–H members, and I noticed a number of them expressing enthusiasm at the idea of their animal being saved from slaughter in this way. One of the young farmers posted a handmade sign on the gate, extolling the animal's virtues and asking, "Wouldn't you love to have her as a pet?"

Our group was successful in purchasing a goat. The local media was bemused at the idea of animal liberationists buying a farm animal, and they filmed as the goat was led away by activists. They also interviewed the girl who had reared this goat. As her dad glowered in the background, she explained that she was glad her animal had been the one purchased by the activists because she liked the thought of him living at a sanctuary rather than being sold to the butcher. Her father's evident anger indicated to me that the purpose of the event, teaching the child to suppress such sympathetic responsiveness, had in this case been thwarted.

Exploiting animals tends to make us feel uncomfortable, even guilty. James Serpell has described the almost universal presence, in cultures that hunt or slaughter animals, of mechanisms for mediating the guilt that such exploitation engenders.[48] Mechanisms that soothe the consciences of those who harm animals take many forms. Many African tribes perform elaborate cleansing and purification ceremonies after killing an animal; others apologize to the slain. The Nuer people of the Sudan justify their consumption of cattle blood by claiming that periodic bleeding is beneficial to the animals' health, while the Ainu of Japan also claim to benefit the bears they eat, by maintaining that bears want to return to the spirit realm from which they came.[49] Western civilization has its own sacred and secular expiatory myths, such as the biblical tale of divinely granted dominion over animals and the scientific denial of animal subjectivity.

All these rituals and myths serve to reduce the guilt feelings of those who harm animals. The general occurrence of guilt-mediating mechanisms around systems of animal exploitation contradicts any notion that humans are by nature indifferent toward animal welfare. People are generally inclined *against* harming animals. If they weren't, there would be no need for social mechanisms that make killing somewhat more bearable; the exploitation of animals would be as straightforward as, say, drinking water or breathing air.[50]

In his study of the slaughter industry, William Thompson notes that "slaughtering and butchering cattle is generally viewed as an undesirable and repugnant job."[51] People who are not inured to the sight tend to find slaughter repulsive. One study on the psychology of slaughter contains quotes from college students who worked on a farm as part of their curriculum. A nineteen-year-old woman wrote:

The first time I went into the slaughter room I had just haltered and pulled a steer into the waiting line. I could tell that the steer sensed what was going to happen to him. He was doing anything to get away. Then when I walked to the slaughter room I was amazed at the amount of blood. It was an awful feeling to look at that steer with its eyes open and his feet pointing up, so I had to look at the ceiling. Mr. —— told me to cut off the head with a saw. I couldn't do it so I left. I guess slaughtering affects me more than the usual person because I raised calves for 4–H at home and became quite attached to them—but I *don't* butcher them.[52]

A nineteen-year-old man wrote, "It's pretty gross. I don't like having the dry heaves all day. Plus, I feel really bad for the cow. It's bad seeing a big animal turned into hamburger."[53]

Those whose livelihood involves harming animals must find ways to manage their feelings, since their immediate reaction to imposing injury or death is almost always negative. Arnold Arluke has documented the prevalence of guilt feelings among those who experiment on animals. In an article published in the trade journal *Lab Animal,* Arluke reported that of the 130 vivisectors he interviewed, about 10 percent immediately admitted to experiencing guilt feelings regarding their work, but after being given ample space to examine their feelings, fully 90 percent expressed what most people would consider "guilty" feelings.[54] One vivisector notes that in his conversations with other researchers, "many had admitted being upset and even had nightmares relating to their work."[55]

A study of the advertisements placed by breeders who supply vivisectors found that the animals are often portrayed as "team-players" who facilitate the researchers' work in much the same way as colleagues or other employees.[56] Advertisement copy describes the animals as research collaborators (mice are said to be "stalking cancer," a guinea pig is called the "unsung hero of bronchial research"), and animals are posed so as to appear to like laboratory equipment such as cages and jars of chemicals. Sexist stereotypes are used to portray compliant animals: "Female animals are shown as subordinate and desiring to please. 'Real anxious to please you' reads the text of an ad that has a drawing of a pregnant hamster in a maternity dress."[57]

In vivisection as well as in each of the other animal exploitation industries we see a definite construction of the animals as willing victims.[58] The prevalence of such images indicates that we are not comfortable oppressing animals. The day after the 1990 March on Washington for the Animals, I heard a National Public Radio reporter discuss a slaughterhouse tour she had taken in order to determine for herself whether the animal liberationist call for vegetarianism had any merit. She declared that she could see in the terrified animals' eyes that they would willingly go to slaughter if they understood the human purpose being served. This fantasy of animals longing to end up dead on our plates is a perennial trope of industry advertisements, including examples such as the long-running Charlie the Tuna campaign (in which the fish repeatedly tries to get hooked), a Domino's Pizza billboard displaying winged bison stampeding toward the viewer over the caption "Buffalo Wings—They Come When You Call," and a recent Chipotle's print ad with a picture of their chicken burrito placed under a banner reading, "For Chickens, It's Like Graduating from Harvard."[59]

Conclusion

It is difficult for humans to exploit animals; but this is not the same as saying it is unnatural. We are by nature capable of exploiting other animals, both technologically—we are able to build tools that allow us to dominate other species—and, more important, emotionally. We have the ability to become emotionally calloused and superficially unmoved by the injuries we impose. So I would not take the position that animal exploitation is contrary to all aspects of our nature. The very fact, however, that the exploitation of animals requires emotional work on our part, that we must *become* detached, shows that for humans the species boundary is permeable. There remains a side of us that is drawn to the protection of nonhuman animals. We rescue wild animals reflexively; we take animals into our homes and care for them as family members. We recoil at the sight of any exploitation to which we are not already inured. We construct fables to salve our consciences against the pain and guilt of causing animals to suffer. Any suggestion that animal liberation represents a misplacement of our affectionate energies must ignore, dismiss, or devalue all of these deep and recurring elements of our human nature. So while it may be an overstatement to say that men's exploitation of animals is unnatural, it is as much or more of an overstatement to say that animal liberation is unnatural.

Just as theistic and rationalistic arguments turn out, upon examination, to be question-begging attempts to excuse men's exploitation of animals, so does any simplistic reference to species membership. Humans in general have too great a tendency to empathize with members of other species to support a characterization of animal liberation as aberrant. Animal liberation efforts are a normal part of human life.

It is possible, nonetheless, to acknowledge and accept our kinship with other species and yet still support men's exploitation of animals—even without reverting to questionable claims of human superiority or divine permission. One can insist that while one part of us may militate against harming other creatures, another part of men's being is predatory by nature. The view that men have a naturally predatory side, and that this side of us should be given precedence over any conflicting tendencies in ourselves or others, is the subject of the next chapter.

2

Men's Predation and the Natural Order

Man is a predator whose natural instinct is to
kill with a weapon.

—Robert Ardrey, *African Genesis*

References to human superiority and to species solidarity distance us from the rest of nature. Rationalistic human superiority arguments claim that we are above all other species, that we have a group of traits making us unique among animals. Allusions to a natural boundary between species are attempts to restrict our affections and sympathies to the human species alone, so that we become emotionally detached from the rest of nature. By contrast, the argument considered in this chapter aims to place us within nature. According to the argument from natural predation, we are one animal species among many, no better, no worse, and we should not try to separate ourselves from the other species. Animals subsist by exploiting members of other species, so as part of nature we should do the same. To cease exploiting animals is to alienate ourselves from the natural order.

The most famous example of this argument is found in Benjamin Franklin's autobiography:

> In my first voyage from Boston to Philadelphia, being becalmed off Block Island, our crew employed themselves catching cod and hauled up a great number. Till then I had stuck to my resolution to eat nothing that had had life; and on this occasion I considered, according to my Master Tryon, the taking of every fish as a kind of unprovoked murder, since none of them had or ever could do us any injury that might justify this massacre. All this seemed very reasonable. But I had formerly been a great lover of fish, and when this came hot out of the frying pan, it smelled admirably well. I balanced some time between principle and inclination till I recollected that when the fish were

opened, I saw smaller fish taken out of their stomachs. "Then," thought I, "if you eat one another, I don't see why we mayn't eat you." So I dined upon cod very heartily and have since continued to eat as other people, returning only now and then occasionally to a vegetable diet. So convenient a thing it is to be a *reasonable creature*, since it enables one to find or make a reason for everything one has a mind to do.[1]

In his ironic final sentence Franklin simultaneously deflates the rationalistic human superiority argument and the very argument from natural predation he just presented. Evidently he was aware of the self-serving quality of the argument from natural predation, but the argument remains common enough to be worth rebutting. It is frequently articulated in hunting literature. The whole world, hunters write, is essentially paradoxical, with good and evil inextricably tied to each other, but at least they, unlike nonhunters and antihunters, are honest enough to admit it and to consciously engage themselves in the paradox of nature. Violence is the way of the world, they claim, so virtue comes not from nonviolence but from acknowledgment of this basic truth. Hunters are emphatic in describing the inescapable violence of nature and life: "Life is a terrible conflict, a grandiose and atrocious confluence"; "We are murderers and cannot live without murdering. The whole of nature is based on murder"; "There is not a man, woman, or child alive who has not caused a blood trail. . . . Life lives off of life"; "A few moments candid contemplation tell you that . . . you are up to your elbows in blood"; and so on.[2] In a world based on violence, advocacy of nonviolence is not virtuous or compassionate, it is hypocrisy rooted in self-deception or blind ignorance, as José Ortega y Gasset states most strongly: "We fall, therefore, [in replacing hunting with wildlife photography] into a new immorality, into the worst of all, which is a matter of not knowing those very conditions without which things cannot be."[3] While nonhunters buy processed meat wrapped in cellophane, protected from any painful awareness of the bloodshed intrinsic to this process, hunters have advanced to a higher stage of consciousness, confronting the truth.[4] This truth is twofold—life depends on bloodshed, and, fortunately, men have a dark side capable of shedding the requisite blood:

> No culture has yet solved the dilemma each has faced with the growth of a conscious mind: how to live a moral and compassionate existence when one is fully aware of the blood, the horror inherent in all life, when one finds darkness not only in one's own culture but within oneself. If there is a stage at which an individual life becomes truly adult, it must be when one grasps the irony in its unfolding and accepts responsibility for a life lived in the midst of such paradox. One must live in the middle of contradiction because if all contradiction were eliminated at once life would collapse.[5]

The final stage of spiritual and ethical growth is not just to acknowledge and accept the blood and horror "inherent in all life" but to enjoy it, as hunting apologist James Swan makes clear: "Hunters do not prefer death to life; rather, they simply seek to participate in the reality of life and embrace it, deriving joy from accepting life as it is."[6]

Hunters have transcended compassion, elevating acknowledgment of the "truth" of inescapable violence to the highest virtue. Ironically, this entire position is based on half-truths and distortions. Swan concludes his book-long defense of hunting by citing Joseph Campbell's "wise" observation that "the trouble with society today is that people have forgotten the basic law of life that 'flesh eats flesh.'"[7] But "flesh eats flesh" is not the basic law of life—most animals are vegetarian. Only about 20 percent of species are carnivorous. Moreover, the preponderance of vegetarian animals is not some anomaly but an essential part of the natural order. The energy essential for living processes ultimately comes from the sun, but while plants can photosynthesize, animals cannot make such direct use of the sun's energy. They make use of the sun's energy through plants, either directly by eating them or indirectly by eating animals who themselves consume vegetation. At each stage of consumption there is some loss of energy. Thus the earth can support more plants than it can support animals who live off of plants, and it can support more herbivorous animals than carnivorous animals. In this sense photosynthesis is more basic than herbivory, while herbivory is more basic than carnivory.

I am not stating that herbivory is more *natural* than carnivory. Both are parts of the natural world at this time. I am stating, contra the proponents of the argument from nature, that exploitation is by no means the only natural relation between species. Statements such as Ortega's "Every animal is in a relationship of superiority or inferiority with regard to every other"[8] can only be based on a self-servingly selective observation of nature, one that blocks awareness of the myriad ways species have adapted through symbiotic mutual cooperation rather than exploitation, not to mention the innumerable instances of mutual indifference, species that neither benefit nor harm one another.

So the question is not whether we should separate ourselves from the rest of nature by not exploiting other species, but whether in striving to be natural we should emulate the exploitative parts of nature or the symbiotic parts. In order to justify his inclination to consume fish, Franklin chooses to identify with the carnivorous fish rather than with those the carnivore preys upon. This is a question-begging choice since both life-forms are equally natural.

We do not identify with nature in general; that would be impossible since there is too much diversity. There are many ways of living that are natural for other species but not for us. Some insect species, for instance, consume their partners after mating. We do not copy this behavior, notwithstanding the fact that it is natural. We do have a choice. All the institutions of animal exploitation that are at issue are institutions we could live without. We do not need hunting, animal farming, or vivisection to live; human life would not cease if these practices were abolished. The strongest form of an argument from nature would be the idea that the exploitation of animals by people is so natural that we really have no control over its occurrence. In that sense it would be beyond moral and political evaluation. But since we do have real possibilities for choosing whether or not to continue these practices, such an argument is not applicable.

The Value of Natural Predation

Another attempted use of nature to justify men's exploitation of animals takes the form of an argument to absurdity:

1. We should protect animals from human exploitation.
2. But then we should also protect them from exploitation by other species.
3. This implies that we should protect animals from natural predators.
4. Since this is absurd, the initial premise enjoining us to protect animals from human exploitation must be mistaken.

This reductio ad absurdum is a frequent rebuttal of animal liberationism. It is employed especially often in defense of sport hunting, as in this argument from Michael Leahy's book *Against Liberation:* "If the abolitionists are so quick to condemn the infliction of a certain amount of necessary pain in the otherwise justifiable cause of field sports why should they not regard life in the wild, with its attendant horrors, as a state to be remedied rather than one to be regarded with mixed feelings of resignation and approval?"[9] The dilemma posed to antihunters is to come out for policing the wild (thus revealing the absurdity of animal liberation) or against such a policy (thus indicating a hypocritical inconsistency).

In responding to this dilemma, animal rights philosophers typically reject general programs to halt natural predation, often agreeing that this would be an absurd policy. But the reductio's conclusion that this justifies sport hunting is avoided by drawing some relevant distinction between human and nonhuman predation. Sometimes the distinction focuses on the different natures of human versus nonhuman hunters, as in "Humans have a choice, but natural predators don't." Tom Regan argued that the goal of wildlife management should be to protect wild animals against those who would violate their rights, but since only humans are moral agents, only humans can violate rights and thus wildlife management policy need only be concerned with stopping predation by humans.[10]

Regan's response is unsatisfactory to many liberationists, relying as it does on such a complete focus on the moral status of the hunter at the exclusion of the prey's experiences (note that the agony of being torn apart is not lessened by the predator's lack of moral agency). Tyler Cowen reveals the essential arbitrariness of Regan's position, noting that "stopping a human killer does not rest on whether or not we consider the killer to be a 'moral agent,' mentally retarded, totally insane, or a vampire."[11] If we protect humans from animal and human killers who are not moral agents, why should we not protect nonhuman animals from such threats?

Other differences between human and nonhuman hunting are suggested. Stephen Clark wrote that "animal suffering is an evil, but not all such evils can be eliminated without introducing worse ones," while Moriarty and Woods doubt whether "removing predators would result in a net decrease in pain in the wild."[12] The unstated premise is that unlike natural predation, human predation can be stopped without introducing worse evils or increasing pain overall.

Stephen Sapontzis's response to the reductio is the most detailed and thorough on record. He concludes that when we cannot stop natural predation without occasioning even more suffering than we prevent, there is no obligation to stop natural predation. On the other hand, when human intervention against natural predation would reduce overall suffering, we should intervene, and there is nothing absurd about such a policy.[13] In neither case is there an inconsistency or absurdity in animal liberation philosophy.

Sapontzis's position might entail a great deal of intervention. Tyler Cowen shares Sapontzis's view that animal welfare requires us to interfere with nature when the costs are low. He argues that "we should count negative impacts on carnivores as positive features" of human policies, concluding that we should invest fewer resources in saving endangered carnivores, the strictures against killing carnivores should be weakened or removed, and in taking animals from the wild for laboratory experimentation we should seek to trap carnivores.[14] Unlike Sapontzis and Cowen, most philosophers of animal rights or animal welfare reject interfering with natural predators in principle and support such interventions only in exceptional cases, if ever.[15]

LOVING NATURE

Responses by animal liberationists to the reductio have not ended the debate between defenders and opponents of men's hunting. The terms of the debate have simply shifted, moving from the practical issue of what sort of interventionist policy is required by animal liberation to the ideological issue of whether animal liberation entails an unacceptably negative evaluation of natural predation. The issue is attitude, not policy.

This shift was occasioned by Ned Hettinger's 1994 article on valuing predation. "By arguing that humans should not join other predators and must not kill animals for basic needs," Hettinger wrote, "animal activists risk being committed to the view that all carnivorous predation is intrinsically evil. On this view, a world without predation would be a better world, other things being equal. This view is one that no true lover of the wild can support, although animal activists frequently do endorse it."[16]

From the standpoint of defending men's hunting, it makes sense to shift the focus away from the interventionist implications of animal liberation toward whether antihunters can truly "love the wild," that is, love natural predation. The liberationist rejection of intervention against natural predation is based on the belief that such a campaign would be counterproductive, the implication being that if we could intervene efficiently we should do so because natural predation is inherently a bad thing. This tacit condemnation of natural predation is no concession to the defenders of men's blood sports. Prohunting theorists must insist that natural predation is a *good* thing in order to justify men's predation on the grounds that it is similar to natural predation. Hettinger recognizes the critical significance of the evaluation of natural predation in the debate over men's hunting: "If what results from animal predation is judged to be good, then the results of human predation on animals must also be judged to be good."[17] Thus Hettinger poses the following dilemma to animal activists: "Either they must argue that animal predation is evil (and show that their arguments do not involve a hatred of nature) or demonstrate that there is some way to value animal predation as a good while consistently and plausibly condemning human predation."[18] This challenge carries weight with antihunters, who like to think of themselves as nature lovers rather than nature haters.

Taking up Hettinger's challenge in their 1997 article on hunting and predation, Paul Moriarty and Mark Woods reject men's hunting on the ground that there are ways of preserving human life that cause less harm than the killing and eating of animals (namely, the consumption of plants). In response to Hettinger, they definitively state that though they oppose men's hunting, they value natural predation: "The removal of predators would mean the removal of something (predation) which we value as a natural process. Even if there were some imaginable case in which the removal of predators would result in the long-term reduction of pain and suffering of sentient beings, we would not see this possibility as sufficient grounds to justify their removal."[19] In Hettinger's sense they would qualify as nature lovers because they do not view animal predation as an evil. This leaves the burden on Moriarty and Woods to explain the relevant difference between human and nonhuman predation. This they do by arguing that, unlike nonhuman predation, men's hunting is not a natural activity.

Moriarty and Woods affirm the value of natural predation while distinguishing it from human hunting. In a recent article, Jennifer Everett responds differently to Hettinger's challenge. Everett acknowledges that animal advocates would tend to find the idea of animals hurting and killing one another "disturbing." But, she argues, this need not imply that animal advocates are hateful of nature: "An animal welfarist can consistently hold that suffering (taken in itself) is not valuable, but that nature, which contains suffering, is valuable, because the values in nature (taken as a whole) outweigh or overshadow the disvalues. Nature, then, let us say is good. It is very good; indeed, it is truly, magnificently, splendidly good."[20] One can value the whole without valuing all of its parts.

Everett deplores the suffering caused by natural predation while acknowledging the value of its role in evolution. Unlike Moriarty and Woods's absolute valorization of natural predation, Everett suggests a merely instrumental, and therefore conditional, affirmation, noting that "if, without predation, ... values would be lost to our world, then predation adds to the value of our world rather than diminishes it."[21]

THE DISVALUE OF NATURAL PREDATION

I oppose men's hunting. But I respond to the challenge posed by Hettinger differently than do Everett and Moriarty and Woods. Unlike those writers, I do not affirm the value of natural predation. I argue here that it is a bad thing, and this turns the prohunting argument on its head: If natural predation is a bad thing, then human hunting that is relevantly similar to natural predation is also bad and should be discontinued.

Until recently in Western thought it was considered obvious that natural predation is a bad thing. A presumption against natural predation can be seen especially in Western theological literature. The first creation story in the book of Genesis, for example, includes a divine injunction that animals only eat plants and concludes with the trope that the whole of this herbivorous creation was seen to be good by God. And the prophecies of Isaiah include his famous image of the wolf living with the lamb, the leopard lying down with the kid, the cow and the bear grazing together, and so forth, all explained thus: "They will not hurt or destroy on all my holy mountain; for the earth will be full of the knowledge of the Lord as the waters cover the sea" (Isaiah 11:9).

In such literature predation is clearly recognized as less than ideal. Indeed, one of the major challenges addressed by Western theology has been the attempt to reconcile the evident disvalue of natural predation with the existence of a God taken to be omnipotent and omnibenevolent. Of all the theodical problems, it is predation that has been seen to pose the most serious threat to God's perfection. Eighteenth-century theologian William Paley remarked that "animals *devouring* one another, forms the chief, if not the only instance, in the works of the Deity, of an economy stamped by marks of design in which the character of utility can be called in question."[22]

All theodical writers feel compelled to address animal predation. And not all believe that predation can be reconciled with God's perfect goodness. For instance, in his theodicy, C. S. Lewis ultimately attributed the existence of predation to the machinations of an evil demon intent on maximizing the amount of torture in the world.[23] And more recently, Quentin Smith's close contact with natural predation led to his conclusion that we live in an evil, godless world:

> Not long ago I was sleeping in a cabin in the woods and was awoken in the middle of the night by the sounds of a struggle between two animals. Cries of terror and extreme agony rent the night, intermingled with the sounds of jaws snapping bones and flesh being torn from limbs. One animal was being savagely attacked, killed and then devoured by another.
>
> A clearer case of a horrible event in nature, a natural evil, has never been presented to me. It seemed to me self-evident that the natural law that *animals must savagely kill and devour each other in order to survive* was an evil natural law and that the obtaining of this law was sufficient evidence that God did not exist.[24]

The biblical representation of predation as less than ideal and the perennial attempts to reconcile predation with God's perfection show that for many Western thinkers predation is obviously bad. This does not show that it actually is bad, but it does indicate where the burden of proof lies—with those who would characterize predation as a good thing.

The arguments given by theodicists who defend God's goodness in allowing predation are structurally identical to the arguments given more recently by prohunting environmentalists who claim that natural predation is good. As I explain below, I find these defenses of predation unconvincing. In both cases the arguments are driven not so much by valid appraisals of natural predation as by a determination to support preconceived conclusions regarding the existence of a beneficent God, in the one case, and the goodness of men's hunting in the other.

There are three major types of argument given in defense of natural predation, based on benefits to the predator, benefits to the prey, and evolutionary progress. The first type of argument is stated by Holmes Rolston III:

> Indisputably, for a prey animal, it is bad to be eaten; death results. . . . The disvalue to the prey is, however, a value to the predator, and, with a systemic turn, perspectives change. The violent death of the hunted means life to the hunter. There is not value loss so much as value capture; nutrient materials and energy flow from one life stream to another, with selective pressures to be efficient about the transfer. The pains of the prey are matched by the pleasures of the predator.[25]

Rolston writes of "value capture," whereas Hettinger says that nature "trades values."[26] Their idea is that in predation value is not lost but just moved about or transferred—one dies so that another may live. This might make sense if predators only devoured one other creature in order to sustain their lives; but of course predators consume many others during the course of their lives, so the exchange is not one for one but hundreds or thousands killed so that one may live. This is not value transfer but value loss. (More sophisticated utilitarian appraisals of natural predation are considered in the next section.)

Predation is indisputably bad for the creature being eaten, but it is just as indisputably good for the predator. So how should we evaluate the overall process? Normally in ethics, when one benefits at the expense of the other, this is considered exploitation—a bad thing; it is not considered some kind of value transfer in which the good achieved by the beneficiary cancels out the loss to the one harmed. This negative evaluation of exploitation normally applies even when the benefit to the exploiter is equal to or somewhat greater than the loss to the exploited one. In this vein Alan Jacobs recently wrote of predation, "I cannot think of it as a good thing that some creatures live only by the dying of other creatures."[27]

Such negative evaluations of natural exploitation can be articulated in terms of an ethical principle enjoining us to consider all points of view. Applying such a principle typically involves imaginatively placing ourselves into each of the positions affected by a practice at issue. According to several widely advocated interpretations of such an approach, if the practice is found unacceptable from any position, then the practice should be rejected on moral grounds.[28] Suppose that we could save five lives by killing one healthy person against her will and harvesting her organs. Should we proceed? One's intuition that we should not can be explained in terms of the principle that since the procedure is odious from the victim's point of view, it is morally unacceptable overall. Recently Mark Rowlands has argued that there is no nonarbitrary reason for excluding the perspectives of nonhuman animals from consideration when we apply this sort of procedure.[29] Place yourself into each of the positions affected by natural predation. From the predator's point of view the practice may be fine, but the prospect of being eaten alive—the prey's point of view—is not something one would choose. This explicates the moral intuition that natural predation is exploitative and is a bad thing overall.

In the course of his analysis Rolston acknowledges the point of view of the prey animal, but he does not take the prey's negative evaluation of predation as a reason to reject hunting. One wonders how deeply Rolston empathizes with the prey, especially given his defiant self-identification as a predator: "Nature is bloody, the top trophic rungs are always raptors, cats, wolves, hunters, and I'm one of those, and unashamed of it."[30] Hunting men tend toward a strong identification with predatory animals, as exemplified in the following comments by Rick Bass:

> What a joy it is . . . to find the carcass of a lion-killed doe freshly cached beneath a spruce tree, with the entrails pulled clear but not eaten. . . . It all makes me feel less alone in the world—and it makes me feel richer. I think many of us are feeling increasingly a certain cultural ostracism, a misunderstanding from a society that is frightened by our passion for hunting. . . . the good thing about this alienation is that it makes the bond between those of us who do hunt that much stronger. . . . that is the feeling I get, too, walking through the woods and finding the faintest remains of a kill. . . . Think how lonely it would be without the big predators. Every generation of man—which is to say, of hunters—has lived, and hunted, with these fellow hunters.[31]

For hunters like Bass the valorization of natural predators is dependent upon a prior commitment to his own hunting, so the attribution of value to natural predation provides no independent support for men's hunting. The defense of men's hunting becomes vacuously circular.

The above conclusion might be disputed by arguing that it focuses too narrowly on the horrible experience of being eaten alive. By examining the entire cycle of predation it can be seen that predation is actually beneficial to the prey as well as to the predators. This is the argument based on benefits to the prey, the second defense of natural predation.

Both theodical writers and hunting advocates have argued that without predation, prey species would be worse off because they would overpopulate and die of starvation. The idea that predation is a net benefit to the prey is supported by downplaying the trauma of being devoured while emphasizing the likelihood of starvation and the suffering occasioned by it.

Regarding the suffering caused by predation, William Paley wrote, "It is only when the attack is actually made upon them that they appear to suffer from it. To contemplate the insecurity of their condition with anxiety and dread requires a degree of reflection which, happily for themselves, they do not possess. A hare, notwithstanding the number of its dangers and its enemies, is as playful an animal as any other."[32] The point that predation does not cause prey animals to suffer constant dread actually undercuts the defense of predation. The more pleasant the day-to-day existence of the prey animal, the more unfortunate is its premature loss of life due to predation.

Paley acknowledges that the attack causes suffering in the immediate moment. The import of this commonsense observation is diminished by defenders of hunting, such as Leahy and Rolston, who see animals as insensitive "brutes" incapable of strong feelings:

> They put stress on the "terror and trauma" of the chase. However, this must be judged in the light of all the qualifications that arise from my analysis of animals as primitive beings. The danger is to be over-impressed by the similarities of the pre-linguistic prototypes of such emotions to those that would be experienced by human beings in similar circumstances.[33]
>
> A safe generalization is that pain becomes less intense as we go down the phylogenetic spectrum and is often not as acute in the nonhuman world.[34]

But in many ways nonhumans are more sensitive than humans and thus may feel certain things more intensely than we do. Any prohunter's blanket generalization that animals cannot suffer acutely should be examined with the same skepticism as the nineteenth-century white slaveholder's belief that blacks were not sensitive enough to suffer from their enslavement.

Whatever their precise degree of sensitivity may be, animals can feel pain and pleasure and thus can be harmed and benefited. The issue here is whether predation is an overall benefit to the prey because the harm of being devoured is outweighed by the benefit of not starving to death. Rolston thinks predation benefits the prey by serving as a mechanism for regulating population levels.[35] Similarly, William Paley rhetorically asked, "Is it then to see the world filled with drooping, superannuated, half-starved, helpless, and unhelped animals, that you would alter the present system of pursuit and prey?"[36]

This image of predators as mercy killers, saving their prey by eating them, is suspicious given that it is never an interpretation offered when humans are the prey. "When a human being is stung to death by killer bees, or sawed in half by a crocodile, or devoured by a man-eating tiger," notes Timothy Anders, "no one suggests that such occurrences are expressions of nature's 'harmony', and no one suggests that the real purpose of the bees, or of the crocodile, or of the tiger was to prevent the poor human being from having to starve to death."[37] One may attempt to distinguish between humans and other animals by claiming that humans have means of regulating our population without being preyed upon while nonhuman animals do not. This claim is weak. Species that are not preyed upon do not universally multiply unchecked until their food supply is exhausted and they die of mass starvation. This would risk extinction; but there are many species that maintain a stable existence while having no natural predators. Note that the logic of the population regulation defense of predation leads to an impossible regress: If species in general need to be preyed upon in order not to overpopulate, then so do predatory species. The zebra's population must be checked by the lion, but the lion's population must be checked by some species that preys on it; this lion eater would also need a predator to keep it in check, and so on indefinitely. The fact that we do not see these infinite regresses in nature shows that successful species that are not preyed upon develop some other means for regulating their population levels.

So it cannot be maintained that predation is generally necessary for population regulation. At best, one could try to show that in certain specific cases a particular predator prevents some degree of starvation for a particular prey species. Even this is not sufficient to show that that particular instance of predation is an overall benefit to the prey. One would need to add (1) an argument showing that a death by starvation is worse than a death by predation, (2) an analysis showing that the prey species would not evolve some other internal mechanism of population regulation over time, and (3) a calculation showing that the benefits predation provides those who are fortuitously saved from starvation by being eaten alive outweigh the harms done to those devoured who were not in danger of starving (such as the young, the temporarily incapacitated, the unlucky, those who can gather food but have trouble avoiding predators, etc.). As Tyler Cowen points out, we cannot presume a priori that a balance of power between predator and prey maximizes welfare.[38] A sound argument showing that a particular instance of predation benefits the prey overall would involve a lengthy analysis including all the elements described. No such analyses exist, indicating that the idea that predation benefits the prey is not a disinterested observation but wishful thinking offered in the hope of pardoning men's hunting.

Arguments that predators benefit the overall health of a particular ecosystem are offered periodically. For example, Mark Hebblewhite studied the Bow Valley of Banff National Park in Alberta, Canada. Wolves made full use of one area of the valley but were partially excluded from an adjacent area. In the areas where wolves remained scarce the elk population was much higher, but willow trees, willow warblers, and beaver dams were not as common (elk browse on willows, leaving less for beavers and willow-dwelling birds). Hebblewhite concludes that "wolves are ecologically important. It (the study) bolsters the importance of conserving species like wolves and other top carnivores."[39] The chain reaction effect of the presence of natural predators is evident here; what is lacking is any argument explaining why one ecosystem is preferable to the other. Such arguments are difficult to sustain convincingly because ecosystems are complicated. Many beings are affected in different ways by a single change (what is good for elk is evidently not so good for warblers and beavers), and it is not obvious how to integrate the varying effects across species and individuals to arrive at a single defensible value judgment.

Even if one could validly conclude for a specific case that natural predation causes greater benefits than harms, this result could not be generalized because every ecosystem has its own particular complexity. Even more to the point, conclusions regarding the beneficial consequences of natural predation in a particular ecosystem show only the *instrumental* value of that predation (it happens to have positive consequences) and do nothing to challenge intuitions regarding predation's *inherent* disvalue (as an instance of exploitation).

The last major argument in defense of natural predation, that of evolutionary progress, proceeds by pointing out valuable traits that have evolved only because of predation: "An Earth with only herbivores and no omnivores or carnivores would be impoverished. The animal skills demanded would be only a fraction of those that have resulted in actual zoology—no horns, no fleet-footed predators or prey, no fine-tuned eyesight and hearing, no quick neural capacity, no advanced brains. . . . [Through predation] the prey not less than the predator will gain in sentience, mobility, cognitive and perceptual powers."[40] The properties selected over time will be those that tend to make a predator successful in acquiring food and those that tend to make a prey animal successful in avoiding being eaten. These properties are thus instrumentally valuable from the perspectives of predator and prey, but this sort of value is not useful as a basis for defending predation as such. It begs the question to assert that predation is a good thing because over time it generates beings with the qualities useful in carrying out predation.

Those who defend men's hunting are particularly liable to jump to the spurious conclusion that predation is good because it generates good predators and prey. Rolston loves the power of the evolved predator: "The wolf is not a big, bad wolf; it is one of the most handsome animals on Earth. . . . We admire the muscle and power, the sentience and skills that could only have evolved in predation."[41] Such adoration of the power to kill requires a dissociation from the perspective of the prey, a dissociation hunters are prone to when defending their sport, as discussed above.

Admiration of the skills of the elusive prey is also evinced by apologists for men's hunting, but this does not mean that they have adopted the perspective of the prey. In contemporary men's hunting, it is the sport that is valued, that is, the competition between determined hunter and evasive hunted and the thrill that comes from taking a skillful opponent.[42] Thus the admiration of natural-born killers and their age-old targets develops from the perspective of the hunter, providing only another circular defense of predation.

The argument from evolutionary progress might be salvageable if the traits valorized can be shown to have value independent of their usefulness in the predational cycle itself. Rolston believes that our very nature as human beings developed through our predatory past: "A world without blood would be poorer, but a world without bloodshed would be poorer too. Among other things, it would be a world without humans—not that humans now cannot be vegetarians but that the evolution of humans would never have taken place."[43] Rolston unquestioningly adopts the old anthropological story that the exigencies of hunting drove the evolution of humans toward technology, communication, and culture itself. We might be here if we had never gone through a period as hunters, but we would not be here as cultural beings. And since the traits of cultural beings have value beyond the facilitation of human predation on nonhumans, this point can be used to ground a noncircular defense of natural predation.

This defense is obsolete. The exact combination of circumstances and practices that led to the development of human culture and our rational capacities is not known. The traditional anthropologies that attributed the development of human rationality to human hunting were unfounded speculations grounded in the presupposition that it had to be men's labor that led to civilization. The masculinist bias of such theorizing is now widely recognized, acknowledged even by defenders of men's hunting, such as Ted Kerasote: "If women anthropologists had been doing most of the research, hunting peoples over most of the temperate globe might have been more accurately labeled 'gatherer-hunter' rather than "hunter-gatherers."[44] The complex process of gathering food, and/or the interaction between mother and child, may actually have been more significant factors in the evolution of human culture and rationality than men's hunting.[45]

Moreover, even if human hunting was instrumental in the development of our culture and rationality, this does not show that hunting generally leads to the development of rational capacities in predators. Indeed, in no nonhuman species has predation yet led to the development of humanlike culture and rationality, and we have no reason for thinking that it ever will do so.

This human evolution defense of predation has also been criticized by noting that one can value the present product of a past process without valorizing the process itself. Past programs of nonconsensual experimentation on humans were not good things, for example, even if they produced some information of lasting usefulness.[46] Notwithstanding the logical gap, Rolston not only defends predation by claiming that it was essential to the development of a distinctively human nature but also defend men's hunting today by interpreting it as a sacramental reenactment of the primordial basis of human evolution. Hettinger summarizes this position: "According to Rolston, we would not have evolved into human beings without the evolution of the human mind and hand to hunt; if our ancestors had remained herbivores, he suggests, there would have been no human culture. Thus, Rolston holds, hunting and eating meat affirms human nature by participating in a process that made us what we are."[47] This is an invalid defense of men's hunting. Suppose, by analogy, that the stylized patterns of motion in tai chi evolved by slowing down and choreographically sequencing arm and leg movements originally used for combat in the martial arts. It would be odd to suggest that we should affirm the present value of tai chi (its usefulness in enhancing physical balance and psychological repose) by attacking each other with our hands and feet, even though for tai chi practitioners that would count as "participating in a process that made us what we are." It is similarly odd to suggest that if capacities for intelligent male cooperativeness, for example, evolved through primordial hunting, that we should affirm the present value of that cooperative capacity by shooting more animals.

The invalidity of this argument for human hunting echoes that of the other defenses of natural predation considered above. Since none of the defenses work, we should revert to the initial presumption that natural predation is a bad thing. For all the reasons articulated by the animal liberationists already cited, it does not follow from this negative evaluation that we should interfere with natural predation. But the negative evaluation does invalidate those defenses of men's hunting based on the premise that natural predation is inherently good. The disvaluing of natural predation maintained here may disqualify me as a true lover of nature according to Hettinger's terms. I prefer, however, to think of my attitude not as a hatred of nature but as an opposition to systems of exploitation, whether those systems are natural or manmade.

The Inevitability of Exploitation

Another form of the argument from nature allows that we could forego animal exploitation but maintains that there is no reason to since we must exploit something—if not animals, then plants: "To live is to consume, to consume is to compete, to compete successfully is to out-compete, i.e., to work to the detriment of something else, be it plant or animal."[48] Since both the exploitation of animals and the exploitation of plants are equally natural, we have no compelling reason to choose one over the other.

Both premises in this argument from nature are faulty. It is not true that in all cases humans must exploit either plants or animals to live healthily. There are many plant parts that can be used without harming the plant itself. Leaves, nuts, and fruits can all be eaten without harming the plant from which they came. Indeed, the reproductive mechanisms of some plant species depend on their being eaten by animals. Also, since animals who are already dead are not harmed by their body parts being eaten, scavenging is not exploitative in the way that hunting and farming are. If these possibilities for nonexploitative consumption seem farfetched, it is worth considering human lives outside modern Western culture. Millions of Jains in India, for example, strive to live without exploiting insects, animals, or plants.[49] Their ideal diet is based around the sorts of vegetation for which the plant is not harmed by being consumed. And with respect to scavenging, note that anthropologists are now exploring the hypothesis that humans did not begin consuming the flesh of large animals through hunting them, as was previously assumed, but rather by scavenging the flesh of already dead animals.[50] Scavenging may be more central to the development of human life than hunting or farming.

The second premise of this argument states that as long as the process is natural, it does not matter how we sustain our lives—exploitation of any sort, animal or plant, is still exploitation. But even if we grant the premise that humans must exploit something or other to be healthy, it does not follow that there are no moral choices to be made. There are degrees of exploitation. When hunters describe nature as intrinsically exploitative, they retain the use of terms with highly negative connotation—"murder," "violence," "horror," and so on—thus still implying that less violence is better than more. It makes no sense to suggest that since some bloodshed in nature is inescapable, we might as well just wade right in and add to it. Remarks such as this—"It is naive of [animal protectionists] to believe that all animal suffering at the hands of humans can be avoided"[51]—are irrelevant if the moral injunction is not to eliminate all imposition of animal suffering but to avoid causing unnecessary suffering.

The moral significance of degrees of violence is also relevant to hunters' moral equation between eating plants and killing animals for food. This equation requires closing one's eyes to quite a bit: the difference in pain between a shot animal and a cut plant, the suffering that hunting at times entails for animals dependent on or close to the one shot, and the fact that meat eaters are typically indirectly responsible for more plant exploitation than vegetarians because of all the plants that hunted or slaughtered animals must eat during their lives.[52] Such closed eyes belie the perennial claim of sensitive sport hunters that they track and shoot animals for meat in order to maximize their honest awareness of nature.[53]

The Nature of Men's Predation

All versions of the argument from nature claim that in significant respects our exploitation of animals is natural. But one may question whether the types of exploitation we perpetrate really deserve to be called natural. No other species cages other animals, imposes disease on them, and then studies the results as we do in vivisection. No other species intensively confines animals to the point that their waste products become ecological hazards, as we do in factory farming. No other species has institutionalized the display of other animals for their amusement, as we do in zoos, circuses, rodeos, and seaparks. Even in hunting, the type of exploitation most often defended as part of the natural order, men are not functioning as truly natural predators do. As I detail in the following, the claim that men's hunting is natural founders at the ecological, physiological, and psychological levels.

ECOLOGY

The managed system of sport hunting practiced in modern North America is often defended on the grounds of ecological utility. According to this argument, the absence of natural nonhuman predators necessitates the regulated use of human hunting to maintain the populations of prey species at healthy, sustainable levels.[54] Though this is one of the most common defenses of hunting, it is fallacious. Deer comprise only about 2 percent of the animals North American hunters kill each year, yet for the remaining 98 percent (doves, rabbits, squirrels, quail, pheasant, ducks, and geese), no one even suggests there are overpopulation problems.[55] And deer hunters cannot realistically portray themselves as "Florence Nightingales with rifles"[56]—euthanizing deer to save them from an agonizing death by starvation—since whether hunting for meat or for trophies deer hunters select the healthy adults for killing, just those individuals most likely to survive a hard winter.[57] Thus human hunters cannot be said to be replacing natural predators, since natural predators are more likely to kill the young, the old, and the unhealthy.[58] Deer hunters might grant that the individuals they kill are not really being helped, but they still maintain that their killing is justified because by helping decrease the herd size they save others from starvation. This idea actually reverses reality, since it is because of hunting that U.S. deer herds are often unnaturally large: In order to boost deer herd size to please hunters, wildlife managers (both public and private) feed deer, manipulate flora, and decimate natural predators.[59] Once the herd has become unnaturally large through such measures, wildlife managers make sure it stays that way, ensuring an annual "harvestable surplus" for hunters by carefully regulating how many does are killed.[60] Even in the absence of natural predators, deer herds that are not hunted by humans tend to reach and maintain a stable population level below the carrying capacity of the habitat and below the levels fostered by states managing wildlife for hunters.[61] For all these reasons it is misleading to defend hunting on the grounds that sportsmen are providing an ecological service by substituting for displaced natural predators.

PHYSIOLOGY

Our physiology indicates that predation upon other animals is not required by our nature but is an option available under certain circumstances. We have the digestive systems of omnivores, not of carnivores.[62] Our teeth and nails are not well suited for tearing apart large mammals; for this we need the aid of tools. We lack the short, smooth intestinal tract of the true carnivore, though our bodies can process flesh to some extent. Vegetarians in the modern West tend to live longer and healthier lives than do meat eaters (the animal-based diet is a major causal factor in our leading killers, cancer, heart disease, and stroke), but it is possible for a human to subsist for a number of decades on a diet of flesh, milk, and eggs.[63] Physiologically speaking, we do not need to prey on other animals, but we can do it with some costs to ourselves. This is not enough to support an argument that we are predators by nature. It merely indicates what we already knew, that we may hunt and eat flesh if we so choose. The ethical question of whether we should do so is still open.

PSYCHOLOGY

The remainder of this chapter concerns the notion, common among defenders of sport hunting, that men possess a hunting instinct. According to what I shall call the atavism argument, man has been a hunter throughout most of his existence, acquiring predatory instincts that cannot have been totally lost in the relatively brief period of time since the development of agriculture. It is suggested that modern sport hunting is an expression of these lingering instincts, and a way of linking civilized man with his prehistoric origins. Various conclusions are drawn from this analysis, including that hunting, being instinctive, is not subject to moral evaluation, that hunting today is necessary for emotional stability, fulfillment, and happiness, and that the abolition of hunting, being the repression of an instinctive need, has led or could lead to various seriously negative consequences such as drug abuse and intrahuman violence.[64] It should not be supposed that the atavism argument uses "man" in a prefeminist generic sense, that is, to mean "human." The argument in both popular and scholarly form has always assumed that men, not women, possess these instincts, an assumption that continues to the present as we see in this quote from a subject in a recent study: "I think the hunting instinct's there, I really do, I think it just goes back right to the times of old, and it is in them, it's in their blood to do it, just as much as it's in my blood to do womanly things it's in their blood to do the manly things, and that's one of them."[65]

There are major problems with the atavism argument. Not only can sport hunting be explained easily without recourse to predatory instincts, but the empirical evidence for the evolution of such instincts is shaky.[66] The presumption that man evolved as a hunter has been challenged by recent anthropological theory, mentioned above, which argues that humans have been foragers, not hunters, throughout most of our existence, gathering plants, insects, and perhaps a few stray small animals, and that scavenging is as likely as hunting to be the first means by which the flesh of large mammals was acquired.[67] Moreover, several writers have pointed out that the occurrence of prehistoric hunting does not necessitate the evolution of predatory instincts.[68] Not all human activities lead to the evolution of corresponding human instincts. Also, the presumption of an inherited hunting instinct is difficult to maintain in the face of the preponderance of nonhunters and antihunters today—a population that is evidently no less well adjusted than hunters themselves.[69] Indeed, as the human population shifts from country to city, the relative popularity of hunting declines. This prompts "wildlife managers," who understand their job in terms of providing sustainable surpluses of designated game animals for the recreational shooting of hunters, to attempt to save their threatened livelihoods through various marketing campaigns promoting the joys of blood sport.[70] Such outreach efforts themselves put the atavism argument into question, as Margaret van de Pitte notes: "For the state and its wildlife managers to acknowledge clearly that the future of hunting depends upon cultivating new hunters from the ranks of children, and the naïve and half-hearted generally, is significant. Such an acknowledgment conflicts with the argument that Hunting (predation) is quite natural to humans."[71]

Another point relevant to assessing the atavism argument is that modern sport hunting is by no means a socially unmediated activity; like human behavior in general, it is conditioned by norms specific to a particular time and place. "This is the reason men hunt," Ortega y Gasset states. "When you are fed up with the troublesome present, with being 'very twentieth century,' you take your gun, whistle for your dog, go out to the mountain, and, without further ado, give yourself the pleasure during a few hours or a few days of being 'Paleolithic.'"[72] North American hunters today do often fantasize that they are acting as their paleolithic forefathers, but the reality is quite different. Modern hunting is hedged by a network of ethical rules and legal regulations. These injunctions are complicated and specific to time and place, they are not instinctive but must be carefully studied, and they greatly condition the modern experience of hunting. James Swan describes the process of hunting for waterfowl in California—how to sign up for the lottery that determines who may shoot, where and when you must go to be assigned a blind, which types of weapons and ammunition are allowed, and the complicated determination of how many of which kinds of birds one may legally shoot ("four per day, eight in possession . . . no more than three mallards, only one of which is a female, only one pintail of either sex, and no more than two redheads and/or canvasbacks"). He concludes: "If I haven't got all these regulations exactly correct, I apologize. I only have a Ph.D. in natural resources, and I have a little trouble reading eight-point condensed-type manuals of regulations."[73]

Observing the multiplicity of rituals surrounding the hunting practices of surviving indigenous hunting cultures, one might argue that since prehistoric hunting was most likely also rule bound, the regulations surrounding hunting today do not preclude its being atavistic. But the specific forms the rules take differ between cultures, and those who deploy the atavistic argument never address the crucial question of which rules so significantly alter the hunting experience that their adoption decisively separates modern hunting from the primal experience. For example, today's apologists for men's hunting presume that prehistoric hunters did not self-impose limits on their means of hunting. They presuppose that early men hunted out of necessity, and that it makes no sense for the truly needy to restrict their means of killing: "It would be as absurd for a hunter in need of food to wait until dawn to kill a deer as it would be for a cougar to wait."[74] Because today's North American hunters are generally not facing hunger regardless of the outcome of their hunt, they have the luxury to apply the rules of fair chase to make the hunting experience a more exciting challenge.[75] How do we know that the envisioned primal hunter, putatively staving off hunger by using any means at his disposal to kill, would be expressing the same "instinctive" disposition as one who self-consciously restricts his means of killing in order to construct the most thrilling hunting experience?[76]

The significant ambivalence hunters feel regarding their killing poses another challenge to the atavism argument. In their discussions of wounding animals and causing protracted deaths, hunters describe such a depth of personal anguish that their oddly placed but frequently expressed desire to minimize the suffering of the animals they shoot must be taken to be sincere:

> One day I finally hit a squirrel with my slingshot, but I only wounded it and then I had to kill it with a stick; it was a nasty, messy business and the squirrel suffered. This made me feel terrible. I still, all these years later, feel terrible thinking about it, and to this day I remain squeamish about killing things. I hate suffering of any kind, human or animal. Don't think because I'm a hunter that this is not so.[77]
>
> I made a poor hit. . . . I get sick when that happens. . . . The foregone conclusion of this book and all experienced hunters is that a vital hit is the only good hit and everything else is bad. Practice, discipline yourself, and strive to make that double lung shot. . . . Be cautious, be sure. The jubilation of a successful kill, quick and clean, is nowhere near as intense as the heartbreak of a bad hit. You don't want it.[78]
>
> I think of this elk tossed off his feet and lying still—one of those careful and lucky stalks ending in the magic bullet, the instantaneous death from a high neck shot. . . . Would that they were all like that instead of the times that I've knelt by their heads, and their breath has grated and their legs have kicked and shivered, their eyes filming over—another life prematurely departed between my hands. The first elk I shot died like that, and I swore that I would never hunt again. I even thought of running away and forgetting the carcass. But I sat by her, holding her head, then finally started my penance.[79]

Hunters do not like the idea of game animals suffering. They would very much like to think that their sport does not hurt animals. This can be seen through the wide range of euphemisms they employ to avoid the word "kill"—"bag," "collect," "control," "cull," "harvest," "manage," "take"—and through their strained arguments for the benignity of shooting, of which the following is just one of many equally farfetched claims: "In most cases, a well-placed, sharp arrowhead causes imperceptible pain, zero hydrostatic shock, and literally puts the animal to sleep on its feet."[80]

When James Swan suggests that "in each of us there is a leopard," or Ted Nugent claims that he is as "much a natural predator as any Canis Lupus or Ursa Horribilus," they are evidently forgetting that wolves, bears, and leopards show none of the compunction over killing their prey that human hunters show.[81] Even if sport hunting were an expression of some kind of predatory instinct, the evidence indicates that human hunters are also disposed against killing and inflicting pain. Thus hunting men are not natural predators, they are conflicted predators. This undermines the atavism argument, since it is not clear that emotional adjustment, happiness, fulfillment, and so on can ever come from expressing a disposition (the predatory "instinct") in such a way that it conflicts with some other disposition (our compassion for animals) that may be just as deep-seated.[82]

Hunters reject the obvious resolution of this conflict—nonlethal stalking practices such as wildlife photography—insisting in various ways that the intent to kill is essential to the hunt. But it is precisely this part of hunting, the killing, that is most difficult to argue is instinctive given our frequent resistance to harming animals. For example: "One of my colleagues, an avid hunter, once told me in exasperation that his 13-year-old son had just ruined his chance to 'get' his first buck. Although the child was in perfect position to shoot the deer, he did not pull the trigger. 'I couldn't do it, Dad,' the boy explained: 'he was looking right into my eyes!'"[83] The first kill is the most difficult.[84] Helping boys "work through this" is part of the process Swan describes as the primary challenge facing hunters today—overcoming guilt.[85] After killing his first animal, hunter Robert Franklin Gish's guilt was so severe he worried for weeks that his mother would die from plague transmitted to her from a flea jumping off the carcass. But his father had been there to "coax" him through the kill: "Later, when I killed my first rabbit with my new Benjamin air rifle . . . I was overcome with a similar pervasive sadness. I shot the rabbit in the back and paralyzed it. And it took another shot to stop its wild cries and suffering. My father coaxed me into the responsibility of finishing it off myself, albeit with tears in my eyes."[86] Evelyn Pluhar's comment is apt: "Such children do not appear to be genetically programmed to kill."[87]

As mentioned in the previous chapter, the portrayal of animal victims as willing participants in their own exploitation indicates a deep-seated uneasiness with the harms we are imposing. Hunters have developed the myth of the willing victim into a point of honor among sportsmen. Sensitive hunters feel that certain hunted individuals, at the crucial final moments of the hunt, will cease fleeing and give themselves up willingly to the hunter. Not all hunted animals do this, and it is a requirement of the most highly ethical hunter that he wait to find the self-sacrificial animal—the willing victim—rather than shoot at those still fleeing. Ted Kerasote thus describes two hunts, one shameful, the other not:

> Just as they caught my scent and began to run, I saw the telltale fork in one beam of the young bull's antlers, threw up the rifle as he bounded across the sage, and pressed the trigger following his bound. I knew instantly that I had shot far over his shoulder. I remained kneeling, smelling their musk and fear on the morning air, and feeling hot shame wash over me, for I had broken an accord: to put everything else aside—especially to whom I would pridefully tell the news—so that walking among elk was allowed by them; to be so calm that they stood momentarily unafraid and perhaps willing to be taken; and, equally important, so that there was enough time to apologize.[88]
>
> In the many miles walked this fall, among all the elk I've seen, she has become the possible elk . . . the elk whom the morning, the snow, and the elk themselves have allowed me to approach. Only the asking remains. "Mother elk," I say. "Please stop." I speak the words in my mind, sending them through the trees and into her sleek brown head. She crosses an opening in the forest, and there, for no reason I can understand, she pauses, her shoulder and flank visible. It is a clear shot, though not a perfect one—I have to stand at full height to make it. But I know I can make it and I say, "Thank-you. I am sorry."[89]

Today's Anglo-European defenders of sport hunting are reviving indigenous hunters' beliefs regarding the willing victim: "Subarctic Amerindians were obsessed with the responsibilities that man and animal had to one another. . . . That he may be killed by a man who was his moral equal was the first law for animals. Thus the animal, when seeing that his meat, hide, and so on was needed by the true hunter, was required to voluntarily surrender itself to the hunter."[90] James Swan explains and defends the belief of indigenous people such as the Huichol Indians of Mexico that if a hunter is purified and acts respectfully toward the hunted species, then he will find willing victims: "The wisdom of native peoples . . . asserts that under the right conditions, the success of the hunter is not just a reflection of skill but the choice of the animal. . . . Among shamanic cultures around the world . . . there is almost unanimous agreement that animals realize the way that nature works and are willing to let humans kill some of their kind for food as long as they agree to care for the rest of the species."[91] Swan applies this idea to his own hunting:

> There was no good reason for that goose to be there. A mile away there were nearly a thousand Canada geese settled in a sanctuary lake. We had no geese decoys and were out in plain site [sic]. Did the bird want to come to us? I have seen ducks fly kamikaze-style into range for hunters standing out in the open, but never geese. They are very wary birds. If the willing-victim sacrifice of animals does exist, then this goose seemed to be living proof. The hunt was offered as a special one to introduce youngsters to hunting. One wonders if the Canada geese approved of what we were doing.[92]

To a nonhunter such as myself this all seems ridiculous, making me wonder: If the animals understand what hunters are doing and approve, why don't they simply slam their bodies into the nearest tree, saving hunters the trouble and expense of stalking and shooting? The hunters themselves are not capable of completely convincing themselves about this—notice Swan's qualifications above, and the self-contradiction in Kerasote's "Thank you. I am sorry" (why apologize if the animal is truly willing?). Kerasote recognizes the possibility of self-deception, yet still cannot completely relinquish belief in the willing victim: "Perhaps the accord really was no more than self-deception on the part of ancient hunters, fostering one of grandest rationalizations of our species, that we were being given a gift because of our mindful behavior. Still, having watched deer and elk stand motionless before me, after I have taken the time to enter their world, I too would disagree with those who say that it has been all a sham. But I may be one of the last who is duping himself."[93] The entire process of hunting—camouflage, quietness, stillness, staying upwind, use of deceptive lures, and so on—presumes that the targets are unwilling.[94] It is the manifest implausibility of the notion of willing victims that makes hunters' commitment to the belief significant. There is evidently a strong desire by sport hunters to believe in the willing victim—after all, we do not see a similar revival of other implausible indigenous beliefs, such as the Huichol idea that killed deer regrow from their buried bones.[95] We can explicate hunters' perennial disposition to see willing victims as the logical conclusion of a reluctance to cause harm. The permission of the hunted individual relieves the hunter of culpability for the harm he imposes on that individual. The desire for exculpation explains not only hunters' contention that prey animals participate willingly in the hunt but also their frequent references to targeted animals as "gifts"[96] and, in the ultimate abdication of responsibility, their occasional assertion that the game animals themselves insist on being hunted:

> Man . . . lessens the nobility of the game animal if he chooses not to kill it. . . . The great and magnificent animal cries out for nobility and respect. The hunter is thus compelled to shoot it.[97]
>
> It is not man who gives to those wolves the role of possible prey. It is the animal—in this case the wolves themselves—which demands that he be considered in this way. . . . Wolves, by nature, count on an "ideal" hunter. Before any particular hunter pursues them they feel themselves to be possible prey, and they model their whole existence in terms of this condition. Thus they automatically convert any normal man who comes upon them into a hunter.[98]

Ortega y Gasset contends, "Every good hunter is uneasy in the depths of his conscience when faced with the death he is about to inflict."[99] This ascription of uneasiness makes sense, for how else can we understand the recurring image of the willing animal victim—an image in such blatant contradiction to the coercive intent of the cattle prod, the vivisectors' cages, the hunters' bullets, arrows, lures, and camouflage—except as a salve to the troubled conscience?

Conclusion

Men's predation is not natural in any morally relevant sense. The most we can say is that our nature gives us the ability to prey on other animals, but this is very far from saying that human nature or the natural order in general can ground a moral justification for men's exploitation of animals.

The need to justify men's exploitation of animals, however, does arise from our nature. Justification is the process of responding to something we feel is wrong by telling a story that makes it seem acceptable after all. Such justificatory stories develop around each of the institutions of animal exploitation, showing that we are not built to view the destruction of other feeling creatures with cold impassivity.

Hunting in particular brings about moral qualms. To be effective the hunter must study the animals he intends to shoot. But as hunting apologist James Swan notes, "The more one learns about wild animals, the more one develops a fondness for them."[100] This learning is intrinsically tied to hunting because the successful hunter's anticipation of the prey's location and movements comes from long observation and, often, selective identification with the hunted.[101] Kerasote, for example, comments on a hunting partner's ambivalence over killing elk: "He has watched too long not to be conflicted when taking . . . their playful lives."[102]

Men shoot animals for sport even though the practice of hunting brings them close enough to their prey to support the awareness that it is not in the animal's interests to be shot and wounded or killed. One study indicates that 20 percent of Americans who hunt in their youth give it up because they become convinced that it is wrong.[103] This 20 percent does not include the many sportsmen who continue to "hunt" but quietly curtail or halt their *shooting,* whose field trips become little more than carrying a gun into the woods with their friends. "As they grow older," Nelson Bryant states, "most men become less intense about hunting, and it isn't always because their reflexes have slowed and their joints stiffened. Some quit altogether. Others engage in token sorties which might or might not result in game being taken."[104] Edward Abbey describes the process and its conclusion: "So why lug a ten-pound gun along? I began leaving my rifle in the truck. Then I left it at home."[105] Kerasote believes that older hunters frequently stop killing because of their time outside with animals: "If a person spends that time really watching, listening, and getting close . . . it becomes harder to look at animals as a 'resource,' or merely meat to harvest, or a certain number of points in a record book. They become endowed with qualities that must be respected. Eventually it becomes impossible to take their lives for shallow reasons."[106]

Men who hunt frequently express regret, remorse, sadness, and shame over the killing they do.[107] The editor of one hunting magazine notes that he doesn't "know any hunter who hasn't felt a sense of sadness after he's shot a deer."[108] Given these feelings in seasoned hunters and the reluctance to kill that often must be overcome in young hunters, the question is not so much whether men should hunt, but why they hunt at all. "The act of . . . shooting an animal as beautiful and vital as the antelope now bouncing lifeless in the back of the truck," Gish notes, "carried with it a strange regret that took on the general outline of the question, 'Why?'"[109] Hunters are not indifferent to the harms they impose; they kill animals because some powerful incentive motivates them to override their regret: "The killing bothers me. . . . what exactly is there about hunting that I like (or need) enough to cause me to tolerate the resulting deaths?"[110]

The perplexing question of why men prey on animals is addressed in the next part of this book.

PART TWO

Understanding Men's Exploitation of Animals

"Don't stop!" a voice beside commanded. It was his mother who rushed past at full gallop. "Run," she cried. "Run as fast as you can!" She did not slow up, but raced ahead, and her command brought Bambi after her. He ran with all his might. "What is it, Mother?" he asked. "What is it, Mother?" His mother answered between gasps, "It—was—He!" Bambi shuddered and they ran on. At last they stopped for lack of breath. . . . Bambi looked around. His mother was no longer there. . . .

The stag looked at Bambi appraisingly and smiled a very slight, hardly noticeable smile. Bambi noticed it however. "Noble Prince," he asked confidently, "what has happened? I don't understand it. Who is this 'He' they are all talking about?" He stopped, terrified by the dark glance that bade him be silent. Another pause ensued. The old stag was gazing past Bambi into the distance. Then he said slowly, "Listen, smell and see for yourself. Find out for yourself."[1]

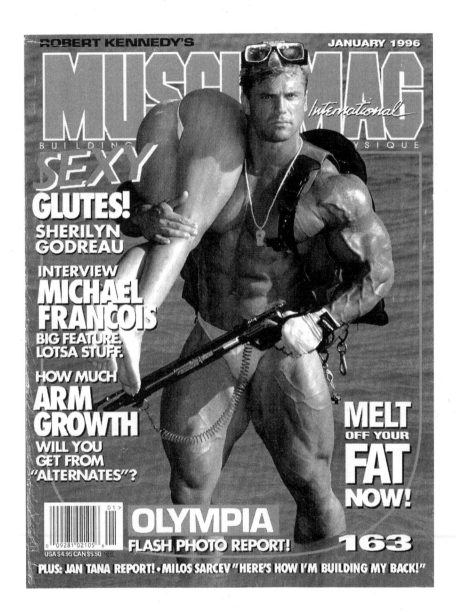

ROBERT KENNEDY'S

JANUARY 1996

MUSCLEMAG
International

BUILDING ... PHYSIQUE

SEXY GLUTES!
SHERILYN GODREAU

INTERVIEW
MICHAEL FRANCOIS
BIG FEATURE.
LOTSA STUFF.

HOW MUCH
ARM GROWTH
WILL YOU
GET FROM
"ALTERNATES"?

MELT
OFF YOUR
FAT
NOW!

OLYMPIA
FLASH PHOTO REPORT!

163

PLUS: JAN TANA REPORT! • MILOS SARCEV "HERE'S HOW I'M BUILDING MY BACK!"

3

The Erotics of Men's Predation

Every hunter remembers his first gun
as much as his first kiss.

—James Swan, *In Defense of Hunting*

In his novel, *The Hound of the Baskervilles,* Arthur Conan Doyle tells a story concerning a cruel nobleman named Hugo Baskerville. Hugo desired a neighboring woman who consistently avoided him. One night he and his companions kidnapped her and locked her in an upstairs room in Baskerville Hall. She escaped by climbing down the ivy on the outside wall:

> Some little time later Hugo left his guests to carry food and drink—with other worse things, perchance—to his captive, and so found the cage empty and the bird escaped. Then, as it would seem, he became as one that hath a devil. . . . And while the revellers stood aghast at the fury of the man, one more wicked or, it may be, more drunken than the rest, cried out that they should put the hounds upon her. Whereat Hugo ran from the house, crying to his grooms that they should saddle his mare and unkennel the pack, and giving the hounds a kerchief of the maid's, he swung them to the line, and so off full cry in the moonlight over the moor.[1]

The woman ultimately died of fear and fatigue, and Hugo himself had his throat torn out by a mysterious large black beast, the "hound of the Baskervilles."

In linking hunting with men's predatory sexuality, Doyle's imagination reflects reality. From the perspective of the man hunting with hounds, the chase is hot, charged with phallic sexuality:

> The sudden immersion in the countryside has numbed and annulled him.
> . . . But here they come, here comes the pack, and instantly the whole horizon is charged with a strange electricity; it begins to move, to stretch elastically.

Suddenly the orgiastic element shoots forth, the dionysiac, which flows and boils in the depths of all hunting. . . . There is a universal vibration. Things that before were inert and flaccid have suddenly grown nerves, and they gesticulate, announce, foretell. There it is, there's the pack![2]

In this chapter I show how contemporary hunting by North American white men is structured and experienced as a sexual activity. The erotic nature of hunting animals allows sport hunting to participate in a relation of reciprocal communication and support with the predatory heterosexuality prominent in Western patriarchal society.

A Passion for Power

Hunters unfailingly describe their relation to their prey in terms of sex and affection. For example, Robert Wegner discusses the "profound love" of deer possessed by Archibald Rutledge, a man who killed 299 white-tailed bucks in his lifetime.[3] In describing hunting, no term in the vocabulary of love is neglected (emphasis added in each case):

For many people throughout history, the most *seductive* voice of Mother Nature at special times of the year has been the invitation to join in the quest to hunt and kill birds, mammals, reptiles, and fish. . . . For the *passionate* hunter who is willing to *fall in love* with the creatures that are hunted, the desire to give something back to nature bears equal passion to the hunt. . . . Hunting, in the final analysis, is a *great teacher of love*.[4]

[Jack] felt that bow hunting made him superior to those who killed by looking through the sights of a powerful rifle. "What did they know," he had said to his girlfriend Candice once, "what *intimacy* did they feel with the animal?"[5]

Critics seem unable to understand the motives that impel what I choose to call the "genuine hunter." That is, the person with a *deep personal bond* to the game he hunts.[6]

The decision to cull was made by *caring* professionals.[7]

Until you have *courted* bluebills in the snow, you have not tasted the purer delights of waterfowling.[8]

Hunting, properly done, is not an outworn cruelty but rather a manifestation of man's desire to reestablish or maintain a union with the natural world. There are various paths to this *marriage*.[9]

Each time we kill a bird, we pledge our eternal troth to it, as at a *wedding* altar.[10]

There is no incongruity in describing the disposition to shoot wild animals to death as loving if one correctly understands the vocabulary being used. "Love" here simply means the desire to possess those creatures who interest or excite the hunter, as Harrison O'Connor describes: "Hunting must be a love affair when, beyond all other emotions, the desire to possess rules. One must reach out for what one cannot quite understand. Whatever animal becomes ordinary must be allowed to pass by. The sight of a magnificent buck I want to feel at a close range. To want to kill him with any less intensity seems murderous to me."[11] Taking possession typically entails killing the animal, eating the flesh, and mounting the head or even the entire body. The identification between loving and possessing by killing and mounting is made in this hunter's comments regarding two ducks he shot and stuffed: "'I saw these mountain ducks and fell in love with them,' says Paul, the tone of his voice matching the expression he wears in the photo with the Dall sheep—one of most tender regard for something precious. 'I just had to have a pair of them.'"[12] Aldo Leopold—hunter, forest manager, and founding father of modern environmental ethics—insisted that men hunt for one reason, "to reduce that beauty to possession."[13] And José Ortega y Gasset, who wrote the outstanding statement of twentieth-century sportsman's philosophy, defined hunting by both humans and nonhumans as "what an animal does to take possession, dead or alive, of some other being that belongs to a species basically inferior to its own."[14]

"Romance" is one of the words most commonly used to refer to hunting, as in the following representative list of titles and subtitles, all from books about hunting: *The Eternal Romance Between Man and Nature, The Romance of Hunting, Romantic Adventures in Field and Forest, Romance of Sporting,* even *Flirtation Camp: Or, The Rifle, Rod, and Gun in California; a Sporting Romance.* Andrée Collard analyzes romantic images of the hunt: "A romantic removes the 'love object' from the reality of its being to the secret places of his mind and establishes a relationship of power/domination over it. There can be no reciprocity, no element of mutuality between the romantic lover and the 'love object.' The quest (chase) is all that matters as it provides a heightened sense of being through the exercise of power."[15] This power difference determines the "basically inferior" status of prey species claimed by Ortega y Gasset.

Hunters' statements confirm Collard's analysis. One sportsman speaks of the "wild romanticism" of Africa and remarks that "as the animal moves into your sights, you are most thoroughly alive."[16] And in his book *In Defense of Hunting,* James Swan describes as "romantic" the lives of the old market hunters ("people who killed ducks, geese, passenger pigeons, and anything else they could for money").[17] Swan explains the source of the appeal of hunting:

> Though fishing and hunting share the common quest for capturing a wild creature, hunting for me has always had a more *seductive* call. . . . Once a fish is hooked, excitement rises to be sure, but once the fish is landed it can be returned to the water to live on. Also, relatively few fish that get off the line before being landed are harmed or killed by being hooked. There is more leniency in fishing. A hunter holds life and death in his hands, with creatures for which we have a closer kinship.[18]

So power over life and death is central to the seductive, exciting romance of hunting. But words like "seduction" and "romance" connote sex as well as power. It is not that "romance" connotes only sex when applied to heterosexual relations and connotes only power when applied to hunting. Rather, hunting and predatory heterosexuality are instances of romance because each is simultaneously sexual and an expression of power.

John Mitchell describes a dinner-table argument over hunting during which a frustrated hunting advocate threw up his hands and said, "Telling you about hunting is like trying to explain sex to a eunuch."[19] Indeed, hunters frequently use sexual allusions to explain their killing: "Hunting includes killing, like sex includes orgasm. Killing is the orgasm of hunting. But like in making love—talking and touching and, you know, looking in the eyes, and just smelling—the long story is the real lovemaking, and orgasm is the inevitable end of it. That is the killing of hunting, but only one part of it."[20] Similarly, James Swan compares the "hunter's high" to the "payoff of an orgasm," and Paul Shepard describes killing as the "ecstatic consummation" of the hunter's "love" for his prey.[21]

Men who defend hunting frequently compare it to sex. According to the atavism argument, discussed in the previous chapter, men who hunt today are expressing a deeply ingrained instinct. In the context of this argument we find comparisons between hunting and sex, such as the following: "One of my basic hypotheses here is that man is instinctively a hunter. He does not hunt for reasons of pleasure, although he has come to associate pleasure with absolute necessity. One may draw an analogy between the pleasures we have learned in the hunt and those we associate with sex."[22] Similarly, according to James Swan hunting is a "basic instinct, like sex, which is implanted in our minds and bodies."[23] He likens the possibility of foregoing the hunt to the possibility of foregoing sexual intercourse. "We can get by without hunting, but is this something we really want to do?" he writes. "We could also drop having sexual intercourse in favor of in vitro fertilization."[24] Swan's rhetoric suggests that both possibilities are equally unnatural, absurd, and undesirable.

The atavism argument was rebutted in chapter 2. My interest here lies in the presumption the argument makes about hunting and sex, namely, that both are so natural as to be unalterable: "[Hunting] is absolutely beyond accepted, formal morality in the way, at essence, that other fundamental human activity, sex, is: sex can bring us pleasure or sadness, but the desire to join with another, whether or not acted on, remains basic and unalterable: by itself it is neither good nor evil; it only is."[25] By naturalizing hunting, this argument attempts to move hunting out of the realm of moral dispute altogether. In this way hunters seek to protect themselves from moral criticism, or, as Mike Gaddis calls it, "persecution":

> Surely the urge and emotion [to kill] spring from instinct as honestly and purely as do the wiles of the chosen quarry. That those instincts should burn more strongly in some is likely a genetic property. Therein is grounds for neither persecution nor apology. In the absence of a kill, there is a void. As the relationship between a man and a woman rarely finds complete expression short of a physical sharing, the hunt is incomplete less possession of the prey. When you boil away the social pretext in either case, the respective behaviors are basic to man's bent for survival and conquest.[26]

Such comparisons of hunting with sex both draw from and reinforce the common view that sexual behavior is innately determined. The naturalization of sex is a reactionary position often promoted specifically to excuse men's sexual violence against women and children, just as naturalizing hunting excuses men's violence against animals. Subsuming sex and hunting under the general heading of a genetically based male "bent for survival and conquest" serves both exculpatory functions simultaneously.

James Whisker compares hunting to sex in order to explain and defend hunting but rejects the literal identification of hunting as a sexual activity. Against theories that analyze hunting as an expression of phallic sexuality, Whisker argues that there are many other phallic symbols besides guns and that, although men do admit to feeling "manly" as a result of hunting, they also derive this feeling from other sports.[27] But the existence of institutions expressive of manliness or phallic sexuality other than hunting says nothing about the nature of hunting itself. Whisker also points out that there are female as well as male hunters. A relatively small number of hunters, less than 7 percent in the United States, are female. Whisker evidently presumes that these women cannot be experiencing their hunting as a form of sexualized domination. But if we reject deterministic/dualistic theories of sexuality, it remains an open question whether some women develop a predatory sexuality (in hunting or elsewhere). To be sure, women's writing on hunting remains relatively free of the frenzied, highly sexualized accounts men frequently give of their hunting.[28] But even if sportswomen do tend to experience hunting differently than do sportsmen, this by itself would not invalidate any given analysis of the nature of *men's* hunting. If some women hunt in nonsexualized ways, this certainly suggests the possibility that some men might also hunt in nonsexualized ways. This abstract possibility notwithstanding, sportsmen's self-descriptions, sampled below, indicate that among them sexual experiences of hunting are common.

The reasons behind Whisker's reluctance to identify men's hunting as sexual are noteworthy. Within sexual interpretations of hunting, he states, the "hunter has been reduced to the position of being a sexually immature, unfulfilled and frustrated and probably mentally ill creature who is in need of therapeutic help."[29] According to Whisker, to see hunting as a sexual activity implies that hunters are fundamentally "unfulfilled and frustrated," that is, they do not gain sexual satisfaction elsewhere. Because he rejects the notion that hunters are sexually dysfunctional, Whisker also rejects the interpretation of hunting as sexual.

Like Whisker, antihunters also at times equate sexualized hunting with sexual dysfunction or deviance. But antihunters are more likely to accept sexual interpretations of hunting and use the equation to stigmatize hunters (hunters are sexually frustrated or impotent; hunting compensates for small penises, and so forth). Neither Whisker's analysis nor antihunting rhetoric of this sort countenances the possibility that eroticized animal hunting may be a sexual expression of *normal* men in hunting communities. As I argue in the next section, sexual descriptions of hunting are not merely metaphoric; for many North American sportsmen, hunting is a sexual experience. By interpreting the sexuality of hunting as sexual deviance, antihunters gain a quick way to demonize a morally repugnant activity, but only at the expense of ignoring the fact that hunting is not perpetrated by a few isolated, abnormal men but is organized and carried out by entire communities of men. Within hunting communities it is the abnormal man who does *not* enjoy hunting. Social scientific research finds no notable differences between hunting and nonhunting men.[30] Hunters are not frustrated and sexually impotent; they typically enjoy both sexual relations with other people *and* the erotics of stalking and shooting wild animals. Within patriarchal social structures the disposition to take sexual pleasure in the domination and destruction of other living beings is a normal part of men's fulfillment.

A comparison with theories of rape may be useful here.[31] Rape is often imaged as the deviant behavior of a sexually frustrated man overwhelmed by a chance encounter with a provocative woman. To sustain this image, certain facts must be ignored: that most rapes are premeditated, that rapists usually know those they attack, that rapes are often carried out by men in groups, that rapists are typically not degenerates or sexual deviants, that more than half of college age men surveyed said they would force sex on a woman if they were sure they could get away with it, and so forth.[32] The last two facts suggest that rape is hardly a deviant activity, yet to acknowledge this conclusion, just as to acknowledge the normalcy of men's erotic enjoyment of hunting, suggests the threatening possibility that there is something seriously wrong with normal manhood in this culture.

The other consequence of the standard image of rape is that it puts the burden on women to control their behavior to avoid "provoking" men into rape. When the man rapes, it becomes "her fault." This is not only a presumption of the legal system but also a common feature of men's phenomenology of rape. As the interviews in the book *Men on Rape* show, rapists often report feeling that *they* were being attacked by their victims and that the rape was a way of regaining lost control or seeking justifiable revenge.[33] I would not deny that some of these men actually feel that they were the disempowered victims, but I would distinguish those feelings from the reality that rape remains a premeditated, unprovoked act of aggression. In a similar way, hunting men often report that they are only responding to some violent depradation initiated by the animal (mountain lions attacking joggers, wolves killing livestock, deer eating our crops, and so on). Hunters make these claims even in situations where the overall context reveals that they themselves initiated the attack. For instance, the 1989 film *In the Blood* tells the story of some of the male descendants of Theodore Roosevelt mounting a hunting expedition to Africa. Once there, the group splits into two parties: one hunts for a trophy-sized cape buffalo, the other decides to bait and kill a large, wily old crocodile known by the locals. A native guide tells the sportsmen that this crocodile has taken some of their livestock. Rumors circulate that the crocodile has killed some children. As the sportsmen carry out their ultimately unsuccessful attempt to kill the crocodile, they construct an image of themselves as benevolent protectors responding justifiably to the crocodile's aggression. Lost in this image is the reality that these white men have come to Africa specifically to kill some indigenous animal, and that once there, they fix on the crocodile not simply because he was claimed to be a threat to the locals but also because he promises to be a challenging adversary, and because crocodiles are protected from sportsmen in most other parts of the world (thus greatly increasing their trophy value and the market value of the crocodile's skin or "pelt").

The Erotics of Hunting

North American white men do not hunt out of necessity; they typically do not hunt to protect people or animals, nor to keep themselves or their families from going hungry. Rather, they pursue hunting for its own sake, as a sport. This point is obscured by the fact that many hunters consume the flesh of their kills with their families, thus giving the appearance that hunting is a subsistence tactic. A reading of the hunting literature, however, reveals that hunters eat the flesh of their kills as an ex post facto attempt at morally legitimating the activity: "Using venison as a basic source of food gives the sport of deer hunting a sound, utilitarian foundation. We must remember that the non-hunting public does not accept deer hunting for either recreational purposes or antler collecting; the non-hunting public, however, accepts hunting when it is done to put deer meat on the table. As an old buck hunter once exclaimed: 'If you don't eat it, don't shoot it.'"[34]

The hunter often portrays himself as providing for his family through a successful kill and "harvest." This posture seeks to ritually reestablish a stereotypical masculine provider role less available now than it may once have been. In reality, hunting is typically not a source of provision but actually drains family resources. Deer hunters, for example, spend on average over forty dollars per pound of venison acquired, once all the costs of equipment, licenses, transportation, unsuccessful hunts, and so forth, are calculated.[35] Hunters are most likely to admit the true reason they hunt when talking to each other, as in the following statement from *World Bowhunters Magazine*: "Nobody hunts just to put meat on the table because it's too expensive, time consuming and extremely inconsistent. Everybody bowhunts because it's fun!"[36]

The "fun" of hunting is doubly sexual, both as a source of erotic enjoyment and as an expression of masculine gender identity. In her ecofeminist critique of hunters' discourse, Marti Kheel cites a number of sportsmen and hunting advocates who understand hunting as an expression of aggressive male sexual energy.[37] A sampling of North American hunters' literature indicates the validity of a sexual interpretation of hunting. The pattern is that of a buildup and release of tension organized around the pursuit, phallic penetration, and erotic touching of a creature whom the hunter finds seductively appealing.

Hunting is experienced as and expected to be a very sensual activity for the hunter.[38] The physical exertion; exposure to the elements; immersion in environments rich in sights, sounds and smells; and the stalking-induced intensification of sensory capacity all contribute. But the warm internal feelings mentioned by hunters go beyond the sensory focus and stimulation entailed by stalking in the wild and suggest an additional, purely sexual aspect of the hunting sensuality.[39]

Indeed, the hunting experience follows rhythms typical of what feminist theorist Martha Vicinus calls the "hydraulic" model of male sexuality.[40] For Ted Nugent, bowhunting follows this pattern—anticipation, desire, pursuit, excitement, penetration, climax, and satiation:

Last season's hunts are still vivid in the mind, but it does little to satisfy the craving.

It's the preparation, the thought process that goes into anticipating the hunt that's the most exciting part.

Their grace and beauty . . . was the essence of the thrill of the hunt. My binoculars revealed their delicate features.

A certain light, cream-colored sheep was calling me.

Him, I wanted.

I had worked myself up to a nervous wreck waiting to shoot.

The heated excitement of the shot.

The shaft was in and out . . . complete penetration.

I was hot. . . . I was on fire.

Oh yeah, a lot of blood here, I'm getting excited now . . . there's no telling what I might do. . . . I'm excited. . . . I am high.

The kill is climactic.

I felt good all over.

It satiated a built-up frustration.

A serious still hunt/stalking maneuver . . . can gratifyingly drain a guy. I like that.[41]

As one southern hunter explains, "Deer huntin' is like the fever. It builds up all year long and then has to be released. It's like buildin' up for 'a piece.' Once ya laid one, you move onto the next one that may be harder."[42]

This is a phallocentric sexuality. The weapon becomes an extension of the hunter's body and the means by which he penetrates animal bodies: "The traditional archer carries his bow lightly and casually, almost as if it's an extension of his body."[43] Decisions of which instrument of penetration to use are made by reference to maximizing the erotic sensation experienced by the hunter, as in this argument for traditional handmade wooden bows and arrows over high-tech factory produced equipment: "Is there any romance in a steel cable or a magnesium pulley? Does an aluminum arrow generate any feeling of warmth for the archer?"[44] For Ted Nugent, the phallus of choice is the arrow tipped with a "broadhead." He nocks the arrow rather unusually, up close to his eye so he can visualize a line down the "shaft" and to the target animal, and at times he paints the shaft of the arrow white to best observe it in flight. The importance of the flight and penetration of his arrows is evident: "I watched the beautiful, romantic arc of the shaft intercept the galloping goat perfectly, right behind the left shoulder, penetrating both lungs."[45]

The various dysfunctions of phallic sexuality all have their counterparts in hunting. In a passage that could easily be paraphrased into a sex manual, Nugent lists the varieties of "target panic," a malady afflicting hunters who become too excited to shoot properly: "The target panic demon comes in many disguises. Flinching, freezing above, below or to one side, failing to come to full draw, releasing the arrow prematurely, not being able to release at all! All kinds of mind-boggling dementia."[46] "Target panic," also known as "buck fever," is common enough among hunters to have generated its own extensive literature.

Targeted animals become objects of erotic desire for the hunter. One night in the middle of a weekend goose hunt, James Swan dreamt "I saw a Canada goose come to me, and then it was lying beside me."[47] Another hunter explicitly identifies his feelings toward hunted animals with sexual desire. "You see the animal and it becomes a love object," he says. "There is tremendous sexuality in this . . . sexuality in the sense of wanting something deeply, in the sense of eros. All quests, all desires, are ultimately the same, don't you think?"[48] And elk hunter Ted Kerasote ends his book by describing this dream:

> I . . . see elk before me, around me, moving everywhere, big dark shapes in the trees, along with their calves of the year. I raise the rifle, wanting to fire, but

also wanting to wait. . . . I walk among them. They aren't afraid, and behind me one of the cows rubs her flank against me. She doesn't smell like elk—dry and musky. She smells washed and clean. When I turn around, she drops her coat and becomes a naked woman, pressing herself to me and pushing me down. Her skin is the creamy color of wapiti rump, her breasts are small. . . . As she bends her head to my chest and tries to take off my shirt, I lift her chin. Her eyes are wet and shining, and I can't tell if she is about to laugh or to cry. I put my hand behind her head pulling her face toward me for a kiss, when I see the elk hide under my nose in the dawn.[49]

Hunters are very aware of the physical beauty of wild animals, a beauty they describe in detail and with longing: "No one can know how I have loved the woods, the streams, the trails of the wild, the ways of the things of slender limbs, of fine nose, of great eager ears, of mild wary eyes, and of vague and half-revealed forms and colors. I have been their friend and mortal enemy. I have so loved them that I longed to kill them."[50] Through killing the hunter gains ultimate control over the animal. In particular, he may now do something to wild animals that they generally do not permit while alive: he may touch them. Thus Thomas McIntyre's exults over a successful kill: "We may look at those antlers now for as long as we wish and whenever we please. We can, if we dare, even put our hands on them. What other memories permit us such liberties? And so, we dance."[51]

Hunters take great pleasure in stroking the fur, antlers, and horns of the large mammals they kill. The erotic nature of this touching is evident from the sensual way that it is done, from the quiet, admiring comments about the animal's beauty that frequently accompany the stroking, and from the words hunters use to describe this aspect of hunting: "The hand touches the gleaming points (or the horn tips), caresses the antler beams (or the burr), and plays with the soft hair on the head. Hunting is a passion better men than I have tried to describe. . . . Were someone to call it an intercourse with nature, I should shake my head at the choice of words, but I shall know what that person gets out of hunting."[52] In this context Plato's characterization of hunting as "nothing more than pursuing the game and laying hands on it" is apt.[53]

In many types of hunting the sexuality of the hunted animals themselves is thoroughly integrated into the pursuit. Hunters make use of the calls and scents of mating animals to track or lure them, to get close enough to kill. Deer hunters, for instance, attempt to bring bucks close to their stands by spreading the scent of a doe in estrus. Jerry Daniels, in *Hunting the Whitetail,* recommends that "you heat your doe scent to 103 degrees to imitate the smell of a 'hot doe.'"[54] Deer hunters are keenly aware of the sexually charged state of the bucks they pursue ("It was November 1, 1986, the rut was as hot as it could ever get"),[55] and they rely on this to make the bucks more reckless than usual and thus easier to kill: "There ain't but one thing that takes a buck's mind off of a human being, or a gun, and that's a doe when he's in rut."[56]

Deer hunters also tend to identify with these bucks; for example, one hunter joked that "all bucks everywhere better watch their nuts today" as he cupped his left hand over his own.[57] The hunters' attribution of aroused states (the "hot rut") to prey animals with whom they identify adds to the overall sexual experience of the sport for the hunter—and not just for deer hunters. Archibald Rutledge suggested that "to call a turkey one will perhaps do best if he will put himself in the place of the bird and will call in such a manner that, if he were in the place of the bird, he would come." Rutledge had such success with one particular turkey call that he "had her christened Miss Seduction."[58]

Hunting and Heterosexuality

In noting the sexuality of hunting, we may start to understand what might otherwise be a puzzling phenomenon, namely, the perception of hunting as a dating situation by hunters such as James Swan:

> I do not remember ever taking a date out hunting in high school, but on a number of occasions we did organize group outings where several couples went out at night spearing carp. . . . One could . . . make a Freudian argument about the symbolism of the spear being thrust into spawning carp. . . . Later, in college, . . . many women students hunted. It was not the kind of date in which most other students on campus participated, but we had a lot of fun.[59]

A Pennsylvania woman describes one such hunting date: "I dated a man who looked forward to that first [day of deer season] with an ardor I wished he would have reserved for me. . . . Before hunting season opened, my boyfriend and I walked the woods of Central Pennsylvania, listening and looking for game. . . . We stopped a lot to kiss."[60]

Sportsmen see their hunting as connected to their sexual relations with women. As reflected in the title *The Man Whom Women Loved* (from a book about big game hunter Bror Blixen), hunters commonly believe that success in hunting animals will gain them affection and sexual attention from women. James Whisker projects this hopeful belief onto prehistory, stating that "man . . . would receive sexual favors from the waiting female as a reward for being a good hunter and provider" and speculating that "the community gave successful hunters sexual rewards, e.g., by offering the most attractive female or a virgin, or the most accomplished lover, to the hunter."[61]

Thomas McIntyre believes that for both male deer and male humans, the possession of large antlers lures females:

> Trophy antlers may have served for the male hunter the very same function they served for the male deer. A female was far more liable to be allured by and to "select" a male who had manifested his ability to provide food, protection, and social rank. . . . Do we also keep the racks of the animals we hunt for similar, unspoken reasons? Probably. Our initial reaction upon entering a trophy room, a present-day cave, filled with antlers reaching to the ceiling is to be just the teensiest bit impressed and intimidated.[62]

Note the specific process by which successful trophy hunters gain sexual access to women, according to McIntyre: by impressing and intimidating others. Similarly, Paul Shepard identifies men's courtship behavior with hunting maneuvers and then speculates about women's reactions to such displays of aggression. "What then does she feel?" he asks. "Humility and adoration perhaps?"[63]

McIntyre gives explicit approval to the use of violence to gain sexual access, excusing men's aggression through the usual biological determinism: "Is this, then, a bad thing? I don't think so. . . . We are all to some extent still motivated by down-home primitive emotions and lusts that all the bullying in the world for us to act 'socially responsibly' is not going to purge from the wicked, wicked human."[64]

Hunters speak admiringly of the imagined sexual lives of the large, antlered males they seek to kill. Ted Kerasote describes rams as "hierarchical and sexually freewheeling: souls who begin their combat early, establishing dominance through their horn size; who won't bond to a single female or even collect a harem."[65] By applying human social categories to the lives of game animals (such as Kerasote's "harem" and McIntyre's "social rank" above), hunters bolster their expectation that somehow, in killing male animals who are sexually active, they also will gain sexual access to females, the presumed dominant sexual status of the targeted animal transferring to the man through the act of taking possession. The general belief is that the antlered male's sexual prowess correlates with his antler size, as in McIntyre's remarks above and Kerasote's statement that the bull elk with large antlers "is the mate a cow wants."[66] By transference, the antlers a trophy hunter has "collected" measure the extent of *his* virile masculinity; antler size in the hunting world matches the function of penis size in popular culture. Antlers are thus the phallic centerpiece of the trophy hunter's attention: "The big boy up front was a huge specimen with maybe 30-inch horns, a truly outsized trophy. His buddy was a respectable 26-inch."[67] These sorts of associations apply in some indigenous hunting cultures as well, as Ted Kerasote's interchange with a native Greenlandic hunter indicates: "About the second [harpoon], Nicolai said one word, '*Usuk.*' In case I had forgotten my Greenlandic vocabulary, he pointed to his crotch. The foreshaft was made from the penile bone of a walrus. Taking a moment to refresh my memory, he pointed to Qitora [his wife] and said, '*Utsuut!*' vagina." Ted and Nicolai then go on to jokingly boast about their relative penis sizes.[68]

The designation of the antlered male as a prized trophy ensures that hunters are aware of the biological sex of targeted animals. In fact, hunters extend the bare maleness of their targets into intense attributions of manly status and power, referring to their targets as the "fallen monarch," "ancient patriarch," "king of the mountain," and so on.[69] Large antlers represent to the hunter the animal's success in surviving years of threats, including harsh conditions, challenges by conspecific males, and the predatory efforts of previous hunters. The hunter's sense of being, developed from his exercise of domination, is felt more fully when the victim is himself imbued with power.[70] The victim must be seen as powerful for the hunter to feel manly and alive in his conquest; thus, hunters construct elaborate rules of fair chase to keep the power difference between hunter and hunted from appearing absolute.[71] The application of manly titles to their antlered prey is part of this process of constructing a victim imaged as powerful.

Interestingly, hunted animals do not lose their status as objects of the hunter's erotic desire when the hunter is self-conscious about the maleness of his prey. For example, Larry Fischer calls one hunter's thirty-five year career of shooting "trophy" deer his "love affair with large, mature bucks."[72] The erotic stroking of the corpse is part of a successful hunt regardless of the animal's sex. Indeed, the antlers themselves are a particular focus of this sensuality. Nor is the phallicism of hunting lessened when the prey is seen as male. Indeed, it takes on homoerotic connotations as in this dialogue exchanged between hunters stalking giraffes: "Give it to him!" "Right in the ass!"[73]

The erotic pursuit of overtly male animals becomes significant when we consider that *hetero*sexuality is explicitly intended in the comparisons between men's hunting and sex. For example, Ted Kerasote, after inadvertently flushing three sage grouse, wonders why his reflexive response was to imagine shooting them. "Does my tracing these grouse across the Wyoming sky, nothing in my hands except my bicycle gloves, lie buried in my hypothalamus like my sexual preference for women?" he asks. "If this part of my brain were a few microns smaller would I prefer men? Would I feel no pleasure at my imaginary tangents intercepting feathered motion in the sky?"[74] Significantly, Kerasote contemplates a theory that if a certain part of his brain were slightly smaller he would *simultaneously* lose his pleasure in hunting and his sexual preference for women. This position moves beyond a mere comparison of hunting and heterosexuality as two structurally similar instincts; the desire to kill animals and a sexual orientation toward women are here seen as coming together in a single package.

For those who defend hunting as an instinctive behavior, the desire to hunt evolved to facilitate food procurement, while the supposed heterosexual instinct evolved to facilitate human reproduction.[75] Thus in principle the two "instincts" remain distinct and separable. Yet the position articulated by Kerasote—that hunting and male heterosexuality are but variant expressions of a single innate quality—remains a common assumption. The bumper sticker "I hunt white tail year round," described by Matt Cartmill as "decorated with drawings of a deer's scut and a woman's buttocks to make sure nobody misses the pun," illustrates just one instance of this viewpoint.[76] According to anthropologist Paul Shepard, the woman draws the hunting man's hostility toward animals onto herself, subtly transforming it in the process into sexual relations between people. For Shepard, heterosexual intercourse and hunting are but two forms of the same phenomenon, which he calls "veneral aggression."[77] This verbal conflation is not unique to Shepard; the *Oxford English Dictionary* provides these two alternate definitions for the term "venery": "the practice or sport of hunting beasts of game; the chase," and "the practice or pursuit of sexual pleasure; indulgence of sexual desire."[78]

The construction of hunting as a heterosexual activity can be reconciled with hunters' eroticizing of targeted male animals if we understand sexual classifications in terms of power rather than biological sex. Feminists have developed an analysis of gender according to which "man" and "woman" are social classes of relative domination and subordination into which individuals are placed at birth based on certain overt biological features. Power difference is thus understood to be primary to gender construction, biological sex secondary. This reverses nonfeminist analyses of gender that legitimate male dominance by theorizing biological sex as primary and power difference as merely an adventitious, natural consequence. A similar reversal of nonfeminist theories of sexual orientation can be made. The conventional categorization is that people are homosexual, heterosexual, or bisexual by virtue of whether they are sexually oriented toward people of the same, different, or either biological sex. Defining sexuality in this way presumes that erotic desire between men and women in this society derives primarily from features of biological sex and only accidentally, if at all, from differences in class power. But if the primary distinction between man and woman is relative class power, then to be sexually attracted to a person *as a man,* or to be sexually attracted to a person *as a woman,* is to eroticize power difference. Thus feminists such as Sheila Jeffreys would reconstrue the concept of heterosexuality:

> Heterosexual desire is defined here as sexual desire that eroticises power difference. It originates in the power relationships between the sexes and normally takes the form of eroticising the subordination of women. In heterosexual desire our subordination becomes sexy for us and for men. Heterosexual desire can exist also in same sex relationships, because women and men do not escape the heterosexual construction of their desire simply by loving their own sex.[79]

The point behind Jeffrey's definitional decision is not simply that the eroticizing of power difference is common in male/female human sexual relationships but also that whether a relationship eroticizes power difference is more significant than whether it is a relationship between two people of the same or different biological sex. The root "hetero" simply means "different"; it is ambiguous regarding what specific difference is at issue. If society adopts the goal that every woman be in a primary relationship with some man, then it becomes sensible to make a basic linguistic distinction between same-sex and different-sex relationships. But if our concern is to understand and oppose structures of unequal power, then the salient issue becomes not who sleeps with whom but whether relationships further male dominance by making it sexy. From this perspective it is important to have a term distinguishing sexual relationships that eroticize power difference from sexual relationships that do not.

The suggestion to use "heterosexual" to refer to relations that eroticize power difference (and by implication, "homosexual" to refer to relations that do not) is based on a politics directly concerned with recognizing and dismantling structures of dominance. For Jeffreys, "heterosexual" refers to the eroticizing of power difference regardless of whether it occurs between members of the same or different biological sex. We who oppose men's exploitation of women and of animals might go beyond this to use "heterosexual" to refer to an erotic of power difference even when it occurs between members of different species.

An understanding of heterosexuality in terms of the erotics of power difference is already demonstrated by sportsmen who openly celebrate a sexuality of male dominance. Hunting men relate their pursuit of male animals to their sexual relations with female humans because both eroticize power difference. Thus we can understand the behavior of Rex Perysian, who, after shooting a boar to death with three arrows, "stood astride the boar and . . . lifted its head by the ears for the camera. 'I'll grab it like I grab my women,' he told his pals. Then Perysian dropped the animal's head and bellowed into the woods, boasting that the kill had sexually aroused him."[80] The biological sex and species of his targets are less essential to Perysian's masculine sexual identity than is the establishment of domination, so the fact that his victim is a nonhuman male does not preempt his comparison with his sexual relations with women. Nor does his mounting of a male animal undermine his identity as a heterosexual male, because he is in the position of dominance. Similarly, men who rape other men in prison are not by these acts deemed homosexual, because, as Christian Parenti explains, "they are not sexually penetrated."[81] Ultimately, a man's sexual identity as "lady killer" and big game hunter fuse, as in the following song lyric from Ted Nugent:

> I am a predator
> That's one thing for sure
> I am a predator
> You better lock your door.[82]

Men are often portrayed as innately predatory, with women and nonhuman animals as their natural prey. Sharing a common status as the designated targets of men's sexualized violence, women and game animals can merge in men's minds, as in Ted Kerasote's dream of shooting-kissing elk-women and in Paul Shepard's remarkable statement that the "association of menstrual blood and the idea of a bleeding wound is inescapable."[83] Although hunters often consciously image their animal targets as virile males, the very same animals may be seen as female outside the immediate context of the pursuit itself. As Carol Adams notes, "Male victims of hunting . . . become symbolically female."[84]

For instance, the character Bambi is a buck in the Disney movie and in Felix Salten's novel. He is represented in the movie as "Prince of the Forest," and this is exactly how sportsmen tend to think of the bucks they hunt. Yet the name Bambi has come to be given exclusively to girls, indicating that the male deer is ultimately feminized by our broader, nonhunting culture.[85] This becomes explicable in terms of Jeffrey's point that the eroticizing of power difference occurs originally and typically in the subordination of women and through Adrienne Rich's observation that "the power men everywhere wield over women . . . has become a model for every other form of exploitation and illegitimate control."[86] Notwithstanding his overt maleness, as a designated target for sportsmen the character Bambi is assimilated to the prototypical target of men's sexual violence, the woman. Thus in discussing the 1989 gang rape and beating of a woman in Central Park, columnist Joanne Jacobs wrote, "The most critical element of this attack was that they were male. She was female. They were predators. She was Bambi."[87] Gender marks relative positions of power as much as it signifies biological sex. In this sense the feminization of the buck can be compared to the practice of referring to sexually subordinated men in U.S. prisons as "gal-boys" or as "she" or "her."[88] Regardless of their biological sex or species, subordination feminizes people and animals.[89]

Although both groups are designated as targets for men's violence, the status of women and wild animals is not identical. Within traditional patriarchal marriage, women's situation can be seen as closer to that of domesticated animals than to that of game animals.[90] Significantly, the term "husband" simultaneously means a woman's spouse and a man who manages livestock for reproduction. The sexual and reproductive lives of cows and pigs are completely controlled by the farmer to further his interests. Thus the common use of terms such as "cow" and "sow" to refer to women shows either women's similar domesticated status or a cultural expectation that such subjugation would be appropriate. Similarly, the application to women of the term "bitch" is significant given that, as Joan Dunayer has explained, breeders have always treated the bitch or female dog "as a means to a useful, profitable, or prestigious litter."[91] The specific use of the word "bitch" to insult assertive women shows the hostility felt towards those members of domesticated groups who do not quietly assume their designated subordinate position.[92]

The names of domesticated animals, almost invariably terms of derision, express the contempt felt by the conqueror for the conquered. In contrast, the names of game animals rarely become terms of derision. Hunters zealously pursue those wild animals they have made into emblems of strength and independence. Deemed *worthy* of being killed, game animals instantiate just the characteristics the hunter hopes to possess by transference through the process of killing and eating. Thus it would be contrary to the purpose of the hunt to see game animals as totally despicable creatures.

So we can understand why parents might choose to name their daughter Bambi: Although the name connotes a creature periodically subjected to men's predatory efforts (who is to that extent in a subordinate position and thus feminine), it also connotes a creature who lives in the wild, that is, generally outside of men's control, and thereby commands a certain degree of grudging respect. The word "fox" is another term transferred from a hunted animal to women. Like "Bambi," the word "fox" is not nearly as derisive as the names of domesticated animals, but it does connote one targeted for aggressive pursuit and ultimate violence. In the United States men apply the adjective "foxy" to women they find sexually desirable and somewhat wily and evasive. Indeed, the "fox" is sexually desirable *because* she is independent and evasive, thus exciting to run down and conquer.[93] Women considered sexually undesirable, on the other hand, are called "dogs," a usage that picks up the already tamed status of those animals (because dogs come when you call them, there is no exciting challenge in shooting them nor any increased masculine status). Challenging and exhilarating, the sport of fox hunting is also extremely violent and orgiastically bloody, culminating in the fox being torn to bits, the body parts being distributed to various participants, and the blood being smeared on novice's faces. The sexual use of the term "foxy" implies an erotic of predation and bloodshed.

Constructing the Erotics of Men's Predation

Hunting and heterosexuality are both structured as institutions of men's sexualized dominance. Their structural similarity allows each to be used to describe the other. Thus heterosexuality describes hunting: "The 'dedicated' waterfowler will shoot other game 'of course,' but we do so much in the same spirit of the lyrics, that when we're not near the girl we love, we love the girl we're near."[94] And hunting describes heterosexuality, as in these two typical nineteenth-century romantic verses:

O let my love sing like a thrush
In the greenwood's blossoming crown
And leap away like a fleeing roe
So that I can hunt it down.[95]

Man is the hunter; woman is his game.
The sleek and shining creature of the chase,
We hunt them for the beauty of their skins;
They love us for it and we ride them down.[96]

Ultimately it becomes difficult to tell whether hunting describes sex or sex describes hunting, as in Ted Nugent's dictum that "life is one big female safari" and the following song lyric by Jon Bon Jovi:

> First you're gonna fall
> Then you're gonna bleed
> For the glory of it all
> That's the story of love.[97]

The many examples of such cross-talk between hunting and heterosexuality reflect the fact that both institutions eroticize power difference. But this discourse is not merely reflective of some independently existing social reality, it is *performative*, each speech act one part of the process of developing and maintaining the erotics of men's predation.

The overt violence of hunting coupled with its erotic stimulation makes its imagery a very useful resource for promulgating a predational sexuality between women and men. For example, Robert Franklin Gish describes the portrayal of one of *Cosmopolitan* magazine's "bachelors of the month":

> There he stood, attorney as hunter, in front of the mounted trophy heads of several species of exotic antelope; his left leg rests on the top of an elephant's foot made into a stool; he leans against a once beautiful tusk of ivory; a zebra's skin adorns the wall. "Mellow minxes" were invited to write to this good "catch." As for him, . . . this particular hunter extends his notion of hunters and hunting to his "feelings about relationships" as well: "I don't want a pushover, mentally or sexually. What's the thrill? There's nothing wrong with a one-night stand, but it's not worth it—what's the point? It's too easy. The challenge and the chase are what's important. That's what always intrigues."[98]

Through this kind of material, *Cosmopolitan* and other similar media encourage women to entertain men's sexual aggression.

Notice that although the primary image in the *Cosmopolitan* example centers on the man as hunter, pursuing both women and wild animals, the man himself is secondarily positioned as the woman's prey through the reference to him as a good "catch." This is not uncommon. The popular book *The Rules: Time-tested Secrets for Capturing the Heart of Mr. Right*, for example, constructs men as predator/prey and women as prey/predator. On the one hand, the overt function of the book (as indicated in the subtitle) is to instruct women on how to "capture" men. Authors Ellen Fein and Sherrie Schneider refer to men as "live prey" and report that they themselves followed the rules "to ensure that the right man didn't get away."[99] As in any hunt, the object is to take possession of the quarry. The authors write of their readers' supposed mounting "desire to own this man" and advise against dating married men because "we do not take what is not ours." Thus the book presumes that women sexually prey upon men. But on the other hand, the working premise of *The Rules* is that the pursuit of others sexually stimulates men, so that if a woman wants a man to fall in love with her she must play hard to get, acting like an "elusive butterfly." The authors essentialize this, calling men's pursuit of women "the natural order of things." They advise women never to initiate sex: "Let him be the man, the aggressor in the bedroom. Biologically, the man must pursue the woman. . . . Flirt when he tries to kiss you or bite your neck. This will turn him into a tiger."[100] The tiger allusion connotes predatory aggression. Fein and Schneider suggest that women should gain sexual satisfaction not by communicating their needs to their partner but by letting "him explore your body like unchartered territory."[101] A charter is a "grant conferring powers, rights, and privileges," including exclusive use; thus the erotic promulgated here is that of the man taking possession of the woman.

Cosmopolitan magazine, *The Rules,* and other such media function to direct women's sexuality along the lines of male domination and female submission. They thus deliver to women in popular form the same message that academics such as Paul Shepard develop in their scientific works, namely, that "the female, whether the target of redirected fury or the sexual prey of the wild huntsman, has not only to deflect his violence but to entertain it."[102] Magazines such as *Playboy* carry out a similar function, teaching their male audience to see men's predation as the essence of normal sexuality. It is worth noting that *Playboy* was initially conceived by Hugh Hefner as just one step beyond its prototype, the existing men's magazines that fetishized hunting: "At the time other men's magazines, such as *Modern Man,* buried their sexual content under pages of he-man stories—how to hunt bears or canoe the Amazon—and masqueraded their nude pictorials as 'art figure studies.' Hefner sensed there was a market for a men's magazine that didn't feel 'wrestling alligators was a more manly pastime than dancing with a female companion in your own apartment.'"[103]

Playboy has not forsaken its roots in the erotics of hunting. The "Playboy bunny" is a sexualized image that identifies women with an animal that is both domesticated and hunted for sport, meat, and as a varmint. And *Playboy* magazine periodically uses hunting motifs in its pictures of exposed women. One feature, titled "Birds of America," creates a series of half-woman, half-bird images by superimposing photos of the lower halves of birds on the models from the waist down. Captions such as "A significant trail blazer in satisfying the appetites of Puritans in 1621, the wild turkey has been responsible for many pilgrims' progress. . . . Disdaining fidelity, she mates with any stray barnyard tom at the tug of a wattle" and "The comely quail is a game bird with come-hither plumage to prove it. Each year she entices scores of avid suitors to hunt for her" blend the status of women and animals as meat, targets for shooting sports, and objects of sexual pursuit.[104] The feature titled "Stalking the Wild Veruschka," in which, according to the caption, the model is "painted to portray the untamed creatures with which she's so often compared," functions similarly.[105] More recently, the following two captions invite the male viewer to see himself as predator and the unclothed female models as prey:

> All creatures great and small can credit evolution for providing camouflaged markings that protect them from predators. Fortunately, Kerri Kendall doesn't need to hide from anybody, because even in her faux catskin suit and cap she would be easy to spot. But don't be fooled by her trusting smile; she's still not an easy target.[106]
>
> Julianna Young has an irrepressible sense of humor. Try to imagine her wearing this bra while swimming in the ocean. Wouldn't any deep-sea fisherman love to reel in such an enviable prize? Talk about your trophies! We'd bet townspeople and tourists would line up three-deep just to watch the photographer record the catch.[107]

A recent cover photograph from *Musclemag International* magazine also uses the image of women as trophy fish (see this chapter's opener). While holding the weapon used to harpoon trophy fish in phallic position, the man slings an evidently slain woman over his shoulder. Inside the magazine, the caption of the cover shot reads, "Eddie Robinson and his wife, Vanessa, having fun at the beach."

Such images and captions both sexualize women's status as prey and further the eroticization of hunting itself, although it is difficult to draw a line between one function and the other. Perhaps it is most accurate to say simply that such media eroticize men's predation, leaving it ambiguous whether the target is a woman or a nonhuman animal (as the images themselves do).

The annual *Sports Illustrated* (*SI*) "swimsuit issue" is worth analyzing in this context. The issues periodically draw on cross-imagery between erotic sport hunting and predatory heterosexuality. For example, in the February 20, 1995, issue of *SI*, five different models are posed so as to blend in with the tropical vegetation of Costa Rica. One woman is placed on a large piece of driftwood, which the caption calls her "perch." And three different pictures show women waist deep in natural pools, apparently emerging from the water toward the male viewer. This is significant because the feature immediately following the swimsuit pictorial is a story in which white men go to Costa Rica to hook large fish and pull them out of the water for trophies. This juxtaposition of imagery indicates that *SI*, like *Playboy* and *Musclemag International*, believes that the image of women as trophy fish (or fish as trophy women?) enhances the erotic appeal of their feature stories.

Sports Illustrated took their propagation of the erotics of predation further in the January 29, 1996, swimsuit issue. Again, women are blended with natural settings such as water, sand, rocks, trees, and animals. But in this issue many of the models are dressed in animal-print bikinis representing species men kill and collect (leopard, tiger, cheetah, lion, zebra, and butterfly). The women are photographed in South Africa, and the swimsuit pictorial immediately follows a feature describing a private South African game park. *SI* has edited the magazine so that it becomes difficult to tell where one story ends and the other begins: The game park and swimsuit features are grouped together under a single title—"Hot Spots"—and the first photo in the game park article shows a female model in a bikini sitting next to a white man surveying the landscape with binoculars. The article remains studiously vague about sport hunting at the game preserve—all the tourists mentioned in the story intend to photograph the wildlife. This emphasis on photographing the animals actually strengthens the magazine's identification of the wild animals with the female models (who are also there to be viewed). Even with hunting downplayed, violence against animals remains a major theme of the story, as the sightseers repeatedly put themselves in positions where they must consider shooting various wild animals in "self-defense."

SI pictorials exploit race as well. Of the five pictures of women of color in the 1996 issue, each portrays a model in an animal-pattern swimsuit and/or a suit with a native African motif. The white women are sometimes posed wearing items of African jewelry, such as a necklace or bracelet. And the metal rings used to constrict and elongate the necks of some African women are featured prominently in several photographs, thus fetishizing the mutilation of women. The series of eroticized photographs of African women with elongated necks works in subtle tandem with this highlighted statement, nominally about giraffes, from the preceding game park story: "Big game is so abundant ... you can order a longneck anytime you want." In this feature, women, animals, and people of color all share a common status as objects placed on display for the white male viewer's entertainment. I say *people* of color rather than *women* of color because immediately following the South African "daring safari" and "swimsuit tour," *SI* has placed a story on the "search for promising young athletes" in Soweto, South Africa. Mirroring practice within the United States, success in sports (a major form of viewing entertainment for white men) is presented as the best path out of poverty and oppression for black men internationally.

The use of such motifs is by no means obsolete. In the winter 2003 swimsuit issue, *SI* again systematically deploys images of race, big game hunting, and trophy fishing to enhance erotic/commercial impact. A Kenya pictorial, in which the swimsuit models are said to "lead a different kind of safari," is accompanied by captions such as "Jessica White shows hunters how to bag their prey without firing a shot," and "On the trail of the human animal in Kenya." African American model Jessica White is posed taking a mud bath, visually associating her with the indigenous animals Westerners can see behaving similarly in any number of nature documentaries—or perhaps witness in person, if they are affluent enough to afford the camp profiled in the pages immediately following the pictorial feature. This issue also includes a feature set on the Aegean Sea off the coast of Turkey in which four of the models are once again posed submerged or half-submerged. Model Sarah O'Hare is shown loosely bound with rope on the deck of a fishing boat, while Bridget Hall is photographed in the grip of three proud local fishermen, suspending her horizontally à la Woman as Trophy Fish.

In her book *The Pornography of Representation,* Susanne Kappeler describes a 1983 photograph of a white Namibian farmer holding a young black man by a heavy iron chain around his neck. The white farmer tortured and killed the black worker, meanwhile forcing his victim to pose for photographs taken by his friends. Kappeler compares this photograph to pornography ("a woman in the place of a black man, the white men in their respective positions . . . unchanged") and suggests that the "picture may remind us of those taken by fishermen and hunters posing with their catch, smiling into the camera."[108] Similarly, Matt Cartmill mentions "the pornographic allure of cheap rod-and-gun magazines, with their snapshot galleries of grinning hunters holding up the heads of big, beautiful deer corpses."[109] In each case white men compose, photograph, and distribute ritualized representations of their class dominance for their mutual amusement and aggrandizement. *Sports Illustrated* blends the iconographies of pornography, hunting, and racial conquest, using each to reinforce the others and in so doing promoting a unified white male identity of sexualized dominance over all disempowered others. One of the Costa Rican photographs, ominously captioned "Patricia Velasquez can paddle but she can't hide," represents women, animals, and people of color through a single image of a camouflaged model; the picture of white man's dominance over these groups is completed by their production, distribution, and consumption of the photograph.

Constructing the erotics of men's predation has material consequences. The *SI* features market their pictorial locations as alluring vacation spots, places that cater to white men's desires to shoot exotic wild animals and/or have sex with fascinating foreign women (the Costa Rica feature begins with the header: "Our raven-haired beauties add to the exotic flavor of Latin America's hottest new destination"). The desire to see certain people and animals of the South turned over to the recreational pleasures of affluent white men is not new. In his 1925 travelogue *The Royal Road to Romance*, Richard Halliburton proclaimed, "The *romantic*—that was what I wanted. . . . I wanted to . . . make love to a pale Kashmiri maiden beside the Shalimar, . . . hunt tigers in a Bengal jungle."[110] Although for the mass readership of *SI*, safaris, tropical trophy fishing, and sex tours abroad remain a fantasy indulged in only vicariously, affluent men increasingly experience such "romance" for real. Exploiting the indebtedness and relative poverty of the global South, foreign businessmen, military leaders, and politicians work with local elites to develop prostitution networks to attract North American, European, Australian, and Japanese men and their hard cash.[111] Global economic inequalities are similarly exploited to turn southern lands into game preserves serving an international clientele. In this way the bodies of indigenous animals, women, and children are made available to affluent foreign men for sexualized domination and penetration.

Domestic hunting in the United States replicates the international scene. State wildlife officials are paid to manage people, animals, and plants so as to provide hunters with annual surpluses of those wild animals they most enjoy tracking and shooting. The casual hunter not heavily invested in trophy collecting may see the hunting trip primarily as a vacation, a chance to get away from the restrictions of work and family life to unwind with the guys and blow off steam in masculine fashion—nominally by shooting at animals but perhaps also by drinking, gambling, passing around pornography, frequenting the local strip clubs that cater to hunters, and so forth. A drawing from Vance Bourjaily's book on hunting celebrates and promotes the common targeted status of geese and local women for men out on a hunting trip (figure 1).[112]

Recognizing the common structure of hunting and heterosexuality as eroticized power difference gives us a deeper understanding of men's vio-

GAMEBIRD

Figure 1. Gamebird

lence. Andrea Dworkin recounts the story of a thirteen-year-old girl who, on a camping trip in northern Wisconsin, was walking alone in the woods when she came across three hunters reading pornographic magazines. The hunters chased her down and raped her, calling her names from the pornography.[113] Dworkin cites this as one example of how pornography is implicated in violence against women. But this situation links not just pornography and rape but also hunting, pornography, and rape. The men were in the woods to consume pornography and to kill deer; when one of the men saw the girl he said, "There's a live one" (she thought he meant a deer). One man beat on her breasts with his rifle. An occasion nominally devoted to killing non-human animals slides easily into a sexual attack against a human female.

A recognition of hunting and heterosexuality as interlinked, socially encouraged forms of men's predation supports a heightened understanding of such events as nine-year-old Cub Scout Cameron Kocher firing a rifle at seven-year-old Jessica Ann Carr, hitting her in the back and killing her as she rode a snowmobile with a friend.[114] Cameron said he was "playing hunter" when he fired the gun. The article mentions that Cameron's father and mother taught him to fish and to hunt for squirrels and rabbits but does not ask where the boy got the idea to hunt human females. The remarkable statement by Cameron's lawyer, that the boy's "feelings of guilt, if they exist, are that he disobeyed his father," I contrast with a more encouraging thought from hunter Sydney Lea. Lea compares the aging hunter's decreasing zeal for killing with "an analogous change in a man's sexual career," concluding, "The diminishment of either predatory instinct isn't irredeemably grim nor even sad. For it is compensated, one hopes, by an increase in moral judgment."[115]

Conclusion

There are many reasons men hunt. Surveys of hunters reveal a consistent pattern of self-described motivations. In descending order of frequency of reporting, hunters give the following reasons for pursuing their sport: love of nature (or the "out of doors"), companionship with other hunters, challenge and suspense, skill development, escape from the daily routine, trophy display, the acquisition of food, exercise, and the thrill of shooting an animal.[116] The analysis of this chapter does not contradict these disclosures; rather, it enables a refined understanding of what they mean. "Love of nature," the most frequently given reason for hunting, amounts to a desire to take possession of that which is imaged as untamed. The "thrill of shooting an animal," as we have seen, includes a specifically sexual component, the erotics of predation.

The reasons for hunting given by sportsmen are not sufficient to explain the institution, however, even when those reasons are supplemented by the analysis of this chapter. On the one hand, most of the benefits cited by hunters are obtainable through activities that do not involve shooting wild animals (getting outdoors with other men, skill development, exercise, acquiring food, and so on). On the other hand, those ends that really do require hunting itself, such as the erotic thrill of tracking and shooting a wild animal, and the seizing of an emblem of independent masculinity through killing, raise a series of additional questions.

We saw in chapter 2 that hunters feel bad when they kill an animal. Notwithstanding the erotic thrill of the chase, the exhilaration of overcoming a worthy adversary, the enhanced masculine status ceded those who take possession of the wild, and all the other allurements of hunting, there is a serious downside to the sport. Young hunters must overcome their empathetic responsiveness, seasoned hunters periodically struggle with their consciences, and retired hunters must live with the memories of all the healthy lives they took. What in the hunt is so important to men that they are willing to override their human disinclination to be the cause of injury and death?

Modern sport hunting is a large-scale institution that continues only through the direct efforts and tacit compliance of many who themselves never hunt. Hunters are a small minority in this society, as they are well aware, and their opportunities to shoot wild animals are conditioned by the opinions of the general nonhunting public and by the plans of policy makers who may never leave the city. Hunters do form a large contingent of those who administer wildlife management regulations. In the end, however, the institution of hunting continues to exist largely through the decisions of people who never directly experience the erotic thrill of tracking and shooting a wild animal. What do they get out of it?

The question of why hunting is so important to both hunters and nonhunters alike can be answered in part by reference to hunting's function in the construction of gender identity. As described above, hunting participates in the promulgation of a predatory heterosexuality in which men are initiators of violence while women and animals are their designated targets. Recognizing the premium this society places on the construction of a gender system polarized along the lines of who initiates violence moves us a long way toward understanding the continued existence of sport hunting. Hunting cannot be dismantled, according to present norms, for it is too useful a tool in the project of convincing us that the essence of manhood is the ability and willingness to destroy others.

This leaves one more question. Why define manhood in this particular way? To answer this question, I turn our attention away from modern sport hunting and onto one of men's oldest institutions of animal exploitation: sacrifice.

4

Sacrifice: A Model of Paternal Exploitation

To what purpose is the multitude of your sacrifices unto me?
—Isaiah 1:11.

In this chapter I analyze one of men's primary institutions of animal exploitation, ritual sacrifice. Animal sacrifice is extremely common across cultures, prompting Christopher Manes to remark, "Such was the scale of institutionalized blood sacrifice for most of religious history that an alien reviewing a videotaped recording of human religion down the ages might sum up worship on this planet in three words: they kill animals."[1]

We think of animal sacrifice as something that people used to do, back when superstition ruled over reason. We believe ourselves too enlightened to accept that our salvation lies in rituals of bloodshed. In chapter 5, however, I show that animal sacrifice has not in fact ended. Rather, we have just given it a new name: animal experimentation. And other current institutions of animal exploitation, such as sport hunting and meat eating, are so imbued with sacrificial structure and ideology that we cannot understand why men exploit animals today without understanding why men have sacrificed animals throughout history.

Sacrifice and Gender

While the procedural details and ideologies associated with sacrifice vary between societies, certain features recur. A human or nonhuman animal is killed; there are ritually prescribed procedures for this killing, as well as for the preparation and disposal of the sacrificial victim's body; there is a public element to the sacrifice; and there is some significant social or spiritual need putatively served by the sacrificial ritual.

Sacrificial rituals have one other element in common cross-culturally: They are performed by men. This generality has been noted by anthropologists for some time but analyzed only recently. Until the work of Nancy Jay, who placed gender at the center of the analysis developed in her 1992 book *Throughout Your Generations Forever: Sacrifice, Religion, and Paternity,* gender was not used to understand sacrifice.

According to Jay, sacrifice functions to establish paternity. This baldly stated thesis is shocking if we are used to thinking of sacrifice literally as "making sacred." The standard theories of sacrifice, and the ideologies typically attached to the rituals, state that sacrifice is done to bring us into closer relation with the divine realm: "But if sacrifice is so complex, whence comes its unity? . . . it always consists in one same procedure . . . This procedure consists in establishing a means of communication between the sacred and the profane worlds through the mediation of a victim, that is, of a thing that in the course of the ceremony is destroyed."[2] In its most concrete form, sacrifice is simply a means of procuring divine favor by providing meat-hungry gods with the taste and smell of burnt flesh. What does the establishment of paternity have to do with that?

Seemingly nothing. But the strength of Jay's position lies in the tremendous range of her supporting examples. Jay shows that sacrifice functions to establish paternity in a great number of cases, including in Roman Catholicism and Greek, African, Hawaiian, and Hebrew religions. In each case, Jay argues, sacrifice "produces and reproduces forms of intergenerational continuity generated by males, transmitted through males, and transcending continuity through women."[3] For instance, in the Roman Catholic Church regular sacrificial practice in the form of the eucharist "has never been separable from clearly defined hierarchical social structure organized in unilineal 'eternal' continuity of descent between males: the Apostolic Succession of the sacrificing priesthood." Jay analyzes the biblical stories in Genesis, highlighting the crucial role of sacrifice in establishing patrilineal descent over and against a system of matrilineal descent. In Hawaiian society, Jay points out, sacrifice is a form of "man's childbirth" in which "the king ritually controls his divine genealogy and reproduces himself and the god without dependence on women's reproductive powers."[4] In ancient Athens participation in the appropriate sacrificial rite was the criterion for membership in the male descent clans. And in the four African cultures Jay considers (the Tallensi, Lugbara, Nuer, and Ashanti), Jay finds sacrificial ritual similarly functioning to establish patriliny.

A striking pattern over such a wide range of examples calls for some explanation. For Jay, the explanation lies in the fact that while the maternal relationship is evident to the eye, manifested through the act of giving birth, paternity is never so obvious. This creates difficulties for societies in which the tracking of paternity is important. Jay argues that in such societies: "What is needed to provide clear evidence of social and religious paternity is an act as definite and available to the senses as is birth. When membership in patrilineal descent groups is identified by rights of participation in blood sacrifice, evidence of 'paternity' is created which is as certain as evidence of maternity, but far more flexible."[5] Jay's explanation leaves two questions unanswered: Why are men motivated to develop rituals for the establishment of paternity, and why is sacrifice the ritual so often developed to serve that function?

In previous chapters I noted some of the many indications that we are disposed against harming animals. Sacrifice is ritualized killing, and as such it tends to be carried out with the hesitations and unease that accompany animal abuse in general.[6] Sacrifice is not a morally neutral act. We do not immobilize large healthy animals, cut their throats, and allow them to bleed to death in a casual, offhand manner. We do this knowing that animals, like us, struggle against death, so we naturally feel some guilt and try to shift the blame. In order to sacrifice animals our inclinations toward protection and against inflicting harm must be managed, quelled, or overridden. We can become desensitized and even get to the point of enjoying sacrificial rituals (many public sacrifices are festive occasions), but this takes work. We must learn to cut off our feelings for the designated sacrificial victims. All this indicates that there must be a good reason to sacrifice; we would not go to all the trouble of managing our sympathies and disinclinations unless something very significant were at stake.

Paternity is what is at stake, according to Jay, and sacrifice is one of the rituals used to establish men as fathers. What is so important about establishing paternity? Why are we so determined to mark fatherhood that we are willing to destroy others in the process?

Some people have the ability to generate new life from their bodies, others do not. Every human culture depends on this life-generating capacity to continue its existence through time, so normally a high degree of status and respect accrues to those possessing this ability. Men cannot gestate, nor can they suckle, so they cannot in these ways contribute to the generation of new life. Thus one possible source of status is not available to men.

Feminist theorists have suggested that under certain circumstances men envy the status accorded women for the crucial life-generating functions associated with their possession of wombs and breasts.[7] Envy is a sort of hostility generated not simply because another possesses something valuable but also because the other is seen to possess something that could or should belong to oneself. If the object of value is scarce, envy can lead to a struggle over its possession. The respect of others is not in principle limited in supply, so the fact that women are respected does not entail that men are not also respected. Status, on the other hand, if it is understood in comparative terms, is necessarily limited. As one goes up in status, others go down relative to oneself. If status is determined by the degree one is respected by others, then a struggle over status becomes a struggle over who deserves respect.

In at least three different ways men who envy women's high status as life-generators can act to improve their relative status. The first way is through compensation, by constructing a realm of male activity to counter the exclusively female activities of gestation and suckling. If women are deemed worthy of respect by virtue of generating life, then men can be deemed worthy of respect by virtue of engaging in philosophy, music, war, hunting, science, or some other putatively valuable activity that is designated as man's work.

The second way men can improve their status is through revaluation. Men may argue that women's contribution to life generation is not as crucial as it first appears. Revaluation can involve devaluing the functions specific to women (gestation and suckling) and/or magnifying functions specific to men (such as fertilization). And finally, men can improve their status through appropriation: taking the inherently valuable functions associated with women's reproductive lives and turning them into male activities. This has only recently become technologically feasible. Now men may take over suckling by replacing mother's milk with formulas developed from the products of men's dairy farms, and men may take over gestation by controlling women's labor in the hospital, incubating fetuses outside the womb, and developing techniques for male pregnancy.

Compensation, revaluation, and appropriation are processes we would expect to see if men are envious of women's status as life-generators. Compensation and revaluation are, in fact, common cross-culturally, and appropriation is evidently proceeding as quickly as the relevant technology can be developed and deployed.[8] This suggests that in many cultures men do experience and act on feelings of "womb envy," a term coined by Eva Kittay specifically to contrast with the Freudian notion of "penis envy." By "womb envy" Kittay means "not merely envy of the specifically named organ but of the complex of a woman's organs and capacities, particularly as it relates to her distinctive childbearing functions," including both gestation and suckling.[9]

Sacrifice is nearly always performed exclusively by men. Correct and regular sacrificial ritual is always characterized as being essential for the continued well-being of the community and thus is, among other things, a realm of purely male activity that men can compare favorably to women's essential reproductive work. This fits sacrifice within compensation, the first possible response to womb envy. Sacrifice also constructs men as fathers. Sometimes the sacrificial rite marks a particular man as the father of a particular son—this is Jay's observation—but as we will see in detail below, sacrifice also ritually constructs men in general as the class responsible for the reproduction of human life. Men tend to give this sacrificially constructed paternity priority over the maternity women develop through their work in gestation and suckling; their "spiritual" labor is split from and valued over what is deemed to be women's merely biological reproduction. In this way sacrifice is also part of the process of devaluing women's reproductive work relative to men's labor.

Jay's research shows that sacrificial ritual typically functions to establish paternity, and the theory of womb envy explains why some ritual is needed for this function. It has not yet been explained why *sacrifice* is so frequently the ritual designated to mark paternity. There are other rituals that could be used to make the paternal relation as obvious as the mother's act of giving birth. One obvious example is the practice of couvade. In this ritual, widespread in South America but practiced in numerous other parts of the world as well, the father mimics the process of giving birth and is treated as if he had physically given birth. Couvade clearly befits public denotations of paternity. The fact that sacrifice would in so many times and places be used as the indicator of paternity suggests that there is something about the nature of blood ritual that makes it particularly effective in this regard. In the following section I explain why sacrifice is so well suited for turning men into fathers.

Sacrifice and Male Birthing

> How terrible for me was, for instance, that: "I'll tear you apart like a fish." ... It was also terrible when you ran around the table, shouting, grabbing at one, obviously not really trying to grab, yet pretending to, and Mother (in the end) had to rescue one, as it seemed. Once again one had, so it seemed to the child, remained alive through your mercy and bore one's life henceforth as an undeserved gift from you.[10]

Men give birth through violence. By threatening to destroy, by demonstrating the will and capacity to destroy, a man constructs a situation in which those who live do so only through his grace. The relatively powerless around him are constantly on the brink of the death he can cause; he sustains their lives—brings them into life—through his decision not to kill them. He thus gives birth to his children deliberately, creating through pure will as is represented in the biblical God's acts of generation by fiat: "Let there be light."

This male birthing is not mythological. There are real acts of violence and real decisions about who to kill and who to spare. Male dominance as an ongoing institution entails a dependence of the powerless on the mercy of those who administer the apparatus of violence. Tales of primordial male birthing—Eve from Adam's rib, Athena from Zeus's head—would be unthinkable in the absence of some material basis for attributing generative powers to men.[11] This material basis lies in men's application and selective withholding of acts of destruction.

Consider a world in which children are always exempted from men's violence. How could men in such a world claim to have generated human life? Since men in this hypothetical society never kill children, these men cannot believe that children exist because of their decision not to kill. Men provide sperm at the onset of an individual human life, but this contribution is relatively insignificant when compared to women's extensive labor in gestation, childbirth, and suckling. Without a precedent of male violence against children, men lose a major social basis for claiming priority over women as the generators of human life.

Yet completed violence against children can render a man childless, defeating his claims to be a generator of human life. So male birth through violence requires a precarious balance: Men's menace toward children must be real, but it must not typically lead to the actual death of the child. The Hebrew story of the Akedah represents one way to accomplish this balance. In the biblical account, Abraham is commanded by God to offer his son Isaac as a burnt offering.[12] Abraham obeys, but just as he takes the knife to cut his son's throat, an angel of the Lord calls out to stop him. Abraham sees a ram caught in a thicket and offers up this animal as a burnt offering in the place of his son.

Jay notes that by this act—the substitution of the ram for the child—"Isaac, on the edge of death, received his life not by birth from his mother but from the hand of his father as directed by God (Elohim); and the granting of life was a deliberate, purposeful act rather than a mere natural process, a spiritual 'birth' accomplished without female assistance."[13] Isaac owes his life to his father because Abraham kills a ram instead of his son. Isaac's dependence on his father's will becomes stronger the closer Abraham comes to actually killing Isaac. Abraham had both the social space (no person could have stopped him from sacrificing Isaac) and the will to kill his son. Killing the ram makes more obvious the father's will and ability to destroy than would his leaving the mountain without spilling any blood at all. Together, the incomplete infanticide and the animal substitution cogently construct paternity through managed violence.

Generalizing from this example, sacrifice can establish paternity when it publicly reveals the father's capacity to kill the child and his decision not to do so. Not all killing of animals by men will function in this way. If the status of children and the animal victims is so dissimilar that it is inconceivable to substitute one for the other, then the killing of those animals communicates no menace toward children. There must be something linking the child with the sacrificial animals for the sacrifice to establish paternity. Any one of the following might suffice: stories or memories of human sacrifice, contemporary examples of men killing children, children and animals sharing a similar property status, or the performance of rituals displaying interrupted or incomplete sacrifices of children by men.

Animal sacrifice establishes paternity by combining with particular sorts of stories, rituals, or practices involving humans. In and of itself, the ritual killing of animals displays men's power over domesticated animals and nothing else. But when the sacrificed animal is a substitute for a particular child, the sacrificer becomes father to that particular child through the substitution; and when a sacrificial animal substitutes not for a particular child but for children or other humans in general, the male sacrificing class becomes responsible for the continued lives of children or humanity in general—in this way constructing a wider type of fatherhood.

In the following sections I analyze Jewish and Christian sacrifice, showing how stories and nonsacrificial rituals work with the sacrifices themselves to allow men to claim credit for the existence of life.

Jewish Sacrifice

Animal sacrifice was an integral part of ancient Hebrew ritual life. Men's ritual killing of domesticated animals superficially mediated relations with the divine, but these sacrifices had implications for human relations as well. The wide range of biblical stories in which humans are sacrificed or nearly sacrificed in the same ways, by the same men, and for the same purposes as animal sacrifice gives animal sacrifice a tone of menace toward those people who might once again be put in the animal victim's place. Also, the circumcision of Jewish boys carries a strong connotation of interrupted killing, given that the same class of men whose cutting stops with the foreskin in the case of male youths did actually bleed their animal victims to death.

HUMAN SACRIFICE IN THE BIBLE

The story of Noah's ark models the process through which men construct themselves as generators of life. At Genesis 6:7 the Lord decides to destroy all human life. Subsequently this decision is qualified; God withholds destruction from a select few by giving Noah precise instructions on how to construct an ark and who to bring on board. Then God "blotted out every living thing that was on the face of the ground, human beings and animals and creeping things and birds of the air; they were blotted out from the earth. Only Noah was left, and those that were with him in the ark" (7:23).

Noah creates in the same way God does, by deciding whom to spare from death. In the story God decides who gets saved, but from the point of view of those struggling to get on the ship as the waters rise, Noah would be the immediate obstacle or means to their salvation. Noah determines who lives and dies, and whether he does so by following God's instructions or through his own initiative is irrelevant. Either way, Noah is the father of humanity because the living world's continuation after the flood is only due to Noah's work in constructing the ark and bringing people, animals, and plants on board.

After the waters subside and the ark passengers alight, Noah's first act is to offer burnt offerings of every clean animal species. The immediate result of this is that "the Lord smelled the pleasing odor" and resolved never again to destroy every living being by flooding.[14] This indicates that proper sacrificial practices are the key to avoiding divine destruction, implying that those charged with administering the sacrifices are the ones who preempt disaster and keep the group alive. The reasons for God's devastating displeasure are vague in the Genesis account, but in the version of the deluge story found in the Gilgamesh epic, the reason for wiping out mankind seems to have been their omission of the creator god's New Year sacrifices.[15]

This correspondence recurs throughout Western sacrificial practice: Ideologically, the men who sacrifice are responsible for life because it is believed that proper sacrificial practice is crucial for the group's survival and well-being; materially, the men who sacrifice are responsible for life because they are the ones here on Earth deciding who not to kill. The ideology, I suggest, is made plausible by the material reality of the selective withholding of sacrificial violence.

Human sacrifice is a recurrent theme in biblical texts. In Deuteronomy whole towns, including all human inhabitants and livestock, are ordered to be sacrificed as a burnt offering should the town turn from the Lord to worship other gods.[16] David impales seven sons and grandsons of Saul "before the Lord" to avert a famine caused by bloodguilt resulting from Saul's slaughter of the Gibeonites.[17] Jephthah sacrifices his daughter to fulfill a vow he had made to God in exchange for military victory over the Ammonites; a group of sailors throws Jonah into the sea to quiet a fierce storm, and so on.[18]

Such stories communicate that human sacrifice is often pleasing to God or even demanded, and that human sacrifice can be effective in averting catastrophe. The sacrifice of children, particularly royal children, often accompanies times of national emergency such as famine or war as a means of ameliorating the crisis.

Human sacrifice is associated with reproduction through the requirement to sacrifice the eldest son. The sacrifice of the firstborn is one of the laws God delivered to Moses: "The firstborn of your sons you shall give to me. You shall do the same with your oxen and with your sheep: seven days it shall remain with its mother; on the eighth day you shall give it to me."[19] This can be interpreted in relation to men's attempts to claim credit for life, especially male life. The first male offspring of each female, human or non-human, is killed eight days after the female gives birth. The female's labor was thus futile. Each subsequent male who lives beyond the eighth day does so because the male head of household forgoes the killing of which he has proven himself capable. Men, not women and female animals, ultimately determine who lives, thus countering the overt appearance that the female contribution to life-generation is primary.

The sacrifice of their firstborn sons by Kings Ahaz and Manasseh is referred to as an "abominable practice" and is said to have provoked the Lord to anger.[20] This is not a repudiation of human sacrifice as such; rather, these kings are condemned because they are sacrificing to the underworld deity Molech rather than to the God of Israel.[21] The ritual killing of humans is regulated in Hebrew Scripture, not prohibited.

God's harsh treatment of Cain, for example, may be read not as divine reaction against killing a person but as punishment for a botched sacrifice. In this story Abel, a keeper of sheep, sacrifices the firstlings of his flock, while his brother Cain, a tiller of soil, offers to the Lord the fruit of the ground. According to Genesis 4:4–5, "The Lord had regard for Abel and his offering, but for Cain and his offering he had no regard." Cain subsequently takes his brother out to the field and kills him. For this the Lord severely punishes Cain.

Cain's killing of Abel is generally interpreted as an irrational fit of jealous rage, and God's reaction as a punishment for killing a person. But Cain's act can be interpreted as an understandable attempt at receiving divine favor. After his favoring of Abel had provoked a reaction from Cain, the Lord had said to Cain, "Why are you angry? . . . If you do well, will you not be accepted?"[22] Since Abel was evidently favored for sacrificing flesh rather than vegetation, it would be reasonable for Cain to interpret "doing well" in terms of blood sacrifice. Having no flock from which to draw animal victims, he kills Abel. Various midrashi (Jewish commentaries) suggest that Cain had watched Adam slaughtering a bull, so he killed Abel in similar fashion by hacking at his neck with a sword.[23] In ancient Israel all slaughter was sacrificial, so if Cain was copying Adam's killing of a bull, he was attempting to offer Abel as a sacrifice.[24] If so, God punished Cain not for killing a person but for killing the wrong person (or perhaps for killing him in the wrong way); note that Abel was favored for offering the *firstborns* of his flock, but Abel was not Cain's firstborn son but his younger brother.

The story of Cain and Abel contains the first mention of animal sacrifice in the book of Genesis. If interpreted as I have suggested, it also contains the first biblical indication of the crucial theme of the interchanging of sacrificial victims. According to Mosaic law, the firstborn son belongs to God, but various substitutions for the son's sacrifice are allowed. At Numbers 3:12 and 3:40 the Levite males aged one month and older are accepted as substitutes for the firstborn sons of all the Israelites, while Exodus 13:13 and Numbers 18:15 indicate that the firstborn son may be redeemed (saved from sacrifice) by paying an appropriate price to the priests.

Animals are substituted for human sacrificial victims in the Passover, described at Exodus 12. God had resolved to kill every firstborn in the land of Egypt. He tells Moses and Aaron that every Israelite family should slaughter a sacrificial lamb and place some of the lamb's blood on their doorposts and lintels on the houses where they eat that lamb; that way, "when I see the blood, I will pass over you, and no plague shall destroy you when I strike the land of Egypt."[25] The role of sacrificial animals as substitutes for human victims is annually communicated to Jewish families through the Passover seder.

The idea that an animal victim may substitute for a human sacrifice is dramatically represented in the legend of the Akedah, summarized above. Abraham's interrupted killing of his son is directly linked to his patriarchal status through the angel's words: "By myself I have sworn, says the Lord: because you have done this, and have not withheld your son, your only son, I will indeed bless you, and I will make your offspring as numerous as the stars of heaven and as the sand that is on the seashore."[26] Interpreting the divine blessing merely as a reward for obedience ignores the substantive content of what Abraham was called to do. It is specifically a near-killing of Isaac that places innumerable offspring into Abraham's patriline. In the story, an angel interrupts the sacrifice at the last moment. But as in the story of Noah's ark, from the point of view of observers such as Isaac, the agency is Abraham's. It is Abraham who must decide whether the voice bidding him to halt is truly an angel of the Lord. Abraham prepares to kill Isaac, and Abraham decides to stop. Since it is through Abraham's grace that Isaac lives, Abraham has established the right to be called father of Isaac and ancestor to all Isaac's descendants.

Abraham's capacity to kill Isaac is indicated by the preparations—woodpile on the altar, binding of Isaac, knife to his throat—but also by the fact that he does actually cut a creature's throat and bleed him to death. The ritual killing of animals serves as a threat to any human being who could be similarly victimized. In Israelite culture, sons, particularly the firstborn, were associated with the animals sacrificed because of legends like the Akedah and the dogma that firstborn sons were owed to God.

In the Akedah an incomplete killing of the son and a completed killing of an animal are immediately interdependent. This story is significant because it associates two types of rituals that are typically not so immediately linked. Excluding Passover, the Israelites sacrificed animals on many occasions in rituals that did not directly represent the animal victim as a substitute for a child. Conversely, the primary ritual of incomplete killing of a child, circumcision, is not typically accompanied by a completed animal sacrifice. But examination of the circumcision ritual reveals that it is associated with completed blood sacrifice in Jewish thought.

JEWISH CIRCUMCISION

Barbara Ehrenreich recently broached the possibility that circumcision developed from human sacrifice. "Circumcision may well be a remnant of a tradition of human sacrifice, with the foreskin serving as a substitute for a whole human victim," she writes. "Some historians speculate that an archaic version of the deity, quite possibly a goddess, demanded human sacrifices and later came to accept the destruction of the male genitals as a sufficient substitute for the whole man."[27] Circumcision as a substitute for human sacrifice is represented in the bizarre story at Exodus 4:24. The Lord, for no apparent reason, tries to kill Moses or his son (the text is ambiguous). Zipporah, Moses's wife, intervenes by cutting off her son's foreskin, at which point the Lord "let him alone." Regardless of whether circumcision originated as an ameliorated human sacrifice, the circumcision ritual does connote the near-killing of the son by the father.

One man who recently circumcised his son himself recommends that every father experience "inflicting upon his child a ritualized blow so intense as to make him shake and recoil, yet so controlled that no damage is done," in order to signify that this will be the worst the child will ever know from his father's hand.[28] This cut is the worst the child will know from his father, but the cut could have gone deeper, the father (or his designated professional circumciser) need not have staunched the blood flow, and the child could have died if the ritual had been directed slightly differently. All this is evident to anyone witnessing the circumcision. The child lives only due to the father's exercise of control over the violence.

Circumcision establishes paternal lineages. From its first mention in Genesis, circumcision is presented as the means for establishing patriliny. God promises to make Abraham the ancestor of a multitude of nations; for his part, Abraham must circumcise himself and institute the practice of circumcising all the males of his line.[29] Ritually, circumcision serves the same function that Jay attributed to animal sacrifice—it marks lines of paternal descent. Circumcision inducts the Jewish boy into the patriliny that is traced back to Abraham: "Only at his circumcision did the boy get a name, being known thereafter as the son of his father, who was the son of his father, and so on, all the way back to the first father, Abraham."[30]

In Jewish circumcision bloodshed is essential to the induction ritual, not the removal of the foreskin. Boys born without foreskins and adult converts who have already been circumcised must still have blood ritually drawn to enter the covenant.[31] The blood of circumcision is believed to have the power to give life. In the circumcision ritual, the father (or, more typically, the mohel, who is the designated agent of the father) inflicts and cauterizes the wound, names the child, and then cites this passage from Ezekiel 16:6: "I passed by you and saw you wallowing in your blood, and I said to you: In your blood, live; I said to you: In your blood, live."[32]

Not all blood is believed to have salvific power. Menstrual blood and the blood of childbirth, for example, are considered impure and polluting. In Jewish thought it is specifically sacrificial blood and circumcision blood that have the power to save. Though the bloods of childbirth and menstruation may seem obviously associated with life, and the blood of sacrifice with death, the associations are just the opposite in rabbinic ideology. A material fact helps make such reversals believable. Sacrificial blood, including the blood flowing from a circumcised penis, can be associated with life because the sacrificial victim needs that blood to live.

Unlike menses and the blood of childbirth, sacrificial blood flows are controlled by men.[33] Men initiate these bloodlettings, and they decide whether to staunch them before death occurs. Men generate life and thus become fathers by making it clear that they are allowing boys to keep the blood they need to live. This can look like men are actually giving salvific blood to boys, a viewpoint that is dramatized in certain versions of the ritual. Traditionally, the mohel cauterizes the wound with his mouth, that is, he sucks blood from the cut penis. He then places some wine on the boy's lips. The imagery here is of two males nourishing each other, entirely bypassing suckling at the mother's breast. The father's agent nourishes the boy by replacing the blood he has lost (wine representing blood). The father receives nourishment by vicariously sucking at his son's wound, which coheres with the notion that men achieve everlasting life by founding a patriline of indefinite length.

Circumcision is a way for men to appropriate credit for childbirth from women. It is important for women to be absent or to have only a peripheral role at the ceremony, lest the overt physical dependence of the child on the woman overwhelm the image of male life giving that is being constructed. In his book on circumcision, Lawrence Hoffman recounts the historical process by which women were more and more excluded from participation in the ritual. Though women had once held their sons on their laps during the cutting, he notes, by the Middle Ages all women, including the mother, were forbidden to attend a circumcision:[34]

> When women still insisted on carrying their sons to the synagogue—and possibly also, once they were already there, holding them during the circumcision rather than giving them up to one of the men—a *ba'alat brit* was instituted. Now she, not the mother, brought the child to the synagogue doors. . . . The circumcision had finally become exclusively male. . . . The only woman who came to the synagogue (the *ba'alat brit*) gave up the child outside the synagogue doors.[35]

The man who holds the boy on his lap during the circumcision is called the *sandek*. Sixteenth-century rabbis characterized the *sandek*'s knees as an altar on which a sacrifice was being offered to God—one of many ways in which circumcision is associated with animal sacrifice.[36] It is worth recounting some of the other connections here.

The circumcision ritual twice refers to the boy as a sacrificial victim, first in a phrase translatable as "Happy is the one whom You offer up as a sacrifice" and later in the mohel's prayer: "Master of the universe, may it be your will that this be considered by you—and thus accepted as according to your will—as if I had sacrificed him before your throne of glory."[37]

The story of Abraham's foundational covenant with God is told twice in the book of Genesis. In the earlier version (at chapter 15) the covenant is marked by an elaborate animal sacrifice. In the later version (at chapter 17) the covenant is sealed not with animal blood but with the blood of circumcision. Circumcision blood, the blood of animal sacrifice, and the blood of the paschal lamb tend to merge in that they are all considered salvific (and they are all let by men). For instance, in one midrash it is stated that not only was the blood of the paschal lamb used at the Passover, but circumcision blood was also applied to the lintels to protect the Israelites from divine destruction.[38]

The circumcision rite is performed in context with blood rituals in which the victim is actually killed. Circumcision has more of a menacing quality than it otherwise would because (1) the same class of men who circumcise also do (or once did) kill animals sacrificially, (2) the circumcised boy is compared to a sacrificial offering in various biblical stories and commentaries as well as in the circumcision rite itself, and (3) the Bible is replete with stories of human sacrifice. In such a context the ritual cutting of a boy is unavoidably perceived as a near-killing, and it is this perception that allows the rite to function as an index of paternity.

Christian Sacrifice

The Old Testament divinity demands the life blood of humans but can be satisfied with partial sacrifices, such as circumcision, and substitutes, such as the paschal lamb and the ram killed in Isaac's place. Christianity rejected both animal sacrifice and circumcision—not because it repudiated Jewish belief in the salvific quality of blood shed by men but because in Christianity this belief took new ritual forms while continuing to ground the establishment of paternity.

The central tenet of Christianity is that God sent his son to Earth to be sacrificed, a sacrifice held to have ultimate saving force. This is a development of, not a break from, the sacrificial belief system of Judaism. The story of Jesus' sacrifice is similar to the Akedah—the primary difference is that in Jesus' case there was no animal substitute at the last moment. In both cases, however, the willingness of the father to kill the son is claimed to generate life.

Christians at times show Jesus as a paschal lamb, and the Akedah and Jesus' crucifixion are both traditionally held to have occurred during the Passover season,[39] a dating that associates Isaac and Jesus with the paschal lamb. The gospel of John states that Jesus was handed over to be crucified on the day of preparation for the Passover, the day on which the Passover lambs are slaughtered.[40] This gospel also states that the soldiers did not break Jesus' bones on the cross, in fulfillment of the scriptural injunction that "none of his bones shall be broken"—an instruction for the butchering of Passover lambs given at Exodus 12:46.[41]

Jesus is repeatedly referred to in the New Testament as a sacrificial offering, often specifically as a sacrificial animal (usually a lamb). "Here is the Lamb of God who takes away the sin of the world!" (John 1:29) is one example.[42] While in Jewish thought animals substituted for human sacrificial victims, Christians reversed the process, replacing animal sacrifice with one final human sacrifice in the form of Jesus Christ. In this change of victims sacrificial ideology was not renounced, it was extended—the logic being that if the ritual shedding of animal blood has salvific efficacy, then human sacrifice must be even more effective; and if human sacrifice works, then it is even better to sacrifice a human who is also God's son. This thinking is evident in the Book of Hebrews, for instance: "For if the blood of goats and bulls, with the sprinkling of the ashes of a heifer, sanctifies those who have been defiled so that their flesh is purified, how much more will the blood of Christ, who through the eternal Spirit offered himself without blemish to God, purify our conscience."[43]

Christian priests ritually reenact the sacrifice of Jesus during the performance of the mass. Bread and wine are turned into the flesh and blood of the crucified Jesus then distributed to the congregation for consumption. Nancy Jay described the connection between eucharistic sacrifice and the establishment of a formal patrilineage of the clergy of the Roman Church—it is through the performance of this reenacted sacrifice that the priests place themselves into a succession traced back to Jesus' apostles.[44]

This is not the only patriline established by Christian sacrifice. The relations between the members of the Christian church, the priests, the founding fathers of the religion, and the divinities are all expressed in genealogical terms. God is referred to as "the Father," Jesus is the son, and Christians are called the "children" of God.[45] Paul refers to himself as "the father" of his converts.[46] Those who believe in Christian doctrine are also called the "descendants" and "offspring" of Abraham.[47]

In the Roman Catholic Church priests are addressed as "father." How does priestly work connote paternity? The sacrifice of Jesus is held to have saved humankind, so those responsible for this sacrifice are saviors, life givers, and fathers. Priests are not seen as the initiators of the sacrifice of Jesus, but by making the flesh and blood of the crucified Christ available for consumption, they bring people today into contact with the salvational act of bloodshed. As mediators between the people and the original saving event, priests at least partially earn the paternal title.

Christian imagery helps give a superficial plausibility to the attribution of life-generating power to Jesus' crucifixion. Jesus is often portrayed as a sacrificial lamb. But Christians themselves are also imaged as a flock of sheep, for instance at John 21:15 and 1 Peter 5:2. In a flock of sheep the destruction of one can save the others. If the flock is pursued by a predator, for example, the offering of one lamb will sate the predator's hunger, thus providing safety for the rest of the flock. Barbara Ehrenreich points out that we humans used to be preyed upon ourselves, and she argues that one basis of sacrificial blood offerings lies in a cultural memory of how the taking of a person or domesticated animal by a predator alleviates the predational threat to the group.[48] Of course in a real situation the offering of an individual gives the group only temporary security, just until the predator becomes hungry again. But in Christian ideology the blood of Jesus is so precious that it saves the rest of the flock for all time.

This attribution of salvation through blood offering only makes sense against the background of a predatory threat. God has been established by the Old Testament as a predatory figure demanding the blood of the firstborn or some substitute. At once and for all time, Jesus' crucifixion satisfied God's blood thirst. Although the priests' work as mediators gives them some claim to paternal status, the real saviors are those believed to have arranged and carried out this ultimate sacrifice, namely, Jesus and God the Father himself (God, like men in general under patriarchy, is both predator and savior). Because Christian priests do not actually perform animal sacrifices or circumcisions, they do not in those traditional ways display power over life and death. This means that they do not exercise the usual means for establishing paternity—the controlled application of deadly bloodletting. But Christian priests do perform baptism, and this ritual, though not entailing the actual spilling of blood, is sufficiently menacing to allow it to function in the usual way as a paternity-marking ritual.

BAPTISM

Early Christians replaced circumcision with baptism.[49] Like Jewish circumcision, baptism is a naming and initiation rite performed by men. Also like circumcision, baptism ritually constructs a near-death experience. In its original form baptism involved total immersion in water, thus creating an image of drowning. Indeed, biblical texts and Christian commentators frequently associate baptism with death. For example, Romans 6:3–4 describes baptism as a death and burial, two gospels refer to Jesus' trial and execution as a baptism (Mark 10:38 and Luke 12:50), the martyrdom of early Christians was called "blood-baptism," and so on.[50] For theologian Karl Barth, threatening the initiate with death is the essential aspect of baptism:

> Baptism carried out [by complete immersion] had in its mode, exactly like the circumcision of the Old Testament, the character of a direct threat to life, succeeded immediately by the corresponding deliverance and preservation. . . . It is impossible to understand the meaning of baptism, unless one keeps in mind that it implies a threat of death and a deliverance to life; nor that, generally speaking, the custom followed in baptism is to be called good or bad as it more or less adequately represents such a process.[51]

By threatening death, the priest can become an instrument of life. The priest guides the initiate back to the surface before he or she drowns, thus positioning himself as savior and life giver. In Christian thought baptism is death *and* rebirth: "The water of baptism is also the source of new life, the means by which man is reborn."[52] Feminist writers have interpreted baptism as a means for men to appropriate birth from women.[53] This interpretation is bolstered by the explicit comparisons Christians make between baptism and maternity. Paul twice characterizes himself as a nursing mother in relation to his converts, and St. Augustine once exclaimed, "Here the maternal womb is the baptismal water."[54] In these comparisons the births given by spiritual men are ceded precedence over the fleshy births of women: "Through [baptism], we are born, not of a creature, but of God."[55] Compare this passage from the gospel of John: "Nicodemus said to him, 'How can anyone be born after having grown old? Can one enter a second time into the mother's womb and be born?' Jesus answered, 'Very truly, I tell you, no one can enter the kingdom of God without being born of water and Spirit. What is born of the flesh is flesh, and what is born of the Spirit is spirit.'"[56]

In Judaism circumcision and the sacrifice of animals are unavoidably linked because both are acts of controlled bloodletting performed by the same class of men. There is not such an obvious association between baptism and the crucifixion of Jesus. Apart from its representation of death and rebirth, the only material connection between baptism and Jesus' sacrifice is the obscure fact that both drowning and crucifixion are deaths by asphyxiation. In Christianity baptism is associated with the sacrifice of God's son through doctrine more than through overt similarity.

Various passages in the New Testament describe baptism as a process of dying and being resurrected with Jesus Christ; for example, Colossians 2:12: "When you were buried with [Christ] in baptism, you were also raised with him through faith in the power of God."[57] The effect of this doctrine is to unite each Christian with Jesus as sacrificial offering. Theologians describe baptismal initiates as "participating in," as being "integrated with," and as "sharing" the death of Jesus.[58] According to Calvin, "Christ by baptism has made us partakers of His death," and Aquinas stated that "baptism incorporates us with the Passion and death of Christ."[59] Once Jesus was crucified, it was through divine intervention that he was brought back to life. In the same way, those who are baptized first die but then are given life through the grace of God. Françoise Cuttaz states that baptism is "as though we ourselves had been nailed with Him and in Him to the Cross," explaining:

> Baptism is "immersion," but it is also "emersion." It is death but also resurrection: it buries us with Christ, only that we may be born with Him to the Divine Life. . . . God pardons by bestowing His life, by bestowing Himself. . . . By incorporating us with the Christ of the Passion, Baptism gives us a share in the merits of the Redeemer. Through this Sacrament, His Sacrifice

becomes *our* sacrifice, His sufferings and death become *ours,* and *ours* too the
supernatural benefits won by them.[60]

The spiritual concept of baptism as death and resurrection is imagined in
its ultimate ritualized form in the following passage from Keith Donahue's
novel, *The Stolen Child:*

> They quickly stripped me of my clothes and bound me like a mummy in a
> gossamer web. . . . Thus bound, I was thrown into the water. . . . The wrench-
> ing juxtaposition of warm air and cool water shocked me most. The gag did
> not come out of my mouth; my hands were not loosed. Submerged, I could
> no longer see, and I tried for a moment to hold my breath, but then felt the
> painful pressure in my chest and sinuses as my lungs quickly filled. My life
> did not flash before my eyes—I was only seven—and I did not call out for
> my mother or father or to God. My last thoughts were not of dying, but of
> being dead. The waters encompassed me, even to my soul, the depths closed
> round about, and weeds were wrapped about my head.
>
> Many years later, when the story of my conversion and purification evolved
> into legend, it was said that when they resuscitated me, out shot a stream of
> water a-swim with tadpoles and tiny fishes. My first memory is of awakening
> in a makeshift bed, dried snot caked in my nose and mouth. . . . The whole
> scene felt like a waking dream or as if I had died and had been born again.[61]

In one biblical passage the great Flood is said to have saved eight persons
and to have prefigured baptism, which now also saves Christians through
water.[62] Noah and his family were "saved" by the flood because everyone else
was killed but they were graciously spared by God. If in baptism the initiate
is nailed on the cross with Jesus, there is a question of whether he or she will
be left to die (like those submerged by the Flood) or saved by God's gift of
eternal life. In theological terms it is God who saves, but here on Earth the
priests control the rituals and thus overtly bestow life by assisting the initiates' emergence from the water before they drown. God resurrected his son
Jesus, according to biblical texts, but priests resurrect initiates by pulling
them safely from the water. God is *the Father* by dogmatic insistence, while
priests merit the title of "father" through their direct administration of the
immersion and emersion of Christian initiates.

Regardless of its connotations of drowning, baptism is not seriously menacing so long as no one ever dies from it. Doctrinally associating baptism
with Jesus' execution somewhat increases the ritual's threatening quality,
but this would naturally remain quite a mild threat so long as the priestly
class itself commits no actual violence. Recall that the threatening quality of

circumcision increases when the priestly class actually kills some creatures by bloodletting. Christian priests perform no routine ritual involving actual violence, but they have a history of periodically sanctioning or perpetrating extreme violence. Examples include the Crusades, the Inquisition, the witch-hunts, numerous anti-Semitic pogroms, and the colonization of the New World. Knowledge of priestly involvement in these campaigns of violence would tend to generate an awareness that priests are capable of and at times willing to kill. This alters the meaning of baptism, enhancing the element of suspense at the moment the initiate is dependent on priestly assistance, a suspense that if consciously articulated might be phrased thus: "Priests do kill at times, will this one kill this time? . . . With his assistance I emerge from the water undrowned; through his grace I live again. . . . Thank you, Father."

Animal Sacrifice in Modern Times

The crucial features of animal sacrifice highlighted in this chapter are its basis in men's envy of women's reproductive capacities and its connection to violence against people. Men kill animals ritualistically in order to communicate a threat toward other people. This threatening behavior, along with actual violence done against selected human subordinates, allows men to claim credit for the continued existence of human life. We live, in other words, because men in power have applied their deadly force elsewhere. In this way men struggle against the respect women are naturally ceded due to their obvious and essential contributions to the reproduction of human society.

Theorizing about religious rituals of animal sacrifice is not of merely historical interest. It has relevance to understanding men's current institutions of animal exploitation—vivisection, hunting, and meat production. Each of these modern institutions has significant elements in common with the classical religious rituals. For vivisection in particular this is more than mere similarity. I argue in the next chapter that animal experimentation *is* a sacrificial ritual.

5

Vivisection as a Sacrificial Ritual

We have not lost faith, but we have transferred it
from God to the medical profession.

—George Bernard Shaw

Those who analyze religious ritual believe that animal sacrifices are no longer performed in modern Western society. A century ago the explanation for the alleged change most likely would have been that people in the past were superstitious and we are not. Today's theorists, however, look for less judgmental explanations for the apparent disappearance of animal sacrifice. To René Girard, for example, the absence of sacrificial rites in modern society is explicable in terms of the development of a judicial system: We no longer need sacrificial scapegoats because perpetrators are punished directly.[1]

Nancy Jay, on the other hand, wrote that sacrifice was concentrated among preindustrial societies and does not "usually survive the introduction of a modern economy with occupational differentiation and monetary media of exchange."[2] This is a generalization, not an explanation. Indeed, Jay's theory of paternal sacrifice generates a puzzle. Given that we live in a society in which men are still driven to establish paternity, and given Jay's demonstration that animal sacrifice is a favored ritual for marking paternity, it is odd that this society would not continue to ritualize the killing of animals. There are possible explanations for this presumed lack of sacrifice. According to Barbara Ehrenreich, for instance, modern warfare is a form of ritual sacrifice that marks patrilines.[3] So one way to solve the puzzle about the apparent disappearance of animal sacrifice would be to postulate that animals need no longer be ritually sacrificed because we have gone back to human sacrifice through the institution of modern warfare.

Such speculations are moot, however, if the underlying presumption about

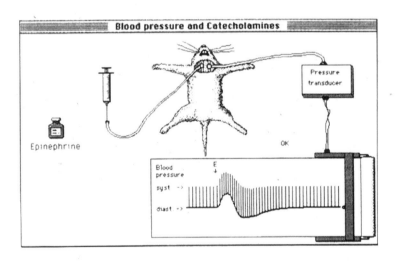

Blood pressure and Catecholamines

the disappearance of animal sacrifice is incorrect. Before concluding that this is a postsacrificial culture, we must examine the institution of vivisection, for this is the practice most plausibly identified as modern society's form of animal sacrifice. In this chapter I show that animal experimentation is indistinguishable from ancient religious rituals of animal sacrifice. The structure, ideology, and function of vivisection, in fact, correspond to those of animal sacrifice. Vivisection is modern society's form of sacrificial ritual. Most significantly, in our society vivisection performs the sacrificial function described in the previous chapter, namely, establishing men as life givers through their exclusive and systematic application of deadly force.

Vivisection as Sacrifice

In its overt organization, vivisection differs little from ancient religious rituals of animal sacrifice. Beyond this structural congruence there is also a direct line of historical continuity between the sacrificial altar and the necropsy table. Indeed, the established technical term for killing an experimental animal is "sacrifice." Arnold Arluke reports that spokespersons from the scientific community have called for scientists to cease using this term, in part because it has "religious and unscientific" connotations. Notwithstanding the serious efforts to delete the term from biological journals and grant proposals, Arluke notes that it "can still be overheard in the laboratory conversations of scientists and technicians as well as in the presentations of scientific papers at professional meetings."[4] This ambivalence over terminology reflects a deeper tension. On the one hand, scientists wish to distinguish themselves from traditional religion, intending to seize for themselves the prestige accorded those who hold the key to salvation. Thus scientists would typically deny any deep connection between religious sacrifice and vivisection, adopting the position that while ancient blood rituals were superstitiously based, what modern researchers do to animals is grounded in empirical reason. On the other hand, vivisectors yearn for the moral approbation of a suspicious public. The term "sacrifice" connotes a religious ritual in which slitting a conscious animal's throat is not only morally permitted but also celebrated as a holy sacrament. Seeking justification for their activities, modern scientists do at times affirm continuity between religious blood rituals and vivisection. One recent example comes from the American Medical Association: "The issue of animal research is fundamentally an issue of the dominion of humans over animals. This issue is rooted in the Judeo-Christian religion of western culture, including the ancient tradition of animal sacrifice described in the Old Testament."[5]

This association of animal research with Judeo-Christian religion is jarring if we think of science purely in enlightenment terms, as the rationalistic repudiation of a superstitious past. But the men who originated professional vivisection did not themselves see the new methodologies this way. They were self-identified Christians who understood their scientific work in theological terms. Scientific methodology, including vivisection, developed largely within the university system, while the university system itself developed from medieval monasticism.[6] Science developed in this context, not as a repudiation of Christianity, but as an extension of its ideology. Francis Bacon, one of the founders of scientific thought, argued that man's dominion over creation, lost at the Fall, could be restored by the arts and sciences: "For creation was not by the curse made altogether and for ever a rebel, but in virtue of that charter, 'In the sweat of thy face shalt thou eat bread,' it is now by various labours . . . at length and in some measure subdued to the supplying of man with bread; that is, to the uses of human life."[7] By "labours" Bacon specifically meant scientific experiments, including dissections and vivisections. Of course Bacon, like all educated white men of the time, was steeped in biblical theology, including the Old Testament affirmation of sacrificial ritual. By classifying scientific experimentation as part of the "labour" required of man at the Fall, he was establishing the required theological context for the reintroduction of a temporarily suspended activity, the ritualized sacrifice of animals. Today's vivisectors may think of themselves as practicing a thoroughly secular activity (and thus consider their use of the word "sacrifice" as a meaningless, slightly embarrassing throwback), but the institution they inherited was founded by men who understood everything they did, including scientific experimentation, in Christian terms.

Vivisection is a form of animal sacrifice. If we understand science in Nietzschean terms, not as a repudiation of Christianity but as just another of its many disputing sects, then it is not surprising that ancient rituals would be reclaimed with minor modifications. Dissidents tend to retain the central elements of the ideological systems they dispute, and Christianity never renounced sacrificial ideology. Modern science may be atheistic or agnostic, but it is not anti-Christian. It retains the essential element of Christianity, its commitment to sacrifice, and promulgates the ancient rituals of sacrifice in something very close to their original forms.

In a 1988 article Michael Lynch described three points of correspondence between animal experimentation and religious rites of animal sacrifice.[8] I go beyond this, describing ten points of correspondence. The correspondences are sufficiently numerous and substantial to warrant classifying animal experimentation as modern Western civilization's form of animal sacrifice. Each of the following features of ancient blood rituals also applies to the scientific sacrifice of animals in vivisection:

1. Sacrifice is the rule-bound manipulation of an animal's body.
2. The rules governing the process must be followed precisely.
3. Sacrificial animals are specially selected for the rite.
4. Sacrifice can only occur at specially designated sites.
5. Sacrifice can only be performed by credentialed officials.
6. Regulations govern who, if anyone, may eat the flesh of the sacrificed animal.
7. Though the animal is destroyed, this is held to be incidental to rather than the real purpose of the sacrifice.
8. Sacrifice is men's work.
9. Sacrifice is claimed to be necessary for achieving some socially significant end.
10. Sacrifice establishes paternity.[9]

Feature 1 is constitutive—an animal must be destroyed or at least manipulated for an action to be considered an animal sacrifice or an act of vivisection. Features 2 to 5 are procedural, indicating that which is necessary to turn an act of animal destruction into a socially sanctioned ritual of sacrifice. The practitioners of religious blood ritual and of animal experimentation are determined that the harms they inflict not be associated with wanton cruelty toward animals. The applications of the terms "sacrifice" and "experiment" are thus based not on what is done to the animals but on who does it, where it is done, which animals are used, and how closely the rules are followed. To count as sacrifice (religious or experimental), the destruction of the animal must be performed or supervised by a priest or by a licensed researcher; the destruction must take place in a temple or in a laboratory; the sacrificed animal must be free of blemishes and contamination and be the right sex, right species, and right genealogy, all as prescribed by religious tradition on the one hand and experimental methodology on the other; and finally, the destruction must be done according to the proper procedures, again as described by religious tradition and by the manuals of experimental technique. The concentration on who, where, and how helps divert the sacrificer's attention away from the what—the harm he is actually imposing. This particular focus helps maintain feature 7: the belief that causing harm is not the real purpose of the sacrifice; it is merely "collateral damage," so to speak. As discussed in more detail in chapter 6, such a diversion of attention benefits researchers by partially relieving the pangs of conscience typically associated with the infliction of harm on animals.

Feature 6 is also procedural, but unlike features 2 to 5, it is not required to turn an act of animal destruction into a sacrifice; rather, it helps determine what type of sacrifice is being performed. Theorists distinguish *communal* sacrifices (which primarily serve to unite people into a community) from *expiatory* sacrifices (which primarily serve to separate people from defilement and other dangers), and they have noted that the eating of expiatory sacrifices is cross-culturally restricted or forbidden. (By contrast, in communal sacrifice the uniting is typically achieved through the shared meal.) Animal experimentation is an expiatory sacrifice, due to its emphasis on ridding us of toxins and disease, and it follows the usual pattern in that the eating of laboratory animals is forbidden.

Features 7 to 9 are ideological; they concern the structure of beliefs regarding sacrifice. Sacrifice is not understood merely as men destroying animals; it is always held to be a special kind of destruction—one that must be performed in order for the group to be secure from danger, and one that must be performed by men in order to be done effectively. This pair of beliefs entails a life-generating, paternal function for men (or at least for one class of men). As described in the previous chapter, the official insistence that men's violent labor contributes as much to the sustenance of society as does women's procreative work does not persist in isolation from material reality. Indeed, it is unlikely that such an overtly improbable dogma could be successfully propagated in the absence of substantial material support. In vivisection, as in sacrifice generally, that support comes from the knowledge that the researcher's tools of destruction could be applied to humans as well as to sacrificial animals. In a real sense, we live only through animal research because in the absence of animal subjects vivisectors would turn their deadly attention in our direction (as they repeatedly remind us).

The details of this material basis for constructing paternity through vivisection are discussed in the latter part of this chapter. The next two sections concern the ideological aspects of modern sacrifice: the image of vivisection as men's work and the portrayal of vivisection as essential for human well-being.

Constructing Vivisection as Men's Work

In a generalization that extends to vivisection, Jay notes that it is "a common feature of unrelated traditions that only adult males—fathers, real and metaphorical—may perform sacrifice."[10] Women have been excluded from the performance of vivisection through three interrelated processes: the exclusion of women from the university, the masculinization of science and vivisection, and the feminization of vivisection's opponents.

Vivisection is the application of the scientific method to the study of physiological processes. The scientific method, and vivisection itself, developed largely within the university system, and that system, as David Noble describes, emerged from medieval monasticism.[11] As the monasteries were viewed as centers of spiritual warfare waged on behalf of the church, so the original universities were founded to train priests to be more effective theological warriors. The university developed as a militaristic institution not only in its goals but also in its internal structure (disputations in the form of knightly jousting, physical punishment accompanying Latin instruction) and its curriculum ("epics and histories full of violence and tales of valor"). According to Noble, women were squeezed out of the mainstream of education as the distinction between warrior and minister of peace collapsed.[12] For centuries universities admitted only celibate men as teachers and students.

Science developed in this context, not as a repudiation of priestly militarism but as a new method for waging theological battle. Francis Bacon referred to the new method of inquiry as a "Masculine Philosophy."[13] From its inception, science was polarized by gender: its practitioners imaged as male, having the capacity and the right to subdue, its subject matter imaged as female, by nature needing and deserving to be subdued.

Only men could practice science because female dispositions hinder the discovery of truth: "Where the Will or Passion hath the casting voice, the case of Truth is desperate. . . . The Woman in us, still prosecutes a deceit, like that begun in the Garden; and our understandings are wedded to an Eve, as fatal as the Mother of our Miseries."[14] The project of science is to restore man's dominion over creation, lost by woman's weakness and deceit, and the practice of science correspondingly requires men to subdue any female tendencies within themselves.

Bacon describes scientific inquiry and application as the subjugation of women: "I am . . . leading to you Nature with all her children to bind her to your service and make her your slave" and "[Recent acquisitions] do not . . . merely exert a gentle guidance over nature's course; they have the power to conquer and subdue her, to shake her to her foundations."[15] The rhetoric of women's subjugation becomes overtly sexual when theoreticians of the new philosophy employ metaphors of exposure and penetration, as in Thomas Sprat's exclamation that the "Beautiful Bosom of *Nature* will be Expos'd to our view" and Nicolas Malebranche's statement that women were intellectually inferior to men because their imagination lacked the "vigor and reach necessary to penetrate to the core of things."[16]

A primary contemporary model for the development of science was the persecution of women as witches. Feminist historians have noted that the witch craze functioned to disempower women as a class and was highly sexualized in its ideology and disciplinary techniques. Women were taken to be guilty of witchcraft more often than men due to the image of an inherently carnal female nature that made them highly susceptible to sexual seduction by the devil. This theory accords with the scientists' concern that female passions lead one to stray from the truth. Inquisitional procedures included stripping women, examining their bodies (including their genitals) for the presence of a "witch's teat," pricking their flesh with a sharp needle to find insensitive spots characteristic of those who concluded a pact with the devil, and ultimately torturing women into confessing to the highly detailed accounts of sexual intercourse with devils provided by prosecutors.[17]

Historians have observed the predominance of inquisitional metaphors in Bacon's description of the new philosophy, highlighting his use of phrases such as "putting nature on the rack," "examine nature herself and the arts upon interrogatories," and "inquisition of nature" and statements such as that "nature exhibits herself more clearly under the trials and vexations of art."[18] Bacon explicitly advocated the vivisection of animals as one experimental technique.[19] He referred to this as using beasts and birds for "dissections and *trials*."[20] For experimentation in general the inquisitional rhetoric may be metaphorical, but in the case of animal experimentation the comparison has deeper significance. As in an inquisition, in a vivisection the subject is confined, immobilized, exposed, and penetrated. Truth is expected to be revealed through the imposition of injury (torture). The injuring and killing of animals as an experimental technique was controversial at the time and remains so. But Bacon had denied that "the inquisition of nature is in any part interdicted or forbidden."[21] This echoes the Inquisition's arrogation of interrogatory techniques, such as torture, that were normally forbidden.

Images of sexual subjugation and penetration continue in modern science. For example, Evelyn Fox Keller cites H. J. Muller's 1926 advocacy of a program of molecular biology: "It is a difficult path, but with the aid of the necromancy of science, it must be penetrated. We cannot leave forever inviolate in their recondite recesses those invisibly small yet fundamental particles, the genes."[22] One male scholar recently remarked, "Laboratories and whorehouses are places in which you do what you like—which has its amusing sides."[23] And nineteenth-century experimental physiologist Claude Bernard, who is generally regarded as the founder of professional vivisection, employed inquisitional terminology in his description of "nature as a woman who must be forced to unveil herself when attacked by the experimenter, who must be put to the question and subdued."[24]

The image of "unveiling" recurs throughout the historiography of science, especially with reference to vivisection:

> Newton seemed to draw off the veil from some of the mysteries of nature (historian David Hume, 1792).[25]
>
> Nature has not up to the present permitted man to raise the veil which hides from him the understanding of vital phenomena (nineteenth-century vivisector François Magendie).[26]
>
> [I am] on the trail of some mysteries, and the veil that covers them is getting thinner and thinner (Louis Pasteur).[27]
>
> Using vivisection, [Galen] tried to unveil the ever intriguing secrets of respiration and heart action, of the functions of the brain and spinal cord (historians Andreas-Holger Maehle and Ulrich Trohler, 1987).[28]

The immediate connotation of "unveiling" as it is used to describe science is the exposing of a woman's body, as in an act of seduction, rape, or inquisition. But a second connotation is the opening of the veil that shields the holiest shrines. In Hebrew religion, for example, the veil protecting the sanctuary could be passed only by priests and only on certain occasions. In doing so, those priests approached as near to God as is possible on Earth, thereby positioning themselves to receive divine secrets. Passing beyond this veil was also associated with animal sacrifice in that one of the occasions for a priest's entering the shrine was to deliver a blood sacrifice. The religious and sacrificial connotation of unveiling was more evident to the early developers of science than to scientists today, given their Christian identities and familiarity with biblical texts. Through the image of unveiling, the act of opening the skin of an animal to observe the still-functioning organs was understood both in terms of a priest entering a holy sanctuary and as a man's exposure and penetration of the female.

Sandra Harding noted that "women have been more systematically excluded from doing serious science than from performing any other social activity except, perhaps, frontline warfare."[29] The masculinity of science derives from its roots in a militaristic/monastic university system, and from the conceptualization of science as a process of sexual subjugation of the female by the male. Thus the traits of the scientist are the traits of the conqueror. This is nowhere more evident than in vivisection, where the scientist's subject matter is a sentient being capable of struggling, rebelling, and/or pleading for sympathy. The vivisector must be willing and able to subdue the subject and to avoid or override any compassionate response he might have to the one being vivisected. The Roman physician and anatomist Galen found the performance of vivisections unpleasant, yet he advised that "the dissection, once started, should proceed just as with a dead animal, penetrating into the deep tissues without pity or compassion," according to Maehle and Trohler.[30]

To the extent that the ability to dominate is seen as a male capacity, the vivisector must be a man. But manhood is not merely a matter of biological sex; it is an ideal that some males achieve more fully than others. Claude Bernard remarked that "the physiologist is not a man of fashion, he is a man of science. . . . He no longer hears the cry of animals, he no longer sees the blood that flows, he sees only his idea and perceives only organisms concealing problems which he intends to solve."[31] The performance of vivisection is also a way to achieve manhood. Experimental physiologist Michael Foster, for instance, noticed that a colleague was "lecturing to women" and advised him not to "do too much lecturing—*it destroys a man* . . . give all your energy to research."[32] On noticing the young Bernard's skill at dissecting animal bodies, François Magendie exclaimed, "Well, you're a better man than I am!"[33] Magendie was famous for his animal experiments. Bernard later established his own reputation as a vivisector, and when Magendie bequeathed his professorship to Bernard he remarked that "at least I know that it won't fall to a molly-coddle."[34] Bernard could only see vivisectors as men. When "four Russian doctoresses" came to work in his laboratory he wrote that "one of them . . . has a heart of steel . . . they are sexless women. It seems strange to me to see students change sex."[35]

While the vivisector typifies manhood, antivivisectionists, whether male or female, are associated with stereotypically feminine traits such as illogic and excessive emotion. The *Lancet* classified the audiences at antivivisectionist lectures as members of "the gentler sex" and "men of illogical minds."[36] During the agitation for antivivisectionist legislation, one member of the House of Lords spoke of "the contempt in which [some on my side] hold the bill and I presume all the milk sops who are parties to it."[37]

Women were predominant in antivivisection activism, a fact that nineteenth-century provivisectionists seized on, using various sexist disparagements to further their cause. This tendency has continued into the present, even showing up in muted forms within historical accounts that purport to be scholarly and neutral. For example, Richard French writes that the "years 1875 and 1876 saw the beginnings of the *hysteria* and sensationalism in the anti-vivisectionist cause."[38] And in Susan Lederer's description of the vivisection controversy in America, women who sought abolition are referred to as "strident" and "shrill," whereas men who sought to continue vivisection are called "moderate" and "impressive."[39]

The gendered politics of the struggle over vivisection have played out in striking ways within the family lives of some of the founders of vivisection. Historian Gerald Geison remarks that "both at home and in his laboratory, Pasteur was the very model of the patriarch."[40] One historian notes that "[physiologist] Burdon-Sanderson's unhappy wife left her own message as to her views by leaving her money to an animal refuge."[41] Claude Bernard's wife and daughters left him; one of the major issues instigating the split was the suffering Bernard caused to animals. Bernard's practice of bringing vivisected animals home for overnight observation and the women's fear for the safety of the family pets may also have been factors. Like Burdon-Sanderson's wife, Mme. Bernard became an active supporter of the animal protection movement. Scholarly accounts of the rift between the Bernards are interesting. Schiller refers to Bernard's wife and daughters as "pathological," while Olmsted says that "Mme. Bernard seems to have had a very narrow intelligence" and claims that she was regarded as a little insane.[42] By contrast, Olmsted writes that Bernard's "untiring kindness, evenness of temper, and consideration" were recognized by all his friends.[43] And Jean Rostand's review of Bernard's famous book on experimental physiology remarks on its "natural nobility and firm virility of expression" and states that in it "we meet not only a scientist but a man."[44]

Claiming the Social Necessity of Vivisection

Given the historical continuity and numerous structural similarities between religious blood rituals and vivisection, and given that scientists themselves call their experimental killings "sacrifices," it is remarkable that Girard, Jay, and all other theorists of sacrifice exclude vivisection from their analyses. In their minds, something decisively distinguishes vivisection from all other ritualized animal killing. Most likely they presume that vivisection is an effective means for achieving its stated ends (developing therapies for human diseases) while other blood rituals are in reality ineffective (Aztec sacrifice did not really make the sun rise, the crucifixion of Jesus did not really yield eternal life for humankind, etc.).

Excluding vivisection from analyses of sacrifice on this basis is problematic, however. Sacrificers in every society give some account of why they perform the ritual. Theorists of sacrifice do not simply accept these official internal accounts as necessarily the best explanation for the origin and continuation of the rite. Nor do they uncritically accept the sacrificer's account as the complete story regarding the social functions served by that sacrificial ritual. The official story may be completely inaccurate or it may be accurate but only provide part of the best overall explanation of why and how that ritual functions. To suspend judgment regarding sacrificers' accounts in other cultures while uncritically accepting the official story regarding vivisection in our culture is an ethnocentrically biased methodology. It may be that the official story ("We are attempting to develop therapies for human diseases") is a complete and accurate account of the function, origin, and development of institutionalized vivisection. But if so, this should be the conclusion of our analysis, not a presumption used at the outset to exclude vivisection from the kind of detailed scrutiny given to ritualized killing in other cultures.

Indeed, a survey of its history reveals that the official account cannot be the entire explanation for animal experimentation. Vivisection was institutionalized before there was any substantial evidence that it might be a useful method for developing therapies for human diseases. As Stewart Richards explains, "Even by 1900 the clinical benefits of experimental physiology . . . were few indeed. . . . All the actors in the vivisectional drama performed as if they accepted the hypothesis of medical utility in advance of the evidence to support it."[45] Even today the official justification for vivisection is often accepted as much on faith as on evidence. Cancer research on animals, to mention just one example, continues unabated despite its failure to significantly improve survival rates after billions of dollars spent and millions of animals sacrificed over several decades.[46]

Until recently, women were the primary healers in European society. Local women healers and midwives, with their empirical knowledge, abundance of practical experience, and extensive herbal pharmacopoeia, were generally more successful in helping the sick than were the university-trained male physicians who spent years studying theology, philosophy, classical languages, and Galen's anatomy texts. This was acknowledged even by prominent male philosophers such as Francis Bacon and Thomas Hobbes.[47] From at least the fourteenth century on, university-trained male physicians have seen themselves as competing with female lay healers, and they have engaged in periodic efforts to eliminate women's healing.[48] The persecution of women as witches played a significant part in the repression of women's healing, in that successful women healers were frequently prosecuted on charges of witchcraft.[49] Noble notes that male physicians played a prominent role in these persecutions, perhaps because this helped eliminate their competition.[50] One of William Harvey's official duties, for example, was to examine women for the presence of the "witch's teat" that would be used as evidence against them by the inquisitors.

The establishment of vivisection as a scientific discipline occurred during the nineteenth century, a time when the status of women was just beginning to partially recover from the witch burnings. Male physicians in Europe and America (so-called regular doctors or allopaths) were facing renewed competition from female lay healers and other "irregulars." The success of vivisectors in establishing their discipline was due in large part to the willingness of regular physicians to associate their profession with vivisection. As I show in detail below, physicians made this association in order to augment their masculine prestige, expecting that this would help them gain hegemony over the healing role.

The performance of vivisection has met with criticism throughout its entire history. In response to these criticisms the vivisector usually claims that his work is essential for human well-being. For example, in response to a Quaker antivivisectionist, Magendie stated that experiments involving vivisection of animals aim at the benefit of humanity—that war is cruel but may be necessary.[51] Until the twentieth century, the preponderance of animal experiments could be classified as basic biological research, that is, they were not designed to test or discover therapies for disease but to gain understanding of physiological processes. Thus when the founding vivisectors claimed their work was necessary for human well-being, they did so in a vague way that pointed to unspecified future benefits. Today the defense of vivisection is more specific. Now vivisectionists argue for continued funding by pointing to past medical interventions such as the polio vaccine and by claiming that specific current diseases such as cancer and AIDS will be "conquered" only if animal experimentation continues.[52]

An extensive literature contests the claims of today's vivisectionists. The points of dispute are whether vivisection was really a crucial part of the process of discovering past medical interventions, whether those medical interventions have been as salutary as is claimed, whether cross-species inferences are valid, whether vivisection of animals is likely to be useful in finding treatments for current human diseases such as cancer and AIDS, and whether non-animal-based research is underfunded relative to its potential usefulness. These points are all relevant to assessing the current claims regarding vivisection and human benefit. Even without a full resolution of these technical points, however, it is clear that there is more behind the establishment of professional vivisection than possible human health benefits, because vivisection was brought into the medical system well before the development of the vaccines and antitoxins that today's vivisectors highlight in their self-justifications.

The International Medical Congress of 1881, held in London, was a crucial turning point in the medical establishment's acceptance of the vivisectionists' utility-based claims. Two days after this conference, the British Medical Association issued a national resolution declaring its "deep sense of the importance of vivisection to the advancement of medical science, and the belief that the further prohibition of it would be attended with serious injury to the community, by preventing investigations which are calculated to promote the better knowledge and treatment of disease in animals as well as man."[53] The conference also was followed by the founding of the Association for the Advancement of Medicine by Research (AAMR), a group of scientists and physicians who lobbied against legislation restricting vivisection and published and distributed brochures defending the practice of vivisection.

The arguments presented in the AAMR literature are highly dubious, relying on distortions of history,[54] references to advances in purely physiological (as opposed to therapeutic) knowledge,[55] advocacy of research programs such as drug testing on animals that beg the question of the validity of cross-species inferences, and the citing of therapeutic techniques that were developed through animal experiments but could just as easily have been developed through other means.[56] Yet according to Nicolaas Rupke, by the late nineteenth century vivisection was "near-unanimously supported by the leaders of the scientific and medical establishment."[57]

Earlier in the century, vivisectors such as Magendie had urged medical men to make themselves more scientific: "For the sake of their own prestige [physicians] should begin by making themselves physicists, chemists, etc."[58] Note that Magendie advocated the addition of science to the medical curriculum as a means of increasing physicians' prestige, not their therapeutic effectiveness. Significantly, a recent study found that a curriculum in basic science actually hinders medical students' abilities to accurately diagnose human diseases.[59] Physicians were concerned about enhancing their prestige and professional image because of the competition they faced from female lay healers and other "irregulars." By making regular medicine more scientific, they intended to make their discipline more masculine and thus more professional (masculinity and professionalism being seen as interchangeable). Science in general and vivisection in particular strongly connote masculinity, as discussed above. Thus as part of their effort to increase the masculine prestige of their profession, elite physicians introduced experimental physiology to medical schools and hospitals, and medical men began promulgating the unsubstantiated claim that animal research (a practice unavailable to female lay healers) was a necessary basis for progress in human healing.[60]

By 1900 the institutional association of medicine with vivisection was a fait accompli, notwithstanding the fact that "the roster of acknowledged practical pay-offs attributed to laboratory researches remained sparse in diagnostics and prognostics and yet sparser in therapeutics."[61] The establishment of biomedical vivisection may not have been therapeutically useful, but it did help to masculinize regular medicine, thus allowing the editor of the *Journal of the American Medical Association* at the turn of the century to argue that a man's success in medicine depended "on his virile courage, which the normal woman does not have nor is expected to have."[62]

Regular medicine today, scientifically based and largely male, sees itself as descending from the vivisectional patriliny of Galen, Harvey, Bernard, Pasteur, and Salk. The medical establishment is one of the staunchest promoters of the notion that our current and future health depends on the vivisection of animals. The American Medical Association's position is that animal experimentation is "absolutely essential to maintaining and improving the health of people."[63] But medical men commit themselves to animal experimentation in advance of evidence supporting its therapeutic necessity, prompting one historian to argue that "the laboratory as an essential part of physiology and medicine is ultimately a self-fulfilling prophecy."[64] Male physicians assume the necessity of vivisection-based medicine to justify their efforts to abolish female lay healing and other "alternative" medicines. Licensing requirements for medical practice, the proscription of midwifery in some states, the restriction of insurance benefits to "regular" medicine, the uniformity of medical school curricula, and other institutional structures supported by physicians function to marginalize healing practices not based in laboratory research. Thus AMA statements such as that without the nineteenth- and twentieth-century programs of animal experimentation, "many millions of Americans alive and healthy today would never have been born or would have suffered a premature death" gain superficial plausibility due to the absence of mainstream healing systems not tied to vivisection.[65] We cannot know whether this society would be more or less healthy overall had the enormous resources allocated to vivisection been used to develop other approaches to healing. But given the masculinity of vivisection, we can be sure that as people come to believe our current and future health depend on vivisectors and the physicians who apply their discoveries, healing for the first time comes to be identified as a male activity.

Medical men are not the only ones who unquestioningly accept the thesis of vivisection's utility. Whether scientist or layperson, most of us have never worked through the voluminous and highly technical literature debating the past and present value of animal experimentation as a research tool. Yet it is an article of our scientific and common sense faith that through animal experiments we have been saved from many diseases. Why is the official account of vivisection's necessity so easily accepted independently of supporting evidence? As with sacrifice in every other society, the salvational necessity of the blood shed by men in laboratories is a cultural given, conditioning our consciousness prior to any utilitarian debate. To understand society's faith in vivisection we must go beyond the largely disregarded technical debates and examine vivisection's material structure as a paternity-generating application of deadly force.

Vivisection as a Sacrificial Establishment of Paternity

As mentioned in the previous chapter, we must distinguish two related meanings of "paternity." In one sense paternity is a relationship between two individuals, one the father of the other. The father is the individual male credited with bringing a specific child into existence. In a broader sense, paternity is a relation between men in general (or a subgroup of men) and living beings in general (or some subgroup of living beings). Men as a class are fathers when they are collectively credited with initiating or sustaining the lives of a group, usually the group of community members in general. In this section I show that vivisection, the modern ritual of animal sacrifice, establishes both types of paternity. Animal experiments are used to establish genealogical relations between specific individuals within the scientific family; and animal experiments are used to allow men as a class to be credited with the generation of human life.

SCIENTIFIC PATRILINES

In both its history and its ideology vivisection has been an activity of men. The men who perform vivisections relate to each other through lines of descent. These lines of descent, or patrilines, are traced by the vivisectors themselves in their informal discussions and professional journals, and by those who write about them in the histories of science and in the science textbooks. Relations of paternity in the sciences are established through discoveries and their applications. The scientist credited with first establishing a theory, method, or significant fact is said to be the father of any subsequent scientists who apply that discovery in their research. The construction of scientific patrilines is a specific instance of the practice of establishing academic patrilines. This practice dates to the inception of the university system itself: "[The relationship of] master with disciples [is] as of fathers with heirs. ... We assert that the true wife of each philosopher is his philosophy from which he begets books like himself according to the forms and cast of his mind, and his disciples are in a fashion his sons" (from a fourteenth-century educational treatise).[66]

In "The Masculine Birth of Time," which is structured as a monologue by an authoritative man addressing a younger man whom he calls "son," Francis Bacon describes the scientific method as a means of establishing a family line that will continue indefinitely:

> [The method] must have in it an inherent power of winning support and a vital principle which will stand up against the ravages of time, so that the tradition of science may mature and spread like some lively vigorous vine. Then also science must be such as to select her followers, who must be worthy to be adopted into her family. ... My dear, dear boy, what I purpose is to unite you with *things themselves* in a chaste, holy, and legal wedlock; and from this association you will secure an increase beyond all the hopes and prayers of ordinary marriages, to wit, a blessed race of Heroes or Supermen.[67]

The researcher's subject matter is positioned in the woman's designated place as the medium through which he generates sons. For both theorists quoted above the man's marriage with philosophy transcends ordinary marriages with mortal women, just as in Christianity the spiritual births accomplished through sacraments transcend women's labor in the flesh. In patriarchal heterosexuality the man is expected to act aggressively upon a passive or even unwilling female, as discussed in chapter 3. Thus the placement of research material in the position of the female bodes ill whenever the man's chosen area of research involves sentient beings, as in vivisection.

The goal of scientists as a class is to pass to the next generation theories and methods sufficient to continue science indefinitely into the future. Throughout the history of science a basic distinction is made between "fertile" discoveries that open new lines of research, thus allowing the number of scientific progeny to increase, and "sterile" discoveries that do not lead to new lines of research and descendants. Following are a few examples of this usage by and about experimental physiologists:

> A great discovery is a fact whose appearance in science gives rise to ideas shedding a bright light which dispels many obscurities and shows us new paths. ... There are new facts which, although well observed, mean nothing to anyone; they remain, for the time being, detached and sterile in science (Claude Bernard).[68]

[Magendie's] activity was not sterile, for the final influence on science was salutary and would be transmitted through the pupils who would carry on the tradition established at the College de France. . . . Many of [Bernard's] isolated observations were fertile for later investigators (historian J. M. D. Olmsted).[69]

Past scientists are great insofar as they persuaded their peers to adopt their ideas and techniques and insofar as those ideas and techniques were fertile in the investigation and resolution of important research problems (Gerald Geison in his study of Pasteur).[70]

In each case fertility is determined by reference to the number of other scientists who use the discovery. At the time of its founding as a scientific discipline in the nineteenth century, vivisection was expected to open up new lines of research at an indefinitely accelerating rate. "It is very certain that for many years to come the problems of physiology demanding experimental solution will increase in something like geometrical ratio," stated E. Ray Lankester.[71] This expectation was borne out; the number of vivisections performed increased at an exponential rate throughout the twentieth century, and correspondingly the number of experimental physiologists has been able to multiply at a rate comparable to that of a population reproducing without check.[72] A typical recitation of the vivisectional patriliny occurs in Joseph Schiller's article in the *Journal of the History of Medicine:* "Claude Bernard of course carries much farther Galen's heritage, which he received through Vesalius, Harvey, Haller, Bichat and Magendie."[73] The American Medical Association traces the genealogy similarly, from Erisistratus of Alexandria to Aristotle to Galen to Harvey to Bernard and finally to twentieth-century biomedical researchers.[74] Galen and Harvey are generally cited as ancestors of today's professional vivisectors, because they were renowned anatomists who performed some experiments on animals. But François Magendie was first to vivisect animals on a routine basis as his primary method of research, and Claude Bernard, his protégé, did extensive vivisectional research and formalized the method in his "seminal" work *An Introduction to the Study of Experimental Medicine.* Thus Bernard and Magendie are generally characterized as the fathers of professional vivisection (as in Olmsted's reference to the observation of animals injected with poisons: "Magendie may rightly be called the father of this branch of medicine").[75] Magendie was aware of his foundational role in establishing a method that would be applied by subsequent generations of vivisectors, stating, "I bequeathe to [our successors] the thyroid, the thymus, suprarenal capsules, the sympathetic nerve, etc., whose functions are totally unknown."[76] Magendie's terminology here is not atypical—the relations between scientists are consistently understood in such genealogical terms, as in Bernard's remark that he studied the history of his chair so as to "learn my genealogy and boast about it on occasion."[77] Bernard referred to his pupils as his "scientific family," and several of his followers described Bernard's attitude toward them as "paternal."[78] Bernard's wife and daughters left him before the end of his life, but some of the work traditionally assigned to women of the family (such as nursing him during illness) was taken over by the young men comprising his scientific offspring.[79]

The vivisectional patriliny is now placed within the broader patriliny of science. Magendie, Bernard, and others are today considered the descendants not just of the early vivisectors but also of all those who founded the scientific method, as in Georges Cuvier's reference to experimental physiologists and other scientists as "the descendants of Archimedes among us."[80] The establishment of this lineage did not happen without struggle. By the nineteenth century science was established as a source of status and a means of access to resources. But it was still an open question whether experimental physiology (as opposed to clinical research, for example) would be accorded the mantle of *the* scientific approach to medicine. Indeed, it was still unclear whether any type of medical research would be considered truly scientific. One historian notes that all nineteenth-century proponents of vivisection "appeal in connection with the experimental method to disciplinary father- and founder-figures, figures who are often ruthlessly recreated and modernised in the author's own image."[81] The father-figure vivisectors align themselves with most often is William Harvey, the seventeenth-century physician and anatomist credited with discovering the circulation of the blood. Nicolaas Rupke argues that the primary purpose of vivisectors' repeated allusions to Harvey and others "was not to show the past importance [i.e., medical utility] of vivisectional work, but to make the Victorian vivisectors the legitimate heirs of the great scientific names of yore."[82]

Nancy Jay wrote, "Ancestor cults . . . are ways of organizing relations among the living. . . . [Ancestors] are also a way of regulating the inheritance of property."[83] In vivisection's case, the property at issue is the resources associated with university chairs, memberships in scientific academies, and so forth. In order to lay claim to this property, vivisectors had to establish patrilineal relations with undisputedly scientific ancestors such as Harvey. Vivisectors would be his legitimate heirs to the extent that they use a method established by Harvey himself. This requires arguing that Harvey employed vivisection as his primary research tool. Thus began a project that has continued for over one hundred years: the reconstruction of Harvey's research, with vivisection highlighted so as to minimize the actual extent of his use of clinical research, anatomy, and thought experiments.[84]

Scientific patrilines are always established via discoveries. A scientist's ancestors are those who discovered the facts and theories he now uses, and those who originated methods he now employs. A scientist's descendants are determined conversely, as those who use theories, facts, and methods he discovered. So a central element in the articulation of scientific patrilines is the attribution of discoveries to individual scientists. This is never simply a matter of chronological priority, of who first suggested the theory, fact, or method. It is primarily a matter of proof; the discoverer is he who first demonstrates the validity of the method or first demonstrates the truth of the theory or fact. Thus struggles over scientific lineage often take the form of disputes over what counts as a demonstration or proof. Those scientists whose techniques are understood to confer proof are well positioned to become founding figures.

In this light we may understand Bernard's principle that "it is to experiment on the living animal that final reference must always be made to reach an understanding of organic properties."[85] Similarly, Magendie consistently maintained that knowledge of life processes demanded experiments on living animals.[86] If discoveries can only be made through vivisections, then Bernard's and Magendie's patrilineal importance as the initial practitioners and advocates of vivisection is assured. Bernard's desire to establish his place in the scientific patriliny would seem to be the best explanation for his gross generalization about the necessity of vivisection, given Brandon Reines's argument that "there is little if any evidence that Bernard actually discovered in his laboratory.... [Bernard] consistently argues that the results of his laboratory experiments led him to search for equivalent natural experiments in the clinical literature, though the natural experiments had been published many years prior to Bernard's animal experiments."[87] Reines concludes that Bernard's "primary commitment was to perpetuate the physiological laboratory."[88]

Regardless of Bernard's personal motivations for declaring vivisection's indispensability, the crucial point is that many other researchers and medical men accepted the principle. Nineteenth-century English physiologist Charles Bell was opposed to vivisection yet performed experiments on animals, explaining, "It must be my apology, that my utmost efforts of persuasion were lost, while I urged my statements on the grounds of anatomy alone."[89] By the twentieth century the performance of vivisection had become a necessary condition for the attribution of a discovery to an investigator.[90]

Historians of science credit vivisectors with biomedical discoveries rather than clinical investigators who defend the same hypotheses, even when the clinical investigation preceded the vivisection.[91] The clinical research is either ignored or discounted. When this cannot be done, historiographers of science frequently invert the actual temporal sequence of the research, giving vivisectors a false chronological priority in order to sustain the dogma that discovery comes only through animal research.[92]

I cite here the history of puerperal or "childbed" fever as just one example of this process of construing vivisection as an indispensable condition for discovery. After the advent of hospitalized childbirth, women began dying of puerperal fever in epidemic proportions. This continued until the introduction of antiseptic routines to the hospital system. One account of this history was given by the president of the Research Defence Society early in this century: "The use of antiseptics, and the modern treatment of wounds, is the direct outcome of the experiments of Pasteur and Lister. Pasteur's discovery of the microbial cause of puerperal fever has in itself enormously reduced the deaths of women in child-birth."[93] Crediting vivisectors Lister and Pasteur with discoveries that saved women from puerperal fever has become standard in medical histories. A more complete history, however, is given by Adrienne Rich in her book *Of Woman Born*. Rich points out that though hand washing by doctors did not become standard practice until 1885 (after Lister's and Pasteur's experimental work), contamination by the attending physicians themselves had been observed to be the cause of puerperal fever for at least ninety years prior to this.[94] Women knew they were more likely to die when attended by physicians than when attended by midwives, and three different men published their own clinically based demonstrations that the disease was carried from physician to patient (Gordon in 1795, Holmes in 1843, and Semmelweis in 1861). Yet the implication that the male physician might be more unclean than the "filthy" midwife was dismissed as outrageous for decades and only reluctantly accepted upon the "discoveries" made in Lister's and Pasteur's vivisectional work.

The possibility that women and men who observe rather than experiment might make a discovery before vivisectors is still rejected out of hand by mainstream historians who describe the puerperal fever epidemic and other episodes of medical history. This resistance to the facts is explicable in terms of the paternal function of medical science. A primary function of science, including medical science, is the construction of paternity. Paternity is constructed in contradistinction to maternity, and thus the mechanism of male birth giving must be distinct from the mechanism ceded as female birth giving. In Western society the controlled application of deadly force is men's work. It is understandable, therefore, that scientists would require the use of violence—vivisection—before they recognize a discovery, given that discovery functions for them as the locus of scientific procreation. Recognizing anything other than male-controlled violence as a means of generating discoveries risks turning medical science from a specifically patrilineal enterprise into a marker of *ungendered* genealogy.

VIVISECTION AS A DISPLAY OF POWER

Vivisection generates individual patrilines, but it also establishes paternity in the broader sense of ceding credit to men as a class for the existence of human life in general. In modern society we are taught that we owe our lives to medical men through the crucial mechanism of animal experimentation. Doctors officiate at birth and at serious illnesses and are given credit for the results. Doctors also have the authority to decide when a person is dead, and thus their word indirectly determines life. Until recently regular doctors were almost exclusively male, making them fathers as opposed to parents. Modern medicine has been highly gendered since its inception, in that it was developed by men in opposition to the female lay healing that predominated prior to the twentieth century. Vivisection is part of modern medicine because the pharmaceuticals and therapies prescribed by regular doctors are always applied to animal bodies first. In the United States (but not in Britain) the connection between medicine and vivisection is even tighter because doctors typically vivisect as part of their training in medical school. Medical men generally believe that it is their basis in science, that is, in vivisection, that validates their status as our society's healers and saviors. Why this official story is so widely accepted at face value is explicable in terms of the model of paternal sacrifice developed in the previous chapter. According to that model, attributions of paternity gain superficial plausibility when fathers demonstrate themselves capable of violence and then withhold that violence from the individuals they could kill. Vivisection is analogous to the complex of biblical blood rituals discussed in the previous chapter in that it also works as a marker of paternity by inflicting actual violence on animals while associating people with the sacrificed animals in various ways. In this society we are prepared to believe that animal experimentation saves our lives through our awareness that we could have been sacrificed in the animals' place.

But vivisection cannot demonstrate men's power over life and death unless the experiments are publicly known. Due to security concerns, laboratories are closed facilities, a fact that might obscure the public nature of vivisection. Vivisections are not displayed to the public as they are being performed, yet the public, though not necessarily aware of the full extent of vivisection, certainly knows that animals are being experimented on and killed in the laboratories. People are made aware of this through the educational system and the mass media. Basic textbooks in biology and psychology describe vivisections, sometimes with text alone, often with pictures. And popular novels and films often feature vivisection as major or minor themes. These are two mechanisms through which vivisection is brought into public consciousness.

Before vivisections were secluded within the laboratory in the twentieth century, they were often done publicly. Especially during the seventeenth and eighteenth centuries, when vivisection was being popularized in Europe, educated gentlemen were likely to encounter open experimental displays. As early as the sixteenth century one Paduan professor of anatomy reported that "high-ranking clergymen took great delight in attending his public vivisections."[95] The clergy were particularly fascinated by this professor's vivisection of pregnant bitches—he would pull a fetus out of the dog's womb and then display the results as he offered the puppy to the bitch, withdrew it, harmed the pup in various ways, and so on. These experiments became classics, often repeated by other experimentalists (including the variations famously introduced by Harry Harlow in the mid-twentieth century and continued by his "descendants" today). They show not only the public nature of vivisection but also the researchers' fascination with the exercise of male control over female birthing.

Another classical experiment type during the development of professional vivisection was the use of the air pump to asphyxiate animals. Various animals were placed in the pump, the air was removed, and notes were taken on duration of survival, the behavior of the dying creature, and so on. In eighteenth-century England such experiments were routinely performed by the itinerants who lectured in public.[96] In the following passage from Benjamin Martin's 1755 dialogue called *The Young Gentleman and Lady's Philosophy*, the male experimentalist uses an air pump to demonstrate to the young lady his ability to generate life by threatening death: "As the Air is more rarified, the Animal is rendered more thoughtful of his unlucky Situation, and seeks in vain to extricate himself.—He leaps and jumps about.—A Vertigo seizes his Brain.—He falls, and is just upon expiring.—but I turn the Vent-piece, and let in the Air by Degrees.—You see him begin to heave, and pant.—At length he rouzes up, opens his Eyes, and wildly stares about him.—I take off the Receiver, and shall now deliver it as recovered from the Dead."[97] The same young gentleman also performs an experiment with electrocution, significantly referring to his animal subject as a victim "sacrificed on this Altar by electrical Fire." The menacing character of his demonstrations is indicated by the young lady's remark: "I hope your explosive Experiments are now at an End; . . . they have so much of the Terrible in them, that I can scarcely conceit I am safe while you show them."[98]

As with sacrifice generally, the salvific effects of vivisection are ideological—a debatable matter of belief—while its destructive effects are overt and unarguable. In vivisection, destruction is primary. The proximate aim of the experimenter is to become capable of inflicting some form of injury or pathology on the experimental subject. It may be most accurate to think of vivisection as a large class of blood rituals. Just as in Hebrew religion there was not one form of animal sacrifice but four or five distinct rituals ranging from running off the scapegoat to burning an entire corpse, so in vivisection there are a plethora of rites distinguishable by their modes of destruction. Every type of injury, disease, or psychosis to which humans are susceptible is imposed on experimental subjects in the belief that somehow this will save us. Vivisectors are in the first instance practitioners of one or more of the following: poisoning, burning, cutting, gassing, starving, asphyxiating, drowning, decompressing, irradiating, electrocuting, freezing, crushing, paralyzing, amputating, decapitating, excising organs, removing parts of the brain, blinding, deafening, socially isolating, inducing addiction, and engendering diseases including cancer, heart disease, stroke, diabetes, AIDS, and so on. Contrary to religious anthropologists, ours is not a society that has abolished animal sacrifice, it is a society with more distinguishable forms of sacrifice than any other culture.

Vivisection's basis in the imposition of injury means that, as Brian Klug puts it in his analysis of the institution, "any self-respecting researcher must be able to cause pain and harm to an animal subject; and to do so without flinching."[99] Since in modern Western culture the ability to administer violence is taken to be a male trait, vivisection has been seen as an essentially male activity as previously discussed. The concern of Bernard and the other nineteenth-century men who professionalized vivisection was to master the technique of imposing injury and pathology, ultimately seeking complete control over the various processes of death. A master such as François Magendie could take the animals under his control to the brink of death and back: "The animal was seized with convulsive tremors, and collapsed as if dead. Wollaston thought it was dead, and begged me to repeat the experiment on another animal. 'I would rather call this one back to life,' I said to him, 'and what is more, make him run as far as you please.' . . . This is what I did."[100]

These are awesome powers. Whether any effective human therapies for the imposed conditions will result from this exercise of power is always an open question at the outset of the research program. And if useful human therapies do emerge, it is also an open question whether those therapies could have been developed through some other, nonsacrificial means. But nonetheless we believe that animal research is crucial for our salvation. The substratum for this belief is the knowledge that vivisectors, so skilled at imposing pathology on nonhuman animals, can also impose pathology on humans. Vivisectors save us insofar as they choose to direct their destructive expertise toward animals rather than toward people.

HUMANS AS EXPERIMENTAL SUBJECTS

As with other forms of animal sacrifice, animal experimentation would pose no obvious threat to human life (and thus fail as a marker of paternity) if humans were without exception protected from experimental sacrifice. This is not the case. Animal vivisection has always been accompanied by at least some human vivisection. The general knowledge of this affects our perception of animal experimentation, turning it into a threat—a form of destruction that we know can be applied to us.

Recently in the United States we have been told of post–World War II researchers' periodic use of unsuspecting hospital patients for radiation experiments. Prior to this the U.S. public heard of the decades during which some black men in the South were used as experimental subjects for the study of the untreated progress of syphilis. We have also learned of the use of American soldiers as experimental material for observing the effects of radioactive fallout from atomic weaponry.

These are some of the specific awarenesses of human experimentation that have developed recently. Earlier, when animal vivisection was becoming institutionalized in the late nineteenth and early twentieth centuries, there was a recurrent fear of being sacrificed in research. Coral Lansbury recounts the nineteenth-century working class belief that "surgeons were vivisecting dogs, cats, and rabbits because they could not vivisect human beings. When the latter were available, they would be used."[101] These fears were grounded in the well-publicized reality that researchers were at times granted experimental access to patients at charity hospitals. The poor also lived in fear that their dead would be taken for experimental dissections, a dread exacerbated by fables of apparently dead men suddenly reviving while under the anatomist's knife.[102]

Susan Lederer has surveyed the incidence of human experimentation prior to World War II. Her study cites a tremendous number of harmful or risky experiments performed on people. These include injecting people with the suspected germs of gonorrhea and syphilis, injecting children with active smallpox virus, infecting patients with leprosy bacilli, producing yellow fever in patients, injecting children with the germs of foot-and-mouth disease, withholding orange juice from children to study scurvy, and infecting infants with the herpes virus.[103] The people used as research material are always those who are socially disempowered in one way or another. For instance, Lederer discusses surgery forced on soldiers, medical experiments done on slaves, jobless men hired for experimentation during the Depression, and nontherapeutic experiments performed on orphans, the retarded, prisoners, and the mentally ill to further the U.S. war effort during World War II. Children were frequently used in experimentation, most typically those in orphanages or the children of the researchers themselves. For example, John Kolmer used experimental polio vaccines on his children and on the children of his secretary, a research program that led to nine deaths.[104]

It is not the actual occurrence of human experimentation that is most relevant to this analysis, but public concern about it. As did Lansbury's study, Lederer's research reveals a significant degree of fear regarding human experimentation. She notes that in the late nineteenth century, human and nonhuman experimentation were seen as intimately related and that "for most of the nineteenth century, suspicion that indigent patients would become the unwitting subjects of therapeutic experimentation in life and the objects of dissection after death persisted among many Americans."[105] Among the African American community, in fact, fears flourished that "night doctors" would kidnap black people for vivisection. Lederer notes that antebellum physicians periodically published notices of their desire to purchase Negroes with particular complaints to test new remedies, and that in the 1890s New York newspapers carried advertisements offering compensation to those who subjected themselves to medical experimentation.[106]

According to Harriet Washington, author of a comprehensive history of experimentation on African Americans titled *Medical Apartheid,* deep distrust and fear of medical professionals and institutions persist among African Americans to this day. This fear was inculcated through the exploitation they have been subjected to by the medical establishment since the antebellum period—dangerous, involuntary, and nontherapeutic experimentation by no means limited to the most infamous case, the Tuskegee syphilis studies. In fact, the pattern of abuse extends from slave times, during which medical experimentation with African Americans was the norm, to today, with recent medical research including cases in which subjects were "given experimental vaccines known to have unacceptably high lethality, were enrolled in experiments without their consent or knowledge, were subjected to surreptitious surgical and medical procedures while unconscious, injected with toxic substances, deliberately monitored rather than treated for deadly ailments, excluded from lifesaving treatments, or secretly farmed for sera or tissues."[107] Notwithstanding the secrecy of practitioners of human vivisection, Washington notes a "periodic hue and cry raised in the popular press" as "media seize upon and decry new experimental abuses with regularity."[108]

The morality of research programs that deliberately produced pathologies in people has been discussed not only in medical journals but also in the popular press. For instance, under the headline "Bronx Family of Six Victims of Vivisection," a 1914 New York newspaper carried a report of children deliberately infected with disease while in the hospital seeking treatment for another condition.[109] Plays and movies also communicated concern over human experimentation. The 1933 Broadway play *Yellow Jack,* based on Walter Reed's yellow fever experiments in Cuba, referred to "human vivisections" and depicted "how doctors and plain men sacrifice lives for other lives," according to one New York critic.[110] Stories such as *Frankenstein* (Mary Shelly, 1818; innumerable film versions from 1908 to the present), *Dr. Jekyll and Mr. Hyde* (Robert Louis Stevenson, 1886; over eighty film versions from 1908 to the present), and *The Island of Dr. Moreau* (H. G. Wells, 1896; filmed in 1932, 1977, and 1996), predict dire consequences of experimentation on the dead, self-experimentation, and human experimentation by physicians who are also depicted as experimenting on animals and human patients. Expressions of this fear pervade our culture. Consider the story of the horrifying results of a scientist vivisecting his own child told in Michael Powell's infamous 1960 film *Peeping Tom.* And the recent *Alien* film series, to cite just one more example, depicts the real enemy not as the aliens themselves but as the corporate and military functionaries who seek to preserve the predatory creature as a vivisectional specimen. In *Alien Resurrection,* the most recent installment in the series, medical researchers working for the military use humans as sacrificial hosts for incubating aliens.

Thus animal experimentation does not occur in isolation from the practice of human experimentation and the fear of becoming an experimental subject. In this context anything done to a research animal communicates an implicit threat of what could be done to a human. The menacing character of animal experimentation is enhanced by researchers themselves and their advocates, who have consistently described vivisected animals as substitutes for humans. For instance, in 1885 William Keen informed a graduating class at the Women's Medical College in Philadelphia, "To grow better we must try new methods, give new drugs, perform new operations, or perform old ones in new ways. That is to say we must experiment. . . . They must then be tried either on an animal or on you. Which shall it be?"[111] A more recent example of this position is provided by vivisection proponent Steven Milloy, who insists that "without laboratory animals, human beings would be the guinea pigs for medical researchers."[112] Compare a poster from the Foundation for Biomedical Research—beneath a picture of a girl lying in a hospital bed with stuffed animals are the lines, "We lost some lab animals. But look what we saved." This is the same doctrine of interchangeability of sacrificial victims seen in the Passover story: Someone must die; will it be you, your child, or an animal substitute? This refrain is no empty rhetoric, for it is repeated throughout the history of modern medicine when researchers try to justify actual experimentation on humans. In explaining the infliction of scurvy on infants, for example, the journal *American Medicine* stated that the absence of an animal model made research on children a necessity, and Walter Reed similarly justified his human experiments in terms of the unavailability of animals.[113]

INCOMPLETE HUMAN SACRIFICE IN MEDICINE

In the modern milieu, shaped by reports of actual human vivisections, fables of what researchers could do to us, and regular assertions by vivisectionists that human and animal subjects are interchangeable, questions such as "Which will you save—your child or a guinea pig?" asked by the Research Defence Society, and "How many cats, or guinea pigs would you or I sacrifice to save the life of our child?" asked by the president of Harvard University, express a specific threat: If researchers are not allowed to sacrifice animals in vivisection, they will sacrifice children.[114] Because vivisectors have sacrificed children experimentally and might do so again, by choosing instead to experiment on animals they are in that sense responsible for the continued existence of the children passed over. In the earlier Western constructions of paternal sacrifice seen in Judaism and Christianity, the capacity of men as a class or of the male priesthood to destroy children was displayed not only by completed animal sacrifices but also by rituals of incomplete human sacrifice such as circumcision and baptism. The same correspondence is apparent in the modern West, where medical men both sacrifice animals experimentally and nearly sacrifice humans through various routine medical procedures that bring children to the edge of death and back.

One such procedure is the neonatal circumcision routinely practiced in U.S. hospitals. Though hospitals' nominal function is to heal, the circumcision of normal infants is not a treatment for injury or illness but the removal of healthy tissue. Since there are no medical grounds for the operation, hospital circumcision of neonates must be understood in ritualistic terms. Medical circumcision retains the life-threatening quality of the explicitly religious circumcisions discussed in the previous chapter, as the following account indicates:

> The silence was soon broken by a piercing scream—the baby's reaction to having his foreskin pinched and crushed as the doctor attached the clamp to his penis. The shriek intensified when the doctor inserted an instrument between the foreskin and the glans (head of the penis), tearing the two structures apart. (They are normally attached to each other during infancy so the foreskin can protect the sensitive glans from urine and feces.) The baby started shaking his head back and forth—the only part of his body free to move—as the doctor used another clamp to crush the foreskin lengthwise, which he then cut. . . . The baby began to gasp and choke, breathless from his shrill continuous screams. . . . During the next stage of the surgery, the doctor crushed the foreskin against the circumcision instrument and then, finally, amputated it. The baby was limp, exhausted, spent.[115]

This quote is from a nursing student witnessing her first circumcision. Parents are generally not allowed to attend the surgery. The enforced privacy lessens the overt menacing quality of the incomplete sacrifice, yet stories of botched circumcisions resulting in mangled penises and even death circulate between parents. And of course parents are the ones left to treat the wound. Ultimately the message communicated to parents in the United States is the same as that communicated to the parents of boys who undergo religious circumcision: Your son lives only due to the skill and forbearance of the circumciser.

Immunization is another example of a medical procedure that functions as an incomplete human sacrifice. Compulsory childhood immunization has a ritualistic quality and structure very similar to the paradigmatically religious initiation rites of circumcision and baptism. At the official level immunization works by deliberately bringing the child to the brink of disease and back. The child is exposed to an attenuated form of the pathogen, with the expectation that this will change the child's immune system so that henceforward he or she will be safe from the associated disease. This is very similar to the ideology of baptism, in which the initiate is killed with Christ and reborn into a new, eternal life. As in the baptism rite the priest must control the immersion (too deep or too long means actual death), so in the immunization rite the physician must control the solution (too active a pathogen means actual disease). A small number of children—ones sacrificed for the greater good—do not survive the inoculation unscathed but actually succumb to the disease. But the vast majority emerges unharmed, a result due to the skill of the physician and his research colleagues in controlling the solution.

Whatever the actual public health benefit of compulsory childhood immunization may be, this should not obscure the ritualistic nature of the procedure. Janice Raymond's remark applies here: "Because medicine has articulated an empirical character and has undergone a process of outward secularization does not mean that it has ceased to operate on cultic, ritual, ecclesial, and theological levels."[116] Empirical studies establishing or challenging the medical utility of childhood inoculations are generally not perused by parents prior to bringing their children into the clinic. Indeed, the parents may not even be aware of the official theory of what immunizations are doing. There is, though, always a parental understanding that the needle is injecting foreign substances into the child's system, substances that may contain either life-sustaining or life-destroying elements. We must have faith because it is beyond the parents' competence to predetermine whether the injected mixture is benign or noxious. If the child survives the injection, it is due to the physician's deliberate exercise of control—he chose a solution that did not kill, even though he has access to fatal mixtures. In that sense the child obviously owes his or her life to the doctor. This sense of the child's dependence on the physician is intensified by the background knowledge of modern medicine's routine sacrifice of laboratory animals and its periodic experimentation on children—medical men are clearly capable of imposing disease, but they chose not to in the case of this child's inoculation.

At the most overt level an inoculation is a puncture wound inflicted by the physician or the physician's assistant. At this level, inoculation is a superficially violent act that must be controlled, like the cutting of the foreskin or the immersion of baptism, if the child is to survive. As with baptism and circumcision, childhood immunization has an initiatory function, at least in the United States, where many states require a battery of inoculations before the child is admitted into the school system. Thus the male-controlled violence of inoculation marks the child's movement from the female-associated domestic sphere into the male-dominated public space of school.

Conclusion

Sacrificial ideology is one of the great constants of Western thought. For millennia this idea has been retained: The blood shed by men generates and preserves human life. No religious, political, cultural, economic, scientific, or technological revolution has resulted in the abolition of faith in men's sacrificial work. New versions of sacrifice have evolved. Israelite animal sacrifice was suspended with the destruction of the Temple, but Christians reshaped Jewish sacrificial ideology, propagating the belief that God the Father's sacrifice of his son saved all humankind. Later, Christian gentlemen revived the actual destruction of animal bodies, moving the rite from the altar to the laboratory but retaining the ancient faith that through the meticulous carving of animal flesh men save humanity.

This continuity is not purely the result of cultural transmission. We believe in sacrifice not simply because we were taught to believe by our elders. The institution of sacrifice makes its own claims credible. How can we doubt that we owe our lives to the priestly and scientific sacrifice of animals when time and again the sacrificers have demonstrated their willingness and ability to substitute humans for the animal victims?

It is not my purpose to argue that the sole function of sacrificial ritual is to establish paternity. Rituals such as vivisection and immunization may be serving other functions simultaneously. In addition, there may be sacrificial rites that do not function to establish paternity at all. This would be consistent with my main point, which is that in those cases in which sacrifice does work to establish paternity, the attribution of fatherhood to the sacrificers is supported by more than just a conventional or traditional association. There is historical continuity between Jewish, Christian, and modern secular forms of sacrifice, but we do not just inherit the notion that men who do ritual violence to animals should be credited with generating life. It is inherent to the logic of Western forms of sacrifice that we owe our lives to the sacrificers' decision to kill animals in our stead.

Nor is this analysis intended to suffice on its own as a critique of vivisection or of other sacrificial rituals. Explaining how an institution works is different from saying that the institution should be abolished. A complete critique of vivisection includes a thorough determination of who benefits and who is harmed by the practice, as well as a discussion of whether the beneficiaries could be justified in thus exploiting the victims. Antivivisectionists argue that we have no right to cage, injure, and kill nonhuman animals for our benefit and that, at any rate, the actual medical benefits of vivisection have been exaggerated, the inefficiencies, invalidities, and iatrogenic harms intrinsic to the practice have been consistently overlooked, and alternative healing systems have been left undeveloped.

The present analysis complements such abolitionist arguments. Arguments about vivisection are incomplete when restricted to ethical questions regarding the moral status of animals and scientific questions regarding the validity and replaceability of animal experiments. Vivisection is not solely about ethics and science; like sacrifice in general it is also about the politics of gender, specifically, the patriarchal commitment to construct men as the primary class of life givers.

As a society we have designated men's controlled application of deadly force as the activity distinguishing male responsibility for life from female responsibility for life. And in a neat and orderly fashion we kill animals to maintain this division of labor. But Western culture is not monolithic. There are oppositional viewpoints with regard both to standard gender roles and dominant norms regarding the treatment of nonhuman animals. Over the last few decades expression of this opposition has become more common. Why this is happening now, and what implications this carries for the structure of manhood and the treatment of animals, are topics addressed in the next part.

PART THREE

Opposing Men's Exploitation of Animals

Two mallards flew up just as we settled into our walking pace. They veered to the left as soon as they cleared the ditch banks. Steve and I both shot, simultaneously. And one duck went down in a long, slow glide. It was clearly a wing shot. Our last shots found the other duck out of range. . . .

When we caught the duck we saw that its right wing was injured, but not all that seriously. The usual thing would be to wring its neck or hit its head hard over the barrel of the shotgun—just plain kill it.

We came to a different conclusion: take it back to the city duck ponds at the Rio Grande Zoo and turn it loose with its kind since many wild ducks flew into those ponds. Maybe its wing would mend. With that contradiction of shooting a duck to save it, and realizing all of the trouble and expense involved, we knew that—for a time at least—our hunting days were definitely over.

We had killed many birds and animals over a period of ten or fifteen years—from adolescence into our early twenties. Perhaps because we had caused death, seen its ugly, permanent transformations, we didn't really like to hunt anymore.

We were brothers in this new feeling about hunting.[1]

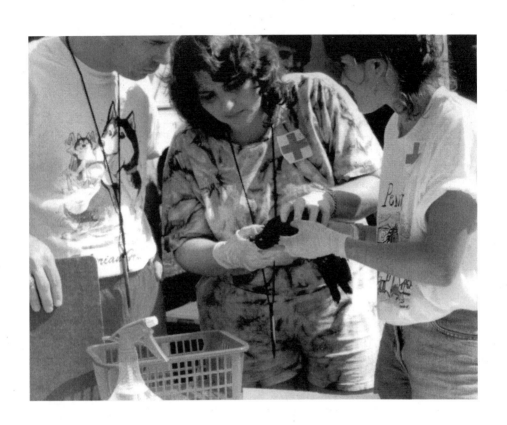

6

The Ethics of Animal Liberation

And when they are slaughtered they make us ashamed of
our work by their terrible cries.

—Plutarch, *Symposiacs*

Animal liberation is based on compassion for individual animals as they are restrained, injured, frustrated, made to suffer, killed, or otherwise harmed through the operations of the major institutions of animal exploitation in the West. In chapter 1 I argued that sympathetic responsiveness to animals is a deep and recurring part of human life, while in chapter 2 I rebutted claims that men's exploitation of animals is part of the natural order. These arguments raise the question of why animal exploitation continues. Chapters 3 to 5 gave an answer to this question in terms of masculine identity and prestige. There is thus an inherent tension between our deep-seated reluctance to cause harm to others and the needs of manhood as it is currently defined.

Humane concern for animals does not necessarily prevail over the tendency toward violence intrinsic to patriarchal masculinity; indeed, history to this point indicates that it typically is subordinated to patriarchal imperatives. Sympathetic responsiveness is natural, but so is our ability to curtail or override our sympathies when we are sufficiently motivated to do so. Additionally, sympathetic feelings do not in and of themselves constitute political opposition to the institutions causing harm. To become counterhegemonic, sympathies must be voiced and they must be understood as challenges to the legitimacy of the exploitative practices. The politicizing of our sympathies is culturally specific; that is, movements for animal liberation arise in some times and places but not others, notwithstanding the ubiquity of the sympathies themselves. This raises our next question: Why now? Why has a movement to abolish the major institutions of animal exploitation arisen within the last few decades?

A full answer to this question would undoubtedly be complex and multi-faceted. Certainly the rise of second-wave feminism would be a likely factor, given the patriarchal nature of animal exploitation as discussed in previous chapters. Also, macro-level developments within capitalism can have an effect on the prevalence of political expressions of empathy, as David Nibert has explained.[1] Without attempting anything so ambitious as a complete theory of why a new animal liberation movement has arisen recently, this chapter opens by offering an account of one process specific to our times that has contributed to the present abolitionism. After detailing how our recent sense of environmental crisis contributes to the opening of social space for the political expression of sympathies for animals, I then move to a discussion of how the resultant moral challenge to men's exploitation of animals is managed.

Environmental Crisis and Sympathy for Animals

Early literature relating environmentalism and animal liberation was often exclusionary and hostile, as evidenced, for example, by Tom Regan referring to Aldo Leopold's land ethic as "environmental fascism" and environmental philosopher J. Baird Callicott calling the concerns of animal liberationists "incoherent," "insensitive," "life-loathing," and "anti-natural."[2] Writers who project a more conciliatory tone, and who might be taken to have offered a reconciliation of the two perspectives, have in my view only brought together with environmentalism a rather attenuated animal protectionism, one marked by a lingering ideology of nonhuman moral inferiority[3] and lacking any explicit mention of the defining goals of animal liberation—abolition of animal farming, vivisection, and sport hunting. I here attempt to explicate the relationship between animal liberation and environmentalism while doing justice to both.

Environmentalism is based on a range of different motivations including self-preservation, concern for future humans, aesthetic appreciation, reverence for life itself, a sense of natural history, and respect for ecological integrity. Though sympathy for individual animals is distinct from respect for ecological integrity, both of these motivations are undermined by the human-centered, or anthropocentric, ideology predominating in the West. Anthropocentrism is the belief that nonhuman nature is of less intrinsic value than human beings and thus may be exploited to further our purposes. The notion that animals are "subhuman" renders strong sympathies for nonhumans inappropriate. Nonhuman animals are not worthy of such attention;

those who persist in showing concern for animal well-being are perversely misplacing their compassions, transferring them from their proper sphere, human life, to an inappropriate realm. So in anthropocentric society we learn to hide, disregard, or prevent altogether our feelings for animals. The anthropocentric viewpoint sees ecological systems of soils, waters, plants, and animals as existing to serve humanity. So ecocentrism—a concern for the land for its own sake—seems out of place. Ecocentric sensibilities are, like sympathies for suffering animals, suppressed. Concern for ourselves and our children, expression of which is allowed (though highly regulated), develops to the exclusion of our other moral capacities.

So animal liberation and environmentalism face a common obstacle. Since anthropocentric ideology forms a coherent whole, a rejection of one part of it brings into question the entire system. As animal liberation develops, anthropocentrism is challenged, which creates possibilities for the development of environmentalism. And conversely, the environmentalist challenge to anthropocentrism makes space for animal liberation. I will give examples of both these processes.

In my own case I developed an animal liberationist consciousness first. Rejecting the institutionalized exploitation of animals still places one outside the bounds of rational normalcy in this culture. My conviction that the feelings and perceptions leading me to vegetarianism and antivivisectionism were valid allowed me to maintain a sense of myself as reasonable. Knowing that the judgment of irrationality was misplaced in my case gave me the capacity to look at others labeled irrational with an open mind. In particular, anyone who argued for expanding the range of morally considerable entities had my respectful attention as a kindred spirit. As I felt I perceived something significant about individual animals that is politically set aside in this society, I presumed that those attributing intrinsic value to individual plants, species, and ecosystems may well also be perceiving some neglected significance. Though not particularly well placed or innately suited for developing environmental consciousness on my own, I have been able to start moving in this direction by attending to the expressions of those environmentalists challenging anthropocentrism.

Conversely, there is evidence that environmentalist challenges to anthropocentrism play a crucial part in the development of animal liberationist sympathies for some activists. This is a two-part process: (1) a sense of ecological crisis undermines confidence in conventional humanistic values, and (2) this weakening of anthropocentric authority allows people to assert traditionally disparaged sympathies for individual animals. As an example of the first part of this process, consider the following comments on the development of a deep environmental consciousness:

> As environment changes, any species that is unable to adapt, to change, to evolve, is extinguished. . . . The human species is one of millions threatened by imminent extinction through nuclear war and other environmental changes. . . . From this point of view, the threat of extinction appears as the invitation to change, to evolve. . . . The change that is required of us is not some new resistance to radiation, but a change in consciousness. . . . A biocentric perspective . . . may give us the courage to face despair and break through to a more viable consciousness, one that is sustainable and in harmony with life again.[4]

The ideological system supporting the hierarchical political and economic structures in the West has been severely shaken by this system's increasingly evident destruction of the biosphere. When faced with the possibility of human extinction, self-preservation, a disposition highly developed under the humanistic ethos, motivates a thorough reassessment of our practices and beliefs. Institutions and values previously so entrenched as to be unquestionable are brought into doubt as we try to figure out the root causes of this crisis. In such a climate, sensitivities of various sorts long buried by the hegemony of anthropocentrism find political expression, first by a few isolated individuals, then in larger numbers as the establishment of organized movements increases our confidence.

There is an apparent paradox in the self-concerned promotion of nonanthropocentric environmentalisms—how can we be affirming the intrinsic value of nonhumans (their value independent of our interests) if we are motivated in the first instance by interest in our own continued existence? It might seem that if, on the one hand, the plea is to act merely *as if* nature mattered, lest we destroy ourselves, then we are still thinking anthropocentrically; yet, on the other hand, if we are truly affirming environmentalism, then we are by definition *not* acting solely out of human self-interest. Apocalyptic environmentalism is common but somewhat puzzling.

The key to understanding the relationship between human self-interest and environmentalism, I suggest, lies in understanding environmentalist consciousness (as well as animal liberationist consciousness) as a *potential* human perceptual/motivational capacity. In many cultural and social settings, we are capable of seeing and affirming the intrinsic value of nonhuman nature, yet we may choose not to, be taught not to, be encouraged not to through various sanctions, or be systematically prevented from doing so by the presence of mechanisms that block the development or application of this capacity. A list of some of the social processes that tend to block environmental consciousness communicates my meaning here: sanctioning the consensus that only humans are intrinsically valuable, erasing or ridiculing environmental consciousness within other cultures or within our own minority traditions, promulgating the notion that we must exploit nature to be healthy, preventing the sorts of knowledge of and relations with non-humans that tend to support environmentalism.

This understanding of environmentalism as a latent capacity that may or may not be actualized brings up the possibility that we may deliberately choose to pursue those courses that tend to develop environmental consciousness. So the path from self-interest to deep environmentalism is not direct and immediate—ending with an enlightened anthropocentrism that is "environmentalist" in name only—but is indirect by at least one step. Self-interested criticism of anthropocentrism entails that we work to remove the barriers to the development of environmentalism (such as the instilled fears and ignorances listed above) and place ourselves in those situations and relations that tend to foster a true environmental consciousness.

The authority of anthropocentric ideology is one of the central barriers to the development of environmental consciousness, so a self-interested rejection of anthropocentric society includes a reevaluation of anthropocentric ideology. The process connecting environmentalism to animal liberation can now more fully be articulated as follows: (1) sense of ecological crisis, (2) a perception of anthropocentrism as a primary culprit and of environmentalism as a necessary remedy, (3) a self-interested decision to seek means to foster environmentalism, (4) an identification of anthropocentric ideology as a major barrier to the development of environmental consciousness, (5) challenges to anthropocentric ideology, and, finally, because anthropocentric ideology is also a major barrier to animal liberationist consciousness, (6) social space is (perhaps inadvertently) created for the development of animal liberation.

The applicability of this framework to some activists is supported by Susan Sperling's study of animal liberationists, though to see this requires a bit of work because she interprets her data differently than do I. Sperling summarizes her understanding of animal liberation as follows:

> A high degree of concern about pollution and technological manipulation of the environment and living organisms is expressed by most adherents of the modern animal rights movement. Many increasingly view our species as

subject to materialistic technological forces antithetical to nature and as facing a potential ecological apocalypse with other species. Animal rights has emerged in recent years as a response to these anxieties about the human relationship to nature much as occurred in the Victorian era.[5]

Sperling notices millenarian tendencies among both today's animal liberationists and nineteenth-century antivivisectionists. Activists of both periods frequently speak of the development and application of technology and modern medicine as a callous expansion, unchecked by social morality, that threatens our imminent destruction. In the Victorian period the threat posed is the dismemberment and destruction of people, particularly the politically vulnerable (women, workers, blacks), through human experimentation and the iatrogenic effects of modern medicine, an ascendant healing philosophy conceived as the invasion and manipulation of inert bodies. Today this iatrogenic threat continues but is joined by the threat of the impending collapse of the life-giving biosphere. Nineteenth- and twentieth-century animal liberationists see their work as part of the effort to turn back these destructive processes, an effort that, if successful, would usher in the millennium, a period of peace and security organized around compassion and respect for living beings.

Contemporary activists quoted by Sperling suggest a significant connection between concerns over environmental crises and the development of animal liberation:

> "The advent of nuclear weapons and environmental pollution have made us realize that science and technology need to be controlled to some extent."
>
> "People are realizing that we can, in fact, destroy the earth and ourselves in the process. . . . I believe that's the arena that was available for the animal rights movement to come forth."
>
> "The specter of a nuclear holocaust, the reality of toxic dumps, of deformed babies, dead rivers, extinct species, have pierced the shroud of numbness and paved the way for questioning authority and wanting to see for oneself. The horrors of the labs and factory farms are no longer hidden."[6]

I am arguing that the sense of imminent ecological crisis destabilizes our confidence in anthropocentric ideology sufficiently to allow the reclamation of compassionate identification with individual animals. Sperling interprets the ecology/animal-liberation relation differently; for her the two are linked *metaphorically*, through animal experimentation apprehended purely as representation. For animal activists, Sperling argues, the vivisection of an animal represents the spoliation of the planet by industrial civilization or the inva-

THE ETHICS OF ANIMAL LIBERATION · 169

sion of the human body by medical science: "Animal experimentation is the key metaphor for the abuses by technological society of living organisms and the ecology."[7] Sperling's idea is that activists oppose animal vivisection not because they care for the well-being of the individual animal subjects but out of concern over iatrogenesis or the environmental crisis. Apparently, animal experimentation is such a potent metaphor for these technological manipulations of humans and the land that we come to see animal experimentation *as* iatrogenesis or environmental destruction, thus concluding that we can actually save ourselves and the planet by abolishing animal research: "The redemption of society is believed literally to hinge on the abolition of the use of animals by science."[8]

Sperling's theory of a purely metaphorical relation between apocalyptic environmentalism and animal liberation is not supported by the crucial evidence, the statements of the animal liberationists.[9] For the activists and writers Sperling quotes, animal vivisection and the environmental crisis are related ideologically, not metaphorically. Animal vivisection does not *stand for* the vivisection of the planet, rather, behind both these practices as well as other systems of domination is a common attitude or mindset. This position is stated explicitly and repeatedly by Sperling's interviewees:

> "We are very concerned about human rights; we are focusing on animal rights. These movements are all related because there's the same basic underlying attitude of supremacy that permits and perpetuates the racist, sexist, speciesist attitudes and concomitant crimes against creatures."
>
> "More people are now aware that the state of mind that would permit the testing of radioactive weapons on monkeys also permits the vivisection of our planet for the same purpose."
>
> "The threat of nuclear annihilation and ecological catastrophe have brought home to a lot of people that Western military-industrial policies, practices and attitudes are pathological and aberrant."[10]

An anthropocentric worldview facilitates the continuation of animal exploitation, so debunking this ideology is one element of animal liberationism. Similarly, environmentalism proceeds only to the extent that anthropocentrism is rejected. So the two movements share a common goal, and this relation is reflected in the activists' comments. Sperling's suggestion that activists see animal liberation as sufficient for or the key to human salvation is not supported by any of her subjects' statements. The statement by Michael Fox that Sperling quotes—that "human liberation will begin when we understand that our evolution and fulfillment are contingent on the recognition of animal rights"—might seem to support her thesis, but only because it has been removed from its immediate context, which is: "I am concerned over the suffering of wild and domestic animals; I am equally concerned, however, for the future of my own species, since the values and actions that destroy nonhuman life and cause untold suffering do no less to humans. . . . Our detachment from nature, our lack of a sense of kinship and continuity with all life underlie the inhumane uses and abuses of animals and the havoc that is being wrought on the natural world."[11] Here again we see the relation clearly stated: animal vivisection not as a metaphor for environmental destruction but as backed by the same anthropocentric values.

Similarly, Sperling vaguely claims that John Aspinall "links salvation from ecological disaster to recognition of the human-animal bond and animal rights," leaving out his explicit explanation of the ideological connection: "The concept of sanctity of human life is the most damaging sophism that philosophy has ever propagated—it has rooted well. Its corollary—a belief in the insanctity of species other than man—is the cause of that damage. The destruction of this idea is a prerequisite for survival."[12] It is in the destruction of this idea—anthropocentrism, the "insanctity of species other than man"—that, notwithstanding the diversity of the values championed, environmentalism and animal liberation provide mutual support.

By interpreting antivivisectionism as a symbolically mediated opposition to ecological destruction, Sperling is denying the grounding of animal liberation in responsiveness to the suffering of real individual animals. Similarly, J. Baird Callicott denies the compassionate basis of our outrage at factory farming and vivisection. For Callicott, these institutions are not objectionable because they cause great harm to animals for the material gains of a few people, rather, their immorality lies in the "transmogrification of organic to mechanical processes." Callicott explains, "The very presence of animals, so emblematic of delicate, complex organic tissue, surrounded by machines, connected to machines, penetrated by machines in research laboratories or crowded together in space-age 'production facilities' is surely the more real and visceral source of our outrage at vivisection and factory farming than the contemplation of the quantity of pain that these unfortunate beings experience."[13] Here Callicott foregoes his capacity to see animals as concrete individuals; for him they are "emblems." But of course, animals are not merely *emblematic* of delicate, complex organic tissue, they *are* delicate, complex, and organic beings. Callicott underestimates the importance of responsiveness to suffering in animal liberationist motivation; even so, I would not completely dismiss his points, since our capacity for compassionate political responsiveness to suffering is conditioned by the frameworks within which the suffering occurs (including, perhaps, whether the suffering is framed by the "transmogrification of organic to mechanical processes").[14]

Consider Peter Singer's critique of Sperling's book. Singer supports his statement that Sperling "fails to grasp what the movement is really all about" by arguing that animal liberation organizations are "seeking above all to prevent needless and unjustifiable suffering."[15] Sperling does unjustifiably minimize the importance of responsiveness, but she also brings to our attention another, interrelated part of "what the movement is really all about," namely, "anxieties about the human relationship to nature." This is not a case of *either* the animal liberation movement is really about concern over animal suffering *or* it is really about renegotiating the human/nature relationship. Animal liberation is about both; and not both accidentally linked but, rather, the questions about our relationship to nature conditioning and facilitating the political expression of our concerns over animal suffering, and vice versa.

We do not struggle to *preserve value* (full stop), we struggle to preserve value *as it is threatened within certain structures.* The intrinsic value of an individual animal's healthy life can face any number of threats—from vivisection to natural nonhuman predation, to name just two. Compassionate responsiveness to suffering motivates protective political efforts in one of these cases but not the other. There is no large-scale animal liberationist campaign to protect animals from their natural predators, notwithstanding the disvalue of natural predation as demonstrated in chapter 3. This is not a point about consistency, or about a potentially arbitrary selectiveness in the application of our sympathies. The point here concerns the historical reality of animal liberation as it has developed to date: The movement is based on compassionate responsiveness to individual animals as their integrity is threatened *by certain human institutions.*

Once conditions have developed that allow political expression of sympathies for particular classes of exploited animals, the salient institutions of exploitation face a crisis of legitimacy. This crisis is engaged ideologically, through the reassertion of debunked philosophies of anthropocentrism and the promulgation of new legitimation myths. Efforts to protect exploitation also concentrate on our sympathetic tendencies themselves. Enormous amounts of social energy are expended to forestall, undermine, and override our sympathies for animals, so that vivisection, animal farming, and hunting can continue. The threat of human sympathy for animals requires institutions of animal exploitation to seek ways to protect themselves from compassionate human opposition.

The remainder of this chapter analyzes mechanisms used to subvert opposition to animal exploitation. Knowledge of the strategies used to block sympathetic opposition to animal exploitation focuses activism, since one way to advance the animal liberation movement is to understand and resist those mechanisms. In the following I distinguish three general sorts of mechanisms: those that forestall the development of our sympathies for animals, those that override our sympathies, and those that render our sympathies void of oppositional implications.

Forestalling Sympathy for Exploited Animals

The awareness that *I am causing harm to an animal* is normally accompanied by hesitation, uneasiness, guilt, and even anguish. Potential opposition to animal exploitation arising from such inhibitions can be forestalled by blocking one or more of the three parts of this awareness: responsibility ("I am causing"), damage due to hurting or killing ("harm"), and the presence of another subject ("to an animal"). This analysis is comparable to the results of Stanley Milgram's research on the conditions under which individuals accept an authority's commands to apply electric shock to a human being. Milgram found that the willingness to follow such commands correlated with the breakdown of what he called "the structure of a meaningful act—*I am hurting a man*."[16] Examples of the three ways in which the meaning of our exploitation of animals is broken down are given in the following.

DENYING RESPONSIBILITY

Humans are loath to accept responsibility for causing harm. One ancient means of denying responsibility for animal exploitation is discussed by James Serpell under the heading of "blame-shifting": "It was ultimately the gods who were to blame [for ancient animal sacrifice], since it was they who demanded the sacrifice in the first place. This is not merely speculation. According to an ancient Babylonian text, the head priest actually bent down to the ear of the slaughtered victim and whispered, 'this deed was done by all the gods; I did not do it.'"[17]

Human responsibility for eating flesh is deferred in our culture by reference to biblical tales of divine permission, such as God's covenant with Noah: "Every moving thing that lives shall be food for you; and as I gave you the green plants, I give you everything" (Genesis 9:3). More broadly, all forms of animal exploitation can be and often are excused in Western culture by highlighting biblical passages such as the following: "Then God said, 'Let us make man in our image, after our likeness; and let them have dominion over the fish of the sea, and over the birds of the air, and over the cattle, and over all the earth, and over every creeping thing that creeps upon the earth'" (Genesis 1:26).[18] The idea of a biblical mandate to dominate animals can be applied in defense of any of the animal exploitation industries. Such an attempt to pass responsibility to God begs the question of our responsibility for affirming a nominally anthropocentric religion. Also, Christians or Jews who might attempt to defer responsibility for animal exploitation to God are acting in bad faith, insofar as they are denying their responsibility for choosing to emphasize one biblical passage over another—for instance, Genesis 2:4–25 (in which animals are created after man to be his helpers) rather than Genesis 1:1–2:3 (in which animals are created before humans and are recognized as good independently of their relations with humans). Passing the blame to God for our exploitative practices is not logically valid, but it does help to ease the conscience.

This theological blame shifting has secular counterparts. Today farmers shift responsibility for their exploitation of animals to the general public by speaking of "consumer demand" for meat as if this technical term referred to an inexorable mass insistence rather than the conditional fact that under present circumstances people will buy a certain amount of meat at a given price. According to a study of the psychology of slaughter, "the most commonly reported justification for slaughtering . . . was that people eat meat, so that slaughtering must be done by someone."[19] As discussed in the following chapter, arguments that shift blame for slaughter from producers to consumers are not sustainable under modern economic conditions, even though many animal advocates themselves uncritically accept this displacement of responsibility.

One additional example of blame shifting comes from our society's treatment of dogs and cats. Stephanie Frommer and Arnold Arluke studied facilities where homeless and abandoned cats and dogs are killed (commonly known as "animal shelters") and found that the workers and those surrendering animals all used blame displacement as a mechanism for minimizing their feelings of guilt. Workers blamed surrenderers for abdicating their lifetime responsibility for their animals, whereas surrenderers blamed landlords, family members, or other third parties for their decision to relegate their pets to probable death—or they blamed society at large for creating a pet "overpopulation problem." Both groups also displaced blame onto the animal victims themselves.[20]

DENYING HARM

Our economic system renders production processes invisible at the point of consumption. This distance between people and production may be self-consciously sustained and increased by an industry when general awareness of that industry's production processes decreases demand for its products. Full awareness of animal suffering can lead to unwelcome public opposition to an industry's operations. Practitioners of animal farming, vivisection, and hunting routinely attempt to minimize awareness of the animal suffering inherent to their industries.

Language is managed by the animal farming industry to remove unsavory associations, since, as John Robbins put it, "the meat business depends on our repressing the unpleasant awareness that we are devouring dead bodies."[21] Animals are not killed or slaughtered, they are "processed" or "packed"; they are not butchered, they are "dressed" or "disassembled." This use of euphemisms is deliberate and self-conscious, as Serpell notes: "A recent edition of the British *Meat Trades Journal* recommended a change in terminology designed to 'conjure up an image of meat divorced from the act of slaughter.' Suggestions included getting rid of the words 'butcher' and 'slaughterhouse' and replacing them with the American euphemisms 'meat plant' and 'meat factory.'"[22]

Similarly, James Swan reports that "fish and game departments are quietly changing the vocabulary of hunting . . . replacing an emotional word such as *kill* with *harvest*."[23] Vivisectors also verbally smooth over the harms they inflict, preferring terms such as "negative stimulation" to "causing pain" and "aversive behavior" to "fear." The killing they do is referred to innocuously as "dispatching," "terminating," or, of course, "sacrificing," the last of which directs attention to the ritual function of the act and away from awareness of the specific harm imposed. I have noticed that scientists always stick to the term "animal experimentation," even (or especially) when discussing the ethics of their profession, as "vivisection" has connotations of harm to the experimental subject but "animal experimentation" does not.

The careful management of terminology can become outright deceit, as when a fur industry spokeswoman spoke of animals trapped or anally electrocuted in order to sell their fur for profit as being "euthanized," a word which actually means "killed painlessly to relieve suffering."[24] Shelter workers, who also misuse the word "euthanasia" to refer to their killing of healthy but unadopted cats and dogs, are clearly laboring under self-deception when they make comments such as the following: "I'm not actually killing the animal.

I'm just giving it an injection. I'm just helping the process speed up. It—I really feel that most of these animals are dying as we speak."[25]

Glib reassurances by animal exploiters are common. After his research program came under scrutiny for animal abuse, Thomas Langfitt told reporters that he and the technicians under his supervision "treat the baboon the way we would treat humans."[26] This comment might mollify the credulous or, for those who understand that Langfitt makes his living smashing the heads of baboons, serve as an indirect threat against people. In this latter respect, Langfitt's remarks further the menacing aspect of animal vivisection previously discussed. In general, however, researcher's efforts to hide the harms they do work against expanding the public understanding of vivisection as an instrument of injury that may be directed against humans. The theory of vivisection as sacrificial ritual developed in chapters 4 and 5 explains how vivisection functions in Western society—why its claims to social necessity are accepted so uncritically and why men in particular would support its continued existence. It is not an account of the intentions of individual vivisectors, who are not necessarily motivated by explicitly patriarchal ends and who may possess no deep concern or understanding regarding how vivisection functions to establish paternity. Apart from the small number of sadists who gravitate toward vivisection as a socially permitted venue for the infliction of torture, vivisectors are ordinary people with mundane aspirations for stimulating work, respectable careers, and so on. Naturally they prefer to minimize annoying, threatening, or conscience-pricking public opposition to their research projects.

Toward this latter end vivisectors seek to block direct observation of their imposition of injury. Laboratories that experiment on animals are generally closed to the public, even when they are publicly funded. Tours of research facilities are typically restricted to the holding facilities, omitting observation of any ongoing experiments. It has not been uncommon for researchers to destroy the vocal chords of the dogs they vivisect, thereby eliminating the nuisance of tortured howling and preempting the possibility of sympathetic response. The eerie result of this process, known as "debarking," is described below: "Recently I visited the compound where animals are 'conditioned' for the ordeal of experimentation at the University of California laboratories at La Jolla. There were well over a hundred dogs, all large: collies, German shepherds, huskies, and others. But there was not a sound from the four rows of crowded kennels: the helpless victims had their vocal chords severed, which rendered them truly voiceless."[27] If we cannot see them or hear them, we cannot sympathize with them, a point well appreciated by Claude Bernard, who remarked that "laboratories are no less valuable to us for sheltering overly impressionable people."[28]

Attempts to conceal the insides of animal labs are organized and thorough. For example, a planned episode of the television series *Quantum Leap* dealing with experiments on primates was opposed by provivisection lobby groups.[29] The fact that this opposition was registered prior to production, before the release of a script, and despite the producer's reassurances ("I've asked [the writer] to show the necessity of using animals for medical research.... We like to lay out both sides and let our audience decide what to think").),[30] reveals that the concern was not with *how* animal vivisection would be treated, positively or negatively, but simply with the fact that experiments on primates would be re-created for television.[31] A similar attitude against laying out both sides is exemplified in NIH director Bernadine Healy's publicly "worrying" over "the success of [animal] rights groups in getting their films and magazines into public libraries and schools."[32] (NIH is a major funder of animal vivisection.)

Hunters also cover up the harms they inflict, for example, by suggesting that death by bullet or arrow is less traumatic than the deaths these targeted animals would otherwise experience. In chapter 2 these denials were cited as evidence that hunters are emotionally conflicted regarding their killing. I would add here that such rhetoric is also part of a deliberate campaign to deflect sympathetic opposition to their sport, as the following quote from a hunting magazine indicates: "If a bullet or broadhead [arrow] damages a vital organ, hemorrhagic shock will send a deer to a swift, painless and peaceful demise. If the general public was aware of this knowledge, their minds could be set at ease and a major argument against hunting would fall by the wayside."[33] But "setting the public's mind at ease" requires omitting the fact that for every deer killed and retrieved by a bowhunter, one is hit and wounded but not retrieved.[34]

Especially by the animal farming industry, for whom every person is a potential customer, there is an ongoing effort to deny the harms done to animals. In response to a growing movement that explicitly advocates vegetarianism based on compassion for animals, meat industry representatives attempt to frame animal farmers as the true animal welfarists: "Our research shows that we can prevent long-term erosion of public support for the livestock industry.... We've got to do a better job of communicating with consumers, and letting them know that we, not the animal rights groups, are the animal welfare experts."[35] This quotation is from the videotape *Animal Welfare*, produced by the National Pork Producers Council and distributed to pig farmers. The narrator of the videotape mentions that newspaper, radio, and television ads are being produced and placed to communicate the message that "livestock producers have always been dedicated to the humane treatment of the livestock in their care; first of all, it's good business. But more importantly, producers know it's the right thing to do." The usual argument is that farmers have a business interest in maintaining the well-being of their "stock" since sick or unhappy animals do not grow as well or cannot be sold and therefore are not as profitable. In fact, today's factory farming systems (that is, farming systems in which animals are kept confined and immobilized for long periods of time) do turn a profit from animals generally unhealthy and in pain, since economies of scale allow the absorption of the early deaths of a small but not insignificant percentage of the animals. Pharmaceuticals are used to keep animals crowded in noxious conditions growing long enough to turn a profit.[36] Even in the most oppressive animal farming industries, such as egg laying by hens in battery cages, animal agriculturalists attempt to deny the harms to the animals. "Generally we try to provide exactly the environment which is most suitable for the bird," states one chicken farmer.[37] Frank Perdue, who keeps 27,000 unhealthy, overstressed, debeaked chickens in a single 150-yard-long building, and whose system kills 6.8 million birds a week, states that these chickens "lead such a soft life."[38] One farmer, who keeps calves tethered for the entirety of their brief lives (so their unexercised flesh has the distinctive veal taste of a newborn), struggles to deny the cruelty: "Some feel that it's rather cruel to the animals to keep them tied in there, but I point out that they're in a controlled environment, they, uh, the weather is, they never get real hot, or in the winter time it's never zero weather, there's no fly problem. And as a result, really, they've got a pretty good life in there . . . although they are chained."[39]

Such statements are part of an industry-wide effort to dim our awareness of the suffering behind animal farming. Advertisements consistently show animals perfectly content to be confined, striving to be hooked, happy to become commodities. The meat, egg, and dairy industries distribute bogus "educational" materials to thousands of schools. One pamphlet shows a grinning steer transported to the "meat packing company." Slaughter is not shown, and the text merely states that "at the packing plant, the 'beef crew' turned beef on the hoof into meat for the store."[40] Killing and dismembering are never mentioned. A coloring book labeled a "factual story approved by The American Egg Board," for example, erases the reality of laying chickens crowded into filthy battery cages by showing a hen standing proudly on a large straw bed with two chicks.[41]

These materials evoke the halcyon picture of the farming family living in harmony and mutual affection with their animals. Even for traditional, less-intensive animal farming, this picture avoids the reality that farmers profit from the slaughter and commodification of farmed animals. The comforting image persists, nonetheless, particularly in children's books. Animals, including farmed animals, are a favorite subject of children's books, but farmed animals are never shown being branded, castrated, debeaked, or slaughtered; they are always portrayed as protected friends. Farms are generally represented as havens, places where we nurture the livestock and protect them from all threats. For instance, the back cover of *The Midnight Farm*, a picture book for children, describes a "reassuring tour of a farm at midnight, . . . revealing the midnight farm through the wonder-filled eyes of a mother and child. . . . Here for parents and children to share is a loving vision indeed—of nature and humanity in harmony, sheltered and protected by friendly darkness."[42] The book's text concludes: "Here in the dark of the midnight farm / Safe and still and full and warm / Deep in the dark and free from harm / In the dark of the midnight farm."

DENYING ANIMAL PRESENCE

In the second Genesis creation story, God created the animals as helpers for the lone first man, then brought them to the man "to see what he would call them; and whatever the man called every living creature, that was its name" (2:19). Today some people call other living creatures "livestock," "game," "pets," "laboratory animals," "meat," and so on, and in so doing they deny the animals' own subjectivity (recall table 1). Projecting human uses for these animals into their definitional essences forestalls sympathy by blocking our awareness that other animals have interests of their own that are systematically overridden by the animal exploitation industries.

Those who take an active role in exploiting animals are particularly prone to the notion that the purpose of an animal's life derives from human interests. As one vivisector put it, "I grew up in the city, but we were very close to a farm community, and my values are farm values. I grew up thinking of animals as *for* something: some were for food, others were pets, . . . each type of animal had its purpose. I think of laboratory animals in the same way: they were bred for research; that's what they're for."[43] Hunter and writer Archibald Rutledge expressed a similar "that's what they're for" philosophy: "Certain game birds and animals are apparently made to be hunted, because of their peculiar food value and because their character lends zest to the pursuit of them."[44]

Animals come to be seen as voids, beings whose inherently empty lives are redeemed only through the imposition of human purposes, as indicated by the laboratory veterinarian's comment mentioned in the introduction: "At least this way they have a purpose." One vivisection textbook defines an "experimental animal" as "part instrument, part reagent, a complicated and incidentally sentient system."[45] The breeders who supply vivisectors further this view of animals as tools with advertisement copy such as "Now available in standard and stripped down model" (referring to guinea pigs with and without hair), "Building a Better Beagle," and "Specific Disease Model Available."[46]

The ability to harm animals on a daily basis without overwhelming distress requires an empathic curtailment that must be carefully inculcated. In his studies of the sociology of animal experimentation, Arnold Arluke found that the novice vivisector's initial response to laboratory animals typically includes affectionate attention and the giving of personal names. Arluke remarks that these young researchers "are still operating with an everyday perspective toward animals and have not yet learned to define laboratory animals as objects." This changes quickly:

> The emotional costs are high when one has a long-term and complex pet relationship with animals that are sacrificed. In such cases, laboratory staff often feel as though they have to kill a friend. A critical phase of the socialization of animal experimenters is going through at least one such relationship. Because of the grief entailed in the death of these pets, people learn through emotional "burns" that some degree of detachment is necessary. After experiencing such a loss or observing others go through it, people may attempt to restrict the extent to which they become involved with animals.[47]

The perception of laboratory animals as data-generating objects soon becomes automatic. For example, an employee of Biosearch, a Philadelphia laboratory at which people expose animals to noxious chemicals and analyze the results, reports that "once you've been here a few days, you lose respect for all living things. Torturing animals is the name of the game."[48] The employee's initial respect for animals (the "everyday perspective" mentioned by Arluke) contradicts the operations of the facility, so it is quickly discarded. The new, more adaptive ways of thinking become habitual, eventually being employed without self-conscious direction. Though the Biosearch employee states that respect for *all* living things is lost, those who exploit animals can learn to be selective with their considerations and affections, withholding them primarily from the animals they harm in the course of their work. An episode of the CBS news show *48 Hours* includes the following revealing statement by Oscar Marino, a toxicologist whose job involves placing poisonous chemicals in the eyes, on the skin, and into the stomachs of rabbits and mice: "Sometimes, you know, I'll be riding along the road and if a rabbit comes out I'll practically kill myself to avoid hitting the rabbit. But, out here, you know, it's kind of different. There's no feeling for these animals here in the laboratory. You know, they're a tool, and that's about it."

The vivisector's psychological need to deny the subjectivity of his victims has taken philosophical form as the theory of animal automatism. In Descartes' original version, all mental properties adhere in an immaterial soul that nonhumans lack; animals are mere machines, very complex, but completely unfeeling. Descartes was well aware of the expiatory function of his view that animals move and make sounds but have no feelings, beliefs, desires or other mental states: "My opinion is not so much cruel to animals as indulgent to men—at least to those who are not given to the superstitions of Pythagoras [that is, vegetarians]—since it absolves them from the suspicion of crime when they eat or kill animals."[49]

Descartes' theory was a boon to seventeenth-century vivisectors, as this eyewitness account indicates:

> They administered beatings to dogs with perfect indifference, and made fun of those who pitied the creatures as if they felt pain. They said the animals were clocks; that the cries they emitted when struck were only the noise of a little spring that had been touched, but that the whole body was without feeling. They nailed poor animals up on boards by their four paws to vivisect them and see the circulation of the blood which was a great subject of conversation.[50]

The popularity of animal automatism has not waned among vivisectors, though today it is expressed more circumspectly. The line now, formalized as "behaviorism" or "operationalism," is that researchers should generally assume that animal behavior results from nonintentional mechanisms. To do otherwise, to talk as if animals might feel or think, is to shamelessly anthropomorphize (since, following Descartes, thinking and feeling are "clearly" distinctively human properties), thereby demonstrating one's lack of the cardinal scientific virtue: objectivity. Descartes' strong thesis is weakened to a form of skepticism: We do not and cannot know that animals think or feel, so to be parsimonious we should just assume that they do not.

Animal automatism is not useful in providing a public justification of vivisection, since the scientifically uninitiated find the theory preposterous.

Nevertheless, animal automatism, even in its weakened form, is useful in allowing professional vivisectors to live with themselves. By purging official discourse of intentional vocabulary, vivisectors can talk among themselves about what they do without any disturbing awareness of the presence of other interested parties. The vivisected animal disappears from view as a conscious subject, beheld only, in Carol Adams's phrase, as an "absent referent."[51] The attempted transformation of sentient beings into manipulated matter and finally into abstract data is violence done to the animals, assisted by violence done to the language:

> The analytic animal is ostensibly an artifact—a product of human intervention. It is actively shaped by human agency, and in some cases literally carved up. Descartes' argument that the animal is no more than a machine becomes a self-fulfilling prophecy, since laboratory procedures assure the removal of the characteristics that make up the naturalistic animal (its life, its holistic and reciprocal presence, and its "subjective" attributes) in the scientific rendering of the phenomenon.[52]

Behavioristic language is one of the laboratory procedures that removes animal subjectivity from human awareness.

Farmers have traditionally recognized animal subjectivity, since managing individual animals typically requires some understanding of their mental states. But with the recent development of factory farming the ideology of animal automatism has been imported from vivisection into farming, as the rhetoric in farm industry literature makes evident:

> The modern layer is, after all, only a very efficient converting machine, changing the raw material—feed-stuffs—into the finished product—the egg—less, of course, maintenance requirements.[53]
>
> Forget the pig is an animal. Treat him just like a machine in a factory. Schedule treatments like you would lubrication. Breeding season like the first step in an assembly line. And marketing like the delivery of finished goods.[54]

Modern factory farming systems require treating animals as machines, so workers naturally begin to think of the farmed animals as unfeeling machines. But this extreme denial of animal subjectivity could well also be a psychologically necessary response to the extra burden of guilt modern farmers bear—unlike traditional farming practices, today's factory farms entail the *unremitting* suffering of the confined chickens, pigs, and cows.

The denial of animal subjectivity is typically accompanied by the notion of human superiority over other life-forms. James Serpell's work is significant in this context.[55] He points out that regarding others as subhuman is a very potent mechanism for emotionally distancing ourselves from them. Moreover, he argues that only in cultures that have domesticated animals do people regard animals as subhuman. From these two observations he infers that we disparage animals *because* we domesticate them—without this disparagement, our sympathies would more seriously interfere with the work of slaughtering an animal who has come to trust us through a previously established relationship of feeding and protection. If he is correct here, then the notion of nonhuman inferiority is a thoroughly political doctrine propagated to facilitate animal exploitation. I noticed in my own case that once I became vegan the idea of nonhuman animals as inferiors seemed not so much false as meaningless. Because I no longer have a personal interest in the continuation of animal exploitation, the question of whether other animals are our inferiors is empty.

Overriding Sympathies for Exploited Animals

There are times at which the comforting denials detailed above cannot be sustained. In particular, those who directly inflict the harms may be too close to the situation for the usual denial mechanisms to work, and those newly exposed to animal exploitation may not yet have had a chance to internalize the ways of thinking and seeing that forestall the pangs of conscience. When denial is not possible, some mechanism for overriding inhibitions against causing harm is necessary.

One arresting example of overcoming inhibitions involved laboratory technicians who, for eight-hour shifts, observed pigs with implanted ventricular assist pumps: "Each pig was observed for approximately three months, and then sacrificed. These 'pig-sitters,' as they were informally labeled, typically developed strong if not profound attachments to their pigs. . . . At the end of the observational period, one of the sitters had to sacrifice the pig. This was emotionally too difficult for a technician to do alone, so several sitters would do it as a group after first getting drunk in a bar across the street from the laboratory."[56] Those who cannot or have not yet detached themselves from "game," "livestock," or "laboratory animals" are still expected to play their roles as producers or consumers in the animal exploitation system. Structures of external incentives encourage or force us to find ways to act against our sympathies, as the following examples illustrate.

EXTERNAL INCENTIVES

The slaughter industry has an extremely high turnover rate. Most new workers last less than a week.[57] The workers who stay do so not because they enjoy or are indifferent to the repetitive killing and dismembering of large mammals. According to William Thompson's study of one slaughterhouse, all those who remained on the job for years told the same story. They took the job directly after high school because it was the highest-paying job available, and they intended to make some quick money that summer and find another job or go to school in the fall. They each, however, fell into what Thompson calls the "financial trap": the development of spending patterns that "simply would not allow them to leave." Thompson recounts one typical story:

> He began the week after his high school graduation, intending only to work that summer in order to earn enough money to attend college in the fall. After about four weeks' work he purchased a new car. He figured he could pay off the car that summer and still save enough money for tuition. Shortly after the car purchase, he added a new stereo sound system to his debt; next came a motorcycle; then the decision to postpone school for one year in order to continue working at the beef plant and pay off his debts. A few months later he married; within a year purchased a house; had a child; and bought another new car. Nine years later, he was still working at the beef plant, hated every minute of it, but in his own words "could not afford to quit."[58]

Thompson suggests that a vicious cycle is at work. The repellant nature of the job leads to its low social status, the workers attempt to overcome this low status through conspicuous consumption, and this consumption becomes contagious as workers avidly discuss and show off their latest acquisitions during breaks. The accumulated debt then forces them to stay at the slaughterhouse given the lack of other jobs paying comparable wages. "Ironically," Thompson notes, "as the workers cursed their jobs, these expensive possessions virtually destroyed any chance of leaving them."[59]

As Jeremy Rifkin explains, slaughterers are typically recruited not by offering above-average wages but by exploiting the dire economic circumstances of the dispossessed: "IBP [Iowa Beef Packers, the nation's largest "beef processor"] and its competitors seized upon the rural poor and the new immigrant groups flooding into the country from Mexico, Central and South America, and Southeast Asia, building corporate empires on the backs of a cheap pool of largely unorganized workers."[60] When desperately poor immigrants are unavailable or unwilling, the animal product industry is not above making use of forced labor. Boomsma chicken farm in Clarion, Iowa, keeps one hundred thousand laying hens in a single shed that stretches the length of two football fields. Workers there sort and package 1.3 million eggs a day, shovel out accumulations of manure, and remove dead hens from tiny cages stuffed full of birds. The owner ran newspapers ads for months but was unable to get people willing to work there. She applied to the Iowa Department of Labor for permission to import workers from Mexico. The department told her to try the local prison. She did, and now the majority of her workers are prison inmates required to work by the Iowa prison system.[61]

Whether prison inmates, new immigrants, or members of the primary labor pool, slaughterhouse employees are drawn from the working class. In vivisection, by contrast, the principal investigators are highly educated professionals working on salary. In their case, the motivation to continue in an occupation requiring the regular imposition of injury and death on animals may be less economic need and more the lure of professional rewards. Desire for career advancement leads the aspiring vivisector to interpret his or her inhibitions as obstacles to be overcome rather than as reasons to oppose vivisection. Although the career vivisector learns generally to avoid situations, behaviors, and ways of seeing that cause uneasiness, such uneasiness, when it does occur (either unavoidably at the beginning of a career or accidentally later on), is seen as a test of one's scientific mettle. Susan Sperling, for example, describes her strongly negative reaction to a series of dissections she performed while a graduate student, characterizing her feeling as "a primitive fear" that she had "committed a transgression."[62] She saw performance of the dissections as a test of whether she was "capable of being a scientist." She passed the test. Notwithstanding her initial feeling of committing a transgression, she was able to continue her graduate studies. Driven by a desire to "succeed and make important discoveries about primate social behavior," Sperling reconciled her career aspirations with her physical revulsion at the direct administration of bloodshed by specializing in primate maternal deprivation, a field that requires "only" the psychological and social manipulation of monkeys, not dissection or brain ablation. Sperling's story exemplifies the process by which a young vivisector discovers which situations are personally repellant or bothersome and then learns how to avoid these situations or mitigate their effects while continuing to climb the academic ladder. The motivation for this effort is plain in Sperling's account: professional success and status and the permission and opportunity to address "interesting" and "important" questions such as "Would the infant langurs become despondent when separated from the mother? Would they exhibit the behavioral and physiological 'depression' that Harlow had observed in his famous studies of separated rhesus macaque infants?"[63]

MYTHS OF NECESSITY

People are generally capable of acting against their sympathies when they believe their lives or the lives of their families depend on it. The animal agriculture and animal research industries exploit this human capacity by propagating the myth that their products are necessary for human health and well-being. Both industries have been largely successful in their efforts to convince the public that we must have their products to survive. This success is due in part to the material logic of sacrifice described in chapters 4 and 5 and in part to the enormous resources both industries have applied to the task of shaping public opinion in their favor.

In this culture, the human consumption of animal products is portrayed as an unremarkable given, leading to a consumer "demand" for meat and dairy that simply must be met; for example: "[Slaughtering] work is honest and necessary in a society which consumes beef."[64] The unquestioned acceptance of meat as a part of the human diet has been fostered by industry propaganda efforts spanning decades. For instance, the meat and dairy industries developed the notion of four essential food groups, with, not coincidentally, meat and dairy being two of them.[65] With this false theory taught in elementary schools, generations were indoctrinated into the myth that we must eat significant quantities of animal flesh or animal products to be healthy. In 1992, the USDA modified the four food groups model, changing it to a "food pyramid," in an attempt to reflect the nutritional research indicating that placing meat and dairy as two equal parts of a four-part diet entails a diet with unhealthy amounts of animal fat. It is healthier to eat larger proportions of fruits and vegetables and smaller amounts of meat and dairy. In fact, the research indicates that the lower one's diet is in animal fat, the healthier one tends to be. As the revisions were being considered, the meat and dairy industries recognized that nutritionally speaking, it is possible to eliminate the meat and dairy categories from the model altogether. Intense lobbying from these economic interests prevented what would have been, to them, a marketing catastrophe: teaching children the reality that they need not eat any animal products to be healthy. So the conclusion of the revisions was a compromised model still including animal products as prominent building blocks in a "healthy" diet, a disingenuous result still retained in the latest version of the food pyramid released in 2005.[66]

The dairy industry has attempted to build its market by portraying cows' milk as a health food, in particular, as a good source of calcium. Their marketing campaign implies that since osteoporosis is a disease involving loss of the calcium needed for strong bones, we should prevent this condition by drinking lots of cows' milk. The reality is that osteoporosis is caused by the consumption of an excessive amount of protein. Protein that cannot be metabolized must be excreted, and this process requires calcium. Since the typical American meat-based diet includes far more protein than can be metabolized, we are constantly using calcium simply to get rid of the extra protein. Vegetarian cultures and cultures that consume much less meat and dairy than do modern Americans do not have a problem with osteoporosis. The dairy industry's promotion of their product as a health food is devious because the consumption of dairy is actually part of a health problem—the overconsumption of animal fat, which leads to higher rates of cancer, stroke, and heart disease, as well as osteoporosis.[67]

Animal vivisectionists similarly claim to be providing for significant human health needs. This story has successfully preempted sympathetic opposition to their routine confinement, injury, and killing of animals, inasmuch as most people who have awareness or concern about animal vivisection tend to oppose only the most egregiously cruel and useless experiments but support the continuation of all the medical experimentation we have been told is "necessary." Vivisectionists respond to any challenges to animal experimentation by publicly pronouncing that we would all die earlier if not for their work, as in the following statement by C. Everett Koop, the former U.S. surgeon general: "When I was born there was no vaccine for polio, no antibiotics, no way to treat diabetes or heart disease. As a result our life expectancy was just 52 years. Today, thanks to animal-based research, that figure is more than 72 years, which means that even those against animal research live to protest at least 20 years longer."[68] Such fear-mongering, though invaluable for maintaining funding and public support, is demagogic given the well-established fact that the increases in life expectancy in the industrialized West have been due predominantly to improvements in public health conditions, not to medical advances (let alone to animal experimentation).[69]

Demoralizing Sympathies for Exploited Animals

Even if our sympathies for exploited animals are engaged, and these sympathies are not overridden by some structure of external needs (real or imaginary), this does not yet entail our morally based opposition to animal exploitation. To yield animal liberationism, sympathies for exploited animals must be understood to validly ground moral opposition to the exploiting institutions or individuals. Sympathy, empathy, compassion, and other forms of "feeling with" another, though often described approvingly, do not carry a positive moral status within them. We recognize the possibility of morally neutral or even iniquitous sympathies (they may be "misguided," "misdirected," "excessive," etc.). This analytic distinction between sympathetic feelings and their moral valuation allows the third and final general means for blocking sympathetic opposition to animal exploitation—our recurrent sympathies for exploited animals may be "demoralized," that is, represented as entailing no abolitionist implications. Two types of demoralization are discussed here: disparaging sympathies for animals (so they provide no moral grounds for abolition) and coopting them (so they can be used to further animal exploitation).

DISPARAGING SYMPATHIES FOR ANIMALS

Even in a culture suffused with animal exploitation, people consistently incline toward empathetic connection with animals.[70] And animal exploiters themselves, much as their emotional lives would be made easier by total detachment, often cannot practically afford the luxury of a complete denial of animal subjectivity. This is due to the fact that the process of exploiting animals usually requires anticipating their actions, and this anticipation is nearly impossible without acknowledging the animals' mental states. Farmers and ranchers must drive their stock to slaughter, and this means forestalling the animals' attempts to escape by understanding their basic desires and fears. Hunters cannot be successful without knowing where and when to find their prey, knowledge that typically proceeds from careful study of and eventual identification with their targets. Vivisectors, notwithstanding their denial of animal subjectivity in official documents such as professional articles and research grant proposals, must tacitly acknowledge animals' mental states in order to proceed with the daily work of collecting data through experimentation—the animals must be moved from their cages, immobilized, fed and watered, and so forth. In his sociological study of laboratory research using chimpanzees, D. Lawrence Wieder found that without an awareness of the animals' subjective states the researchers could not effectively manage the chimps throughout the course of the experiment.[71] Similarly, author and animal trainer Vicki Hearne notes that trainers routinely attribute emotional states such as loves and worries to their dogs and horses, and that this unselfconscious recognition of subjectivity is crucial to their success in "eliciting interesting behavior" from the animals.[72]

Acknowledging animals' subjective states is not the same thing as sympathizing with them, but it is only one step away. Animal exploiters precariously balance the practical need to understand animals' thoughts and feelings with their own emotional need not to care too much about the harm they are doing to the animals. Exploiters must also concern themselves with the constant potential for opposition to their activities arising from public sympathies for animals—sympathies never completely subverted by industry denials and myths. Both these concerns over inconvenient sympathies are addressed by belittling the emotions themselves, intending that these feelings never be taken seriously as the basis of individual action or public policy. An example of this is the characterization of antihunters as "Bambi-lovers." Many people have been emotionally affected by the movie *Bambi,* and it is true that the movie is biologically inaccurate (deer, for instance, do not really speak). But the suggestion that opposition to hunting stems solely from exposure to unrealistically anthropomorphic depictions of animals derides sympathies for targeted animals by implying that they are always irrationally based.

Sympathies are derogated in gender-specific ways. Women's expressions of sympathetic concern are expected and tolerated, but they are not respected; rather, they are dismissed as typical female hysteria. Men, on the other hand, are often not allowed to express such feelings. For example, on one occasion at the Labor Day pigeon shoot in Hegins, Pennsylvania, a boy, about eight years old or so, was crying at the sight of pigeons being blown out of the air and then having their heads pulled off by "trapper boys." As this boy turned away in tears, his dad grabbed and twisted his head, forcing him to face the shooting, saying, "You *will* watch."[73]

In the vivisection industry, founded by men and still male dominated, compassion for animals traditionally has been simultaneously feminized and derogated:

> As a young graduate student, he was running an experiment with rats. The experiment was over, and he was faced with the problem of what to do with the animals. He approached his advisor, who replied, "Sacrifice them." . . . "How?" asked my friend. . . . "Like this," replied the instructor, dashing the head of the rat on the side of the workbench, breaking its neck. . . . My friend, a kind man, was horrified and said so. The professor fixed him in a cold gaze and said, "What's the matter, Smith, are you soft? Maybe you're not cut out to be a psychologist!"[74]

In this environment "softness" is not allowed, so men who would be scientists must establish their hard callousness, and women who would be scientists must be like the men.[75] Bernard Rollin describes the process of turning our ordinary caring dispositions into a vice to be expunged: "My friend, like countless other embryonic scientists, physicians, and veterinarians, was starting with a sense of moral concern for the animals, with respect for them as ends in themselves, as living creatures. This, however, is seen as sentimentality, squeamishness, lack of professionalism, etc., and so values are transvaluated, as Nietzsche says, and what is ordinarily a virtue—compassion and sensitivity—becomes a vice."[76]

This conventional association of scientific capacity with masculine callousness can become a liability, however, when vivisectors, like hunters and animal farmers, choose to deflect outside criticism by depicting themselves as compassionate animal welfarists. In an article published by the trade journal *Lab Animal*, Arnold Arluke recommends that vivisectors no longer continue the traditional suppression and denial of their sympathetic hesitations regarding the infliction of injury and death.[77] Arluke advises vivisection facilities to begin supporting the expression of these feelings and to help manage and "redefine" them through stress management workshops and individual counseling. Apparently, many vivisectors somehow believe that feeling guilty about their work means they may be doing something wrong. But Arluke encourages institutions to remedy this moral naïveté by teaching vivisectors that "guilt is really an indicator that the lab workers' consciences are alive and well." Arluke makes clear that improving vivisection's public image is the ultimate point of bringing vivisectors' uneasiness out of the closet: "If [institutions] acknowledge and attend to the types of uneasiness that I discussed earlier, it is possible that scientists and technicians may become more human in the public's eye."[78]

Insofar as deep and recurring hesitations are not recognized as the basis for compassionate social change, they are degraded. Thus Arluke's strategy continues to degrade the human disinclination to harm animals, no longer as a feminine vice, but now as a commendable stress to be therapeutically managed in the course of animal exploitation business as usual.

COOPTING EMPATHY

Arluke's suggestion to publicize vivisector's moral qualms to improve the profession's image exemplifies one way in which empathy may be coopted by the institutions of animal exploitation. The public relations value of portraying animal exploiters as animal lovers is significant. Beyond this, there can also be a practical benefit to encouraging sympathetic identification with exploited animals. In vivisection laboratories, "cowboys"—lab technicians who disparage animals and manage their research subjects through over-

whelming force and intimidation—are being replaced by "animal people,"
who communicate with laboratory animals, particularly primates, bond
with them, and attempt to provide for their emotional and social needs
as well as their basic physical needs (to the extent that this is possible for
animals who are caged and systematically injured).[79] One American vivisection lab, which does AIDS and other research on chimps, invites volunteers
from the community into the facility to provide the young chimps with the
"love and stimulus" necessary for their normal development and growth.
James Mahoney, the laboratory's chief veterinarian, explains in an HBO
documentary the thinking behind this policy: "We do have a strong intention to bridge the gap between us, so that when we *do* do the research, they
don't resent us, they don't hate us, they don't distrust us. And even if we do
something unpleasant to them, they'll forgive us. That is our intention."[80]
The volunteers who come into this laboratory to play with the chimps are
largely, perhaps exclusively, female. Here women's stereotypical nurturance
is being used to better facilitate an exploitative process organized and led by
men. The affective sexual division of labor is not strict, however, since we
see on the video that Mahoney also himself cuddles the chimps, tells them
he loves them, and so forth. These images humanize the researcher, and
the relationship with the chimps thus established facilitates their continued
experimental exploitation in the ways Mahoney describes—they are healthier,
more normal, and easier to manipulate.

In hunting, as previously discussed, the men who track and shoot animals
see themselves as true animal lovers. As James Swan notes, the "nature hunter
. . . must develop an acute sympathy with the animals he hunts. He must not
only have a good deal of knowledge about them, he must have a feeling for
them."[81] This sympathetic identification allows the hunter to anticipate the
targeted animal's behavior and thus position himself appropriately for the
kill. Sympathy for the prey, though constantly threatening to motivate the
hunter's ultimate abdication of blood sports, is in the meantime carefully
managed as an invaluable tool of the chase.

Hunters, witnessing the dwindling of their demographic base through
urbanization and the recent upswing in public expressions of animal rights
consciousness, perceive themselves as a shrinking, embattled minority. How
long will they be allowed to continue their shooting sports? One expression
of this concern is voiced by Ted Kerasote, who recommends that hunters
renounce their traditional sexism and begin welcoming women into their
ranks: "Until women restore their sympathies to hunting's fundamental life-
giving, life-respecting aspects, and have a hand in reducing its elements of

machismo and competition, hunters will be fighting an uphill losing battle. It is women who will vote hunting out of existence."[82] Kerasote's hope is that the recruitment of putatively compassionate women will counter the generally accurate understanding of hunters as evincing a will to dominate, in that way preserving the nonhunting majority's toleration of blood sports for another generation. This hope may be moot if a change in men's attitudes toward women as hunters is insufficient to entice them into the practice or if women hunters are unable to convince the public of their basically compassionate attitude toward the animals they shoot.

In the third major institution of animal exploitation, meat production, we also see the dual-purpose cooptation of empathy. This is exemplified in the work of Temple Grandin, an autistic woman who designs slaughterhouse facilities and equipment. Her professed design methodology is to empathetically imagine the animals' point of view, constructing the abattoir so that at each step in moving from transport vehicles to the killing floor the animals are calm and composed, ultimately walking straight to their deaths without direct coercion. In a recent article, Anna Williams points out that recruitment of the farmed animals' own subjectivity as a means of facilitating the smoothest possible path to their demise is not new. Physical coercion is expensive, requiring substantial labor inputs, and the resultant bruises significantly lower the retail value of the carcass. Hence, as Williams shows, the mechanized slaughter industry has since its inception implemented various deceptive devices to transform the animals' resistance into unwitting compliance—blinders, decoy animals, trap doors, and the like.[83] Williams describes Grandin's "stairway to heaven" as just the latest in a series of innovations through which "an appreciation of animal sentience fortifies, rather than interrupts, production": "A curved entrance into the packinghouse and a conveyor . . . transports animals to their deaths on the kill floor. Its raised sides and serpentine shape distinguish Grandin's entrance. The sidewalls block out distracting sights and sounds while the curved route exploits the animals' tendency to circle. Faced with this structure, cattle effectively walk themselves into the packinghouse."[84]

The value such technologies provide to the industry is not restricted to efficiency gains; they also produce opportunities for slaughterers to portray themselves as animal welfarists who hire designers such as Grandin to help reduce the stress levels of farmed animals approaching death and dismemberment en masse. Grandin and her publishers actively assist in the construction of her humane image. The jacket of her latest book, *Animals in Translation,* for example, informs the reader that Grandin is "one of the most celebrated and effective animal advocates on the planet" and quotes reviewers extolling her remarkable empathic abilities and the use to which she puts them:

> Temple Grandin was born with the ability to live in the animal world, completely understanding their environment.
> Temple Grandin takes us deep inside the minds of animals. Her observations of dogs, cats, cows, pigs, birds, fish, and horses are meticulous and humane.
> Temple Grandin has done many wonderful things for this world, things that have made a tremendous difference in the lives of animals and people. . . . If only we could understand animals as smoothly as she does.[85]

Inside the book, Grandin speaks of her empathy for animals, how she likes to kiss cows (the animals she "loves best") on the nose, when she "started to fall in love with animals" (high school), and her feeling that "people and animals are supposed to be together."[86] She also boasts that "half the cattle in the United States and Canada are handled in humane slaughter systems I've designed."[87] This means that Grandin's machinery kills twenty million of her best beloved each year, an impressive accomplishment for one of the planet's most effective animal advocates.[88] Grandin reports that she is often asked how someone who loves animals so much can work in the meatpacking industry. She resolves this dissonance via the standard blame displacement—"I don't see the human race converting to vegetarianism anytime soon"—and by reasoning that since we brought farm animals into existence, we owe them a decent life and a decent death.[89]

Regardless of Grandin's professed humane motivations, she is hired because her technical innovations save money for slaughterers. She has worked in animal exploitation industries long enough to be well aware of this, and example after example in her book indicate that human economic interests, not the well-being of exploited animals, drive industry decisions. Two examples follow:

> Prods will get an animal moving, but they're stupid things to use because they can panic the animals and make them rear up, which is dangerous for the workers. Prods always stress an animal, and when an animal is stressed his immune system goes down and he starts getting sick, which means higher veterinary bills. Plus stressed animals gain less weight, which means less meat to sell. Dairy cattle who've been handled with prods give less milk. . . . Stress is horrible for growth, period, which means stress is horrible for profits. . . .
> Not too long ago I got a call to go out to a meatpacking plant where the animals were getting big fat bruises on their loins. The loin is the area in between a cow's rib cage and its rear leg. It's the most expensive part of the animal,

because that's where the steak is located. So nobody wants their cattle getting bruised loins. A bruise means bleeding inside the muscle, and the bloody area has to be cut out in the butchering process, which means less meat to sell.[90]

Mirroring the situation in vivisection and hunting discussed above, we see that also in animal farming empathy for animals can be coopted, subverting its abolitionist implications and putting it to use as a mechanism for boosting the industry's humane image while simultaneously improving its efficiency.

Conclusion

> To make a new world the American animals
> know there must be sacrifices. Every evening
> a prayer is said for the spies who've volunteered
> to be petted in the houses of the enemy.
> "They are savages," one reported,
> "let no one be fooled by their capacity for loving."
> —Stephen Dunn, "The Animals of America"

Our capacity for loving animals underlies the ethics of animal liberation. Yet as this chapter has shown, our affections for animals are not inevitably applied toward dismantling the institutions of animal exploitation. The politicizing of sympathies for animals is culturally contingent; thus, notwithstanding the omnipresence of these sympathies, movements for animal liberation arise only infrequently. And when they do, exploitative industries deploy a range of means to forestall, override, disparage, or coopt our sympathies, attempting to counteract the movement before it reaches the critical strength sufficient for enacting abolition. Thus the animal issue may be seen as a struggle between the inclination to preserve entrenched institutions and the plain implications of our compassion. How animal advocates engage this struggle is the subject of the next and final chapter.

7

The Politics of Animal
Liberation

> We want power.
> —Wayne Pacelle

The ethics of animal liberation are simple and generally moving: Our natural and normal sympathies motivate an ethical injunction against causing unnecessary harm to animals. This immediately entails the immorality of sport hunting and, coupled with the articulation of our actual nutrition and health needs, undermines the legitimacy of animal farming and vivisection.

The straightforward nature of animal liberation ethics, however, does not mean that the politics of animal liberation are equally clear-cut. The main strategies adopted by the animal advocacy movement seem straightforward enough: make the ethical case against animal exploitation through education and the mass media, push for enforcement of existing anticruelty laws, lobby for passage of new legislation that offers animals greater protection. In order to avoid counterproductive or self-defeating activism, though, we need a specific understanding of what these approaches entail, including how they are actually applied and whether they are likely to be successful given the structure of the institutions of animal exploitation.

The focus of our legal system is highly individualistic, encouraging us to frame justice issues in terms of specific acts of personal malfeasance. This framing is not the most relevant for animal liberation, however, given that the animal abuse challenged is not caused by individual acts of sadism but by corporate entities (the animal farming industry, the medical establishment, the wildlife management system) underwritten by the ideology and practice of male dominance. But the animal liberation movement often uncritically adopts society's identification of the individual as the primary site of good and evil. The first section of this chapter analyzes the displacement of focus from the corporate to the individual in a particular case, the promotion of vegetarianism as direct action. I argue that the way vegetarianism is portrayed by some animal advocates supports the notion that animal farming is driven by the dietary choices of individual consumers, thus propagating the very myth the industry uses to justify its continued existence.

Our consciousness-raising efforts can also be problematic. Sexism is one of the primary means the mass media use in the competition to draw people's attention. Additionally, sexism is still operative in the social process of determining whose opinions are worthy of serious consideration. In striving to gain media attention and to be taken seriously as social critics, animal liberationists at times defer to or actively use sexist practices. In the second and third sections of this chapter I analyze several examples of this tendency and challenge the use of sexism as an animal liberationist tactic.

At its most basic level the animal liberation movement seeks power via control of the individual, pursued through either moral persuasion (promoting personal conversion to veganism) or state-imposed restrictions (anticruelty laws, etc.). The main argument of this book is that with respect to animal exploitation, individuals are not the problem. Individuals are fine, in that our normal sympathetic responsiveness to animals is sufficient to motivate the abolition of animal exploitation. The problems are structural, involving entrenched economic interests and, more deeply, a system of gender based on white male dominance over disempowered others (women, children, people of color, animals). In the final section of this book I describe an approach to animal liberation that is antisexist and renounces the attempt to manipulate or otherwise gain power over individual human beings.

From Virtuous Vegetarianism to Radical Subversion

As animal farming becomes more intensive—confining huge numbers of animals into smaller and smaller spaces for larger and larger portions of their lives—the suffering experienced by the exploited animals increases. The sheer scope of the torment occasioned by intensive animal farming makes it one of the primary issues of concern for animal liberationists.

Modern intensive animal farming also takes a great toll on the environment. Farm animal production is a major source of pollution. Much of the enormous amount of manure produced by the billions of farm animals exploited each year in the United States, for instance, ends up polluting rivers and ground water. The U.S. farm animal system requires tremendous amounts of energy, thus depleting oil, coal, and gas reserves, contributing to the environmental damage done by mining and drilling and hastening the global warming effects produced by burning fossil fuels. To feed a vegetarian population would require one-third less total energy. Cows produce methane, a greenhouse gas, so this is another way in which animal farming contributes to global warming. The production of a pound of steak has the same greenhouse effect as a twenty-five-mile drive in a typical American car. Animal farming also requires huge amounts of water; in fact, more than half of all water consumed for all purposes in the United States goes to livestock production. (Consider that in California, 5,214 gallons of water are required to produce a pound of beef, but only 25 gallons are needed to produce a pound of potatoes or a pound of wheat.) Agriculture geared toward a vegetarian diet requires much less land than does meat production. A typical American meat eater requires 3.25 acres of land a year (this includes the land to grow the plants eaten directly, plus the land to grow the food for the cows, chickens, pigs, and other animals whose flesh or products are eaten), while a vegan requires only one-sixth of an acre to eat for a year. Finally, large tracts of tropical rain forest are cleared to provide grazing for cattle. These animals are then sold to affluent countries to become fast food. Each hamburger produced from beef imported from Central or South America involves the destruction of fifty-five square feet of rain forest.[1]

Respect for animal well-being and for environmental integrity both lead to the conclusion that the current animal-based agriculture system is unacceptable. Upon realizing this, animal liberationists and environmentalists often adopt dietary changes so as not to be implicated in a destructive system. Animal advocates publicize both the ecological costs of animal-based agriculture and the great suffering experienced by factory-farmed animals. Often these writings also include detailed descriptions of the pernicious human health consequences of a diet oriented around animal products.[2] The combination of ethical arguments based on ecological and humane considerations with prudential arguments based on human health is powerful. Most animal liberationists are either vegetarian (eating no animal flesh) or vegan (consuming no animal products). Lately, many environmental activists have been moving in the same direction.

It is evidently hypocritical to oppose animal exploitation while continuing to eat the flesh of slaughtered animals. This motivates vegetarianism—we abstain from meat and other animal products to avoid the feeling of cognitive dissonance between our activism and our daily choices. But a key question remains: Does vegetarianism, in addition to allowing us to live with ourselves, also provide real benefits for animals and the land?

Animal liberationists often speak as if the practical efficacy of vegetarianism is beyond question. A truism of the movement is that going vegetarian or vegan is the "best thing one can do for the animals." There are entire animal advocacy groups dedicated exclusively to converting people to vegetarianism and veganism. As in the Friends of Animals slogan, "Spare an Animal—Eat a Vegetable," the simple idea is that as people cease eating meat, fewer animals will be processed by the system. Thus we have the power to reduce the oppression of animals simply by being conscientious about what we eat.

This picture of personal power is alluring, but it may not be sustainable in the face of the reality of the meat production system. The scale at which meat is produced is so vast it is not clear whether an individual's choice to become vegetarian is even noticeable. Production decisions are not made at the level of the individual. I may go from eating ten chickens a year as a meat-eater to eating zero chickens a year as a vegetarian, but that does not mean that ten fewer chickens are slaughtered. The philosophical literature devoted to thinking through the likely consequences of an individual's vegetarianism generally works from two premises: (1) an individual's vegetarian choices are inefficacious—simply not noticed by agribusiness, so production levels are unchanged, and (2) vegetarian collectives of a large enough size *are* noticed and do reduce meat production. Given these presumptions, the goal for utilitarian advocates of vegetarianism becomes bridging the two premises—finding some way of analytically linking the inefficacious individual to the efficacious collective. Suggested means include pointing to a ripple effect by which the individual's vegetarianism influences others to abstain from meat and analyzing the effects of the individual's vegetarianism as one equal part of the collective's effect.[3]

Another approach was developed by Peter Singer.[4] He affirmed the second premise, assuming that at some point the number of vegetarians does reach a threshold at which production levels drop. One person who stops eating chickens has no effect on the number of broiler hens slaughtered, nor does the vegetarianism of five people or even five hundred. But suppose that ten thousand people becoming vegetarian does affect production levels—perhaps one fewer one-hundred-thousand-bird shed is constructed. Now, most of us are not the precise individual who tips the scales, but somebody is, according to Singer, and therefore that person's vegetarian choice makes a huge difference in the overall levels of animal suffering. Since each of us is equally likely to be the one who crosses that threshold, each of us has a small chance of making a huge difference. In becoming vegetarian, I may not be directly saving ten chickens, but if I have a one in ten thousand chance of saving one hundred thousand birds, then the expected utility is the same as if I did (1/10,000 times 100,000 equals 10 birds saved). The principle holds regardless of the precise numbers. Large numbers of vegetarians cause large drops in production levels, so each member of the vegetarian group can legitimately take partial credit for reducing animal exploitation through his or her dietary choice.

Singer's argument relies crucially on premise two regarding the efficacy of vegetarian collectives. But this premise is shaky. If an extremely large vegetarian collective formed, comprising, say, one hundred million Americans, then of course animal agriculture would be affected. Consider the dramatic drop in production levels in the United Kingdom due to consumers' fear over beef being contaminated by mad cow disease. Unfortunately, such scares do not necessarily lead to vegetarianism on a massive scale, only to a search for other animal products or other sources of meat. At present in the United States we have and can only expect vegetarian subcultures on the order of several million individuals. These sizable but still minority vegetarian collectives are assumed to affect meat production levels by utilitarian arguments such as Singer's, but is this assumption correct? According to meat industry propaganda, animals are slaughtered in order to meet an externally generated demand. Thus if demand drops noticeably, so does production. But this picture distorts reality. Production levels are established through a complex of factors, of which consumer desire is but one. Moreover, demand itself is managed by the industry to bring it into correspondence with independently established production levels.

To excuse its cruelty, industry would have us believe the opposite, that demand for meat is prior to supply. Typical in its crude essentialism is slaughterhouse designer Temple Grandin's self-serving account: "The fact that humans evolved as both plant and meat eaters means that the vast majority of human beings are going to continue to eat both. Humans are animals, too, and we do what our animal natures tell us to do. That means we're going to continue to have feedlots and slaughterhouses."[5] As any vegetarian can attest, however, there is no "animal nature" at our core hungering for the flesh of other animals. Demand for meat does not exist in isolation from meat production, nor does it determine production levels according to any simple linear relation. Consider the following chapters in the history of beef. By the 1870s buffalo had been exterminated from the Great Plains, allowing ranchers to graze their cattle. Many of the ranchers then made their initial fortunes by selling beef to the government to feed to natives who were starving because their subsistence base, the buffalo, had been destroyed.[6] Here the development of the productive base for beef directly created its "demand." Moreover, in the twentieth century, meat production increased drastically, but not because individuals were clamoring for more and more flesh. David Nibert and Bill Winders report that U.S. agricultural policies emerging from the New Deal resulted in continuous overproduction of corn, wheat, and soybeans. Farmers and the state then promoted meat production and consumption as a way to utilize this surplus of grains.[7] Another relevant example comes from World War II, during which the Department of War determined to feed U.S. servicemen huge quantities of beef because they believed that was essential for maintaining their fighting ability.[8] Here policymakers' deep, unexamined presumptions connecting meat, male virility, and aggressive capacity were a large contributing factor in the determination of production levels.

Animal agriculture boosts demand through propaganda such as the four food groups model of nutrition, discussed in the previous chapter. Today, as the deleterious effects of flesh consumption gradually reach public consciousness, a small minority of Westerners are moving toward vegetarianism. The animal agriculture complex reacts to sustain demand in a variety of ways. The establishment of McDonald's fast-food restaurants in Russia, India, and other new markets outside the West indicates one response. Transnational businesses do not passively allow consumers to determine how much will be bought and sold—just as the tobacco industry responds to steadily declining cigarette sales in the United States by working to open up markets in the global South, so the animal agriculture industry is positioning itself to maintain sales of flesh notwithstanding the vegetarian decisions of a few million humane and/or health-conscious Anglo-Europeans. The so-called diseases of affluence (cancer, heart disease, stroke, diabetes, and other conditions associated with excessive consumption of animal fat) are now being exported to urban workers of the global South via the provision of fast-food hamburgers.[9]

Since the production of meat is driven as much or more by supply-side considerations as by independent consumer demand, it becomes difficult to show that meat boycotts (vegetarianism) actually affect the industry. This does not deter animal liberationists from advocating vegetarianism, however. For example, in his article on "Five Arguments for Vegetarianism," William Stephens argues that even if an individual's dietary choices are too minimal an influence to realistically lessen the injustices of animal agriculture, we should still abstain from meat as an expression of virtue, a mark of moral integrity.[10] Similarly, PETA advocates vegetarianism even when the consequences for animals are negligible or potentially negative. For example, PETA's vegan campaign coordinator, Bruce Friedrich, contacted Oklahoma City federal building bomber Timothy McVeigh two months prior to his scheduled execution, exhorting him to switch to a vegan diet. McVeigh demurred. Given the short time he had left to live, it is evident that veganism by McVeigh could not affect production levels. And the ripple effect, in this case, was more likely to be negative than positive. Nonetheless, Friedrich made the effort to convert McVeigh, reasoning thus: "I don't know what it means for the vegan movement if Timothy McVeigh, in his final days, adopts a vegan diet. But I think it would be very positive for his soul."[11]

Emphasizing moral integrity in abstraction from utilitarian considerations preserves a moral case for vegetarianism, regardless of the result of uncertain reckonings concerning the wider impact of an individual's dietary choices. But it is risky to detach virtue from consequences in this way. If virtue is achieved by boycotting a pernicious industry even when that boycott is not likely to be efficacious, then virtue is not outwardly directed—looking toward dismantling an oppressive industry—but is inward-looking, a matter of achieving personal purity by protecting oneself from culpability for the oppression.[12] We might then form vegetarian subcultures so that we are not morally tainted by the evil going on "out there." Such a vegetarian separatism is not analogous to separatist strategies in other social justice movements. In black nationalism and feminist separatism, for example, the oppressed themselves leave white supremacist patriarchy, so by their very leaving they end oppression, at least that directed toward themselves. If you and I walk out of the meat-eating culture, on the other hand, animals are still slaughtered.

The step from the injustice of animal agriculture to personal vegetarianism is problematic: To avoid simply walking away from injustice, we must attend to the likely consequences of our actions, but it appears that even in conjunction with several million other vegetarians our dietary choices might not appreciably stem the traffic in animals. Given the problems with this crucial step from injustice to boycott, we might consider the arguments against animal farming afresh. Ecological and humane considerations strongly indicate the injustice of contemporary animal agriculture. What most directly follows from this is not vegetarianism, but the abolition or complete reform of animal agriculture. Interestingly, once we bracket the vegetarian conclusion, the argument from human health concerns is no longer morally distinct from the other two arguments. What I put in my body may be a matter of prudence (a personal choice rather than a moral imperative), but when industries market products known to cause disease, that is a justice issue. Given the numbers of people presently dying of cancer, heart disease, stroke, and so on, and the causal connections between these deaths and the consumption of a meat-based diet of the sort marketed by agribusiness, the meat industry is now in a position morally analogous to companies that continued marketing baby formula in the global South after it was established that the formula was grossly increasing infant mortality there. So the argument regarding human health now fits in with the others, each one showing in a distinct way that animal agriculture is unjust and therefore should be abolished or radically restructured.

The first obligation to end injustice lies with the perpetrators. Animal farmers would like us to believe that they are not primarily responsible for slaughter, that they are only giving the people what they want, but the reality is different. Agribusiness produces both meat and demand for meat. So the ecological, humane, and nutritional arguments against meat are most properly directed to those on the production side, entailing that they should stop what they are doing. A vegetarian conclusion can too abruptly shift the focus to individual dietary choices that are not the root of the problem but are a function of the system itself. The issue then becomes salvaging one's personal virtue rather than insisting on institutional change.

If agribusiness will not stop the injustices on their own (and unfortunately, there is no reason to think that they will do so), then it becomes the public's responsibility to insist that they stop. As such, radical change is initiated not by agribusiness executives or stockholders and their supporters in government—the people presently driving the system—but by those who the industry would prefer to position as passive recipients of their decisions concerning food production. In other words, radical social change is bottom up; it is "subversive," meaning overturning from underneath.

Unlike virtuous vegetarianism, the focus of such radical subversion is not on me and my behavior, or on you and your behavior, but on the animal agriculture system itself. This entails a praxis going well beyond the formation of vegetarian enclaves. In addition to advocating vegetarianism, we confront the animal agriculture system directly, insisting that they stop the production and marketing of meat, dairy, and eggs. Production, not consumption, becomes the center of activist attention.

As we continue our efforts to expand consciousness regarding meat, we should remember that vegetarianism is only one implication of the injustice of animal agriculture, and that implication is indirect. More immediately, that injustice calls for interventions directed against the meat industry. A recent example of such direct intervention comes from Britain, where the confinement of calves in crates is illegal. When people there realized that dairy farmers were circumventing the law by transporting calves to the Continent to be confined, they blockaded the transportation system at the points of export. So long as agriculture continues to act unjustly toward human and nonhuman animals and nature, we should confront this system at its roots, at the points of financing, production, distribution, and marketing, not merely at the point of consumption. We should videotape the slaughter process and show the tapes publicly—not to disgust people into meat abstention (a common response to such tapes but one likely to be short-lived) but to hold the industry responsible for the harms they are imposing on animals for profit. We should counter every lie the industry propagates to boost sales (milk does not "do a body good"—cows' milk is good food for growing calves, not for people, and in fact, most minority Americans are unable to digest the milk sugar lactose).[13] We should insist that the U.S. government cease subsidizing animal agriculture, protest the construction of new burger joints, and sue the meat producers and retailers for compensatory and punitive damages for the noxious human health consequences of their products. We could march into a McDonald's, not to shame the customers into leaving (where would they go?) but to pointedly ask management why they are not selling a vegetarian burger (next we can ask them why they're selling any meat at all). These are just a few examples of antimeat activism; many more can and are being added to this list as we focus on production as well as consumption.

The efficacy of such actions may or may not be furthered by activists choosing vegetarianism. For blocking a lorry carrying farmed animals for export, a meat-eater's body is as good as a vegetarian's. But many activists, especially those of us with long-term commitments to the abolition of animal exploitation, find that vegetarianism or especially veganism naturally ground our political work.[14] We may choose veganism to detach our interests from those of the industries we criticize, to avoid appearing hypocritical, or to stand as an example of the possibility of living robustly without the products of animal abuse. This is not a veganism of personal purity, it is a veganism of political contingency.

As animal activists our awareness of the scope and intensity of suffering inflicted on animals within the meat production system generates a valid sense of emergency, the feeling that we must do something now to stop the slaughter. The highly entrenched status of animal agriculture, though, makes us wonder what can be done. In this situation it is understandable that the one thing we do have control over, what we put into our bodies, would be touted as a significantly powerful tactic in and of itself, as in the recent Friends of Animals slogan "Veganism is Direct Action." But we should take care that our humane desire to influence the system not lead us into faulty analysis and prematurely false hopes. In fact, veganism is not direct action; by definition direct action is intervention at the point of injustice without mediation of political authorities and without relying on the capitulation of the perpetrators. Examples of direct action include purchasing animals from farmers and placing them in sanctuaries, destroying equipment or facilities used in animal agriculture, blocking vehicles transporting animals to slaughter, and so on. Veganism as a tactic is *indirect* action because it is based on the hope that if we stop buying meat, they will stop killing animals.

This hope may be more or less well grounded, depending on historically contingent facts regarding the number of new vegetarians, the responsiveness of supply to demand, the availability of other markets to replace the vegetarians, and so on. We may certainly hope for the day when animal agriculture collapses due to the sheer number of people who refuse to consume its products. In the meantime, though, even if our vegetarianism does not yet save a single animal, we may still recognize its value in complementing and supporting the many other, more radically subversive ways we work to dismantle animal agriculture.

Sexism in the Movement I

In the United States the propensity to eat flesh is stimulated by a range of factors, including advertising, nutritional propaganda from industry, the convenience of fast food, artificially low prices resulting from government subsidies, and cultural associations of certain meats with affluence and masculinity. The last factor continues to have a significant impact. One of my male students told me that he had once considered changing to a vegetarian diet. He said that he felt reluctant to mention this to his grandfather because he believed the response would be, "You going to stop going out with girls, too?" Remarks such as this indicate a connection between meat eating and norms of heterosexual masculinity. As Carol Adams has shown in *The Sexual Politics of Meat,* associations between meat and manhood are deep and significant. We eat meat, according to Adams, because the culturally entrenched image of man-as-hunter makes meat a manly food. In sexist society, what is manly is deemed good, so while men eat meat to feel manly, women eat meat because it's "good" food.

Those who market meat make use of these connotations (consider, for example, products such as the "Manwich" and steakhouses that run macho contests to determine who can eat the biggest slab of beef), but they do not create them. Hunting and animal sacrifice predate capitalism, as do the masculine connotations of meat. These deep associations affect animal liberation activism. Liberationists are feminized by their activism: vegetarian activists because of the gendered connotations of diet, activists in general because the institutions challenged by the movement—vivisection, hunting, and meat production—are major centers for the construction of patriarchal masculinity.

In response to this feminization we periodically see compensatory efforts by male animal liberationists. Cleveland Amory, founder of the Fund for Animals and author of *Man Kind? Our Incredible War on Wildlife,* referred, tongue-in-cheek, to antihunting activists as "namby-pamby Bambi lovers."[15] This passing acknowledgment of the feminization of animal liberationists is in ironic contrast to the masculine style Amory adopted in his scathing critique of hunting and trapping—his book is confrontational, sarcastic, and peppered with attributions of cowardice. The framing of the book also reassures readers of Amory's manhood. The cover photo shows Amory with his arm wrapped around a wolf's neck. The wolf, ears back, looks away from Amory while Amory himself gazes sternly into the distance. The image is of domination and control, not mutuality or affection. Amory opened his book with a violent (and facetious?) fantasy regarding the starting of a Hunt-the-Hunters Hunt Club. And to remove any lingering doubts in the reader's mind regarding his masculinity, Amory ended his book by quoting the opinion that "it takes a world more guts to love nature and admit it than to kill a helpless animal at a safe distance."[16]

Amory is not an isolated case. Male animal advocates strive in a variety of ways to preserve a manhood threatened by their participation in the movement. These compensatory moves warrant scrutiny due to their potential for distorting animal rights theory and prompting the adoption of dubious tactics. In the following I consider the standard philosophies of animal rights in the context of these gender dynamics.

Carol Gilligan has described justice and caring as two distinct moral frameworks, or orientations, to ethical concerns.[17] The justice framework is characterized by abstraction, the application of general rules of conduct, an emphasis on restraining aggression, and a concern for consistency and the fair resolution of conflicting claims and interests. The caring framework, on the other hand, is characterized by its focus on the concrete and particular, its emphasis on the maintenance and extension of connection, and by its concern for responsiveness and the satisfaction of needs. Two prominent theorists, Peter Singer and Tom Regan, have framed animal liberation as a justice issue, though, I suggest, it may more appropriately be understood in terms of caring.

Regan's and Singer's arguments against animal exploitation are structured, fundamentally, as comparisons between the treatment of humans and the treatment of other animals. According to Regan, we harm animals to benefit others, and although we do not do this to humans (generally speaking), there is no relevant difference between humans and animals to justify the dissimilar treatment. Thus animals, in comparison with humans, are treated unfairly. For Singer, we are unfair to oppose sexism and racism while tolerating speciesism, when again there is no relevant difference between humans and other animals to support the distinction. For both Regan and Singer, and other writers within the justice framework, the basic moral judgment concerns the discrepancy between the treatment of humans and the treatment of other similar animals. What is called into question is the fairness, or what they more often refer to as the consistency, of a society that treats two relevantly similar groups of individuals in such totally different ways.

The emphasis on comparing the treatment of humans and the treatment of other animals matches neither my motivations nor those of others in the animal liberation movement. My opposition to the institutionalized exploitation of animals is not based on a comparison between human and animal treatment but on a consideration of the abuse of the animals in and of itself. In his recent *Introduction to Animal Rights,* Gary Francione captures this direct responsiveness when he explains why we would object to "Simon the Sadist," a man who burns dogs for pleasure:

> The primary reason why we find Simon's action morally objectionable is its direct effect on the dog. . . . Simply because the dog can experience pain and suffering, we regard it as morally necessary to justify our infliction of harm on the dog. . . . An integral part of our moral thinking is the idea that, other things being equal, the fact that an action causes pain counts as a reason against that action. . . . Imposing harm on another sentient being is wrong in itself.[18]

We need not refer to hypothetical examples to see this sort of immediate reaction against the infliction of harm. In each of the major institutions of men's animal exploitation, hunting, meat production, and vivisection, I respond directly to the animals' plight as they are injured and killed. In objecting to these practices I am not comparing the treatment of humans and animals and thinking "this is unfair because humans are protected from such usage." I am appalled by the myriad abuses in and of themselves—shooting, trapping, poisoning, hooking, and asphyxiating wild animals; branding, castrating, forcibly impregnating, tail docking, debeaking, confining, and slaughtering farmed animals; and burning, cutting, gassing, starving, asphyxiating, decapitating, decompressing, irradiating, electrocuting, freezing, crushing, paralyzing, socially isolating, and imposing disease on animals in laboratories—these acts are abhorrent because of what they do to the animals. My moral condemnation of the acts arises directly from my sympathy for the animals and is independent of the question of whether humans are protected from such abuse. To the extent that humans are also treated in these ways I object to that, too, but again, out of sympathy and not considerations of fairness.

Consider the following statements by others who oppose institutions of animal abuse:

> The production-line maintenance of animals, . . . is without a doubt one of the darkest and most shameful chapters in human culture. If you have ever stood before a stable where animals are being fattened and have heard hundreds of calves bleating, if you can understand the calf's cry for help, then you will have had enough of those people who derive profit from it. I eat meat but rarely veal. . . . I could never bring myself to slaughter a cow. This is very difficult to do to any animal that one has taken care of for a long time.[19]
>
> Ninety percent of all pigs are now raised in indoor, near-dark, windowless confinement sheds. . . . I respond on an emotional level with horror at what each individual pig is subjected to and sympathize with each pig, whose extreme sociability is evidenced by these animals' increased popularity as pets. . . . As a lactating mother, I empathize with the sow whose reproductive freedoms have been denied and whose nursing experience seems so wretched. As a consumer and a vegetarian, I visualize this information when I witness people buying or eating "ham," "bacon," or "sausage."[20]
>
> I was one morning, while studying alone in the Natural History Museum, suddenly disturbed by a frightful burst of screams, of a character more distressing than words can convey, proceeding from some chamber on another side of the building. I called the porter in charge of the museum, and asked him what it meant. He replied with a grin, "It is only the dogs being vivisected in Monsieur Beclard's laboratory." . . . Therewith he left me, and I sat down alone and listened. Much as I had heard and said, and even written, before that day about vivisection, I found myself then for the first time in its actual presence, and there swept over me a wave of such extreme mental anguish that my heart stood still under it. . . . And then and there, burying my face in my hands, with tears of agony I prayed for strength and courage to labour

effectually for the abolition of so vile a wrong, and to do at least what one heart and voice might to root this curse of torture from the land.[21]

These memoirs reveal no comparison between human and animal treatment; upon seeing or hearing how the animals are abused, there is an immediate reaction directed against that treatment, and based on that reaction, a moral judgment and decision to act.

Regan and Singer believe that for most people sympathetic responsiveness to animals is an insufficient basis for the development of an animal liberation perspective. They feel that abstract, justice-based argumentation—which they call "reason"—is necessary to augment people's sympathies. In fact, Regan questions whether an ethic of care can "go far enough":[22]

> What are the resources within the ethic of care that can move people to consider the ethics of their dealings with individuals who *stand outside* the existing circle of their valued interpersonal relationships? . . . Unless we supplement the ethic of care with some other motivating force—some other grounding of our moral judgment—we run the grave risk that our ethic will be excessively conservative and will blind us to those obligations we have to people for whom we are indifferent.
>
> Nowhere, perhaps, is this possibility more evident than in the case of our moral dealings with nonhuman animals. The plain fact is, most people do not care very much about what happens to them. . . .
>
> And thus it is that a feminist ethic that is *limited to an ethic of care* will, I think, be unable to illuminate the moral significance of the idea that we (human) animals are not superior to all other animals.[23]

To remedy this supposed limitation of the caring approach, Regan suggests the marshaling of "consistency" arguments such as those mentioned above.

Singer does "not think that an appeal to sympathy and goodheartedness alone will convince most people of the wrongness of speciesism."[24] He believes that humans have evolved instinctive capacities to respond sympathetically only to a few individuals closely similar to or associated with themselves.[25] Thus reason, in the guise of formal argumentation for a principle of equal consideration, must be applied for consideration to be extended to other clans, races, and species.

Given their low estimation of the human capacity to sympathize with nonhumans, we can understand why Regan and Singer might feel that their justice-oriented approaches to animal liberation are essential. If people do not care for animals, supporters of animal liberation cannot presume that such affections are present in those they are trying to persuade. At best, they can assume the presence of some concern for humans and use this concern as a fulcrum, trying to impel their interlocutors to animal liberation through charges of inconsistency. This is precisely Regan's and Singer's justice-based strategy.

I can understand how one might conclude that people do not care about animals, given the existence of such horrendous institutions as vivisection, factory farming, and sport hunting. Regan's and Singer's accounts, however, involve an overly simplistic understanding of the limitations of people's sympathies. For Regan it is a "plain fact" that people do not care about animals, whereas for Singer it is a genetic fact. On the contrary, I contend that this state of affairs is not "plain" but rather elaborate, and it is not genetic but socially constructed. As we saw in the previous chapter, the industries of animal use go to great lengths to subvert our sympathetic inclinations toward animals. Animal exploitation thrives not because people fail to care but in spite of the fact that they care.

The disposition to care for animals is not the unreliable quirk of a few but is, rather, the normal state of human beings. As Andrée Collard put it, "Our common bond with animals is *natural* (of nature), *normal* (of the norm), and healthy (*whole*some)."[26] If we shift our attention away from animal exploitation to other cultural phenomena, we see the strength and depth of the human-animal bond. As described in chapter 1, many areas of human life reveal the widespread tendency toward the sympathetic protection of nonhuman animals and away from the infliction of injury and death: animal rescue efforts, pet keeping, children's literature, the variety of mechanisms for managing guilt over harming animals, and so on. And empirical studies such as Stephen Kellert's support a picture of humans as beings most frequently oriented toward affectionate and protective relations with nonhuman animals.

Regan's and Singer's rejection of sympathy as the moral basis of animal liberation occurs in conjunction with a recurring tendency for men to deny any strong affectionate or emotional basis for their animal advocacy. Many male animal liberationists go to great pains to deny that their activism is motivated by love. Don Barnes, for example, a researcher who renounced vivisection and became an animal liberation activist, insists, "I'm not an animal-lover. Some animals I like, others I don't like. To say I'm an animal-lover is the same as saying I'm a nigger lover."[27] Wayne Pacelle, while executive director of the antihunting group the Fund for Animals, told hunting writer Ted Kerasote, "I don't feel bonded to any particular nonhuman animal. I like them and I pet them and I'm kind to them, but there's no special bond between me and other animals."[28] Similarly, Peter Singer opens his book on *Animal Liberation* by explaining that though he and his wife are opposed to speciesism, "we were not especially 'interested in' animals. Neither of us had ever been inordinately fond of dogs, cats, or horses in the way that many people are. We didn't 'love' animals."[29]

To acknowledge love is to bring emotion into the discussion, and many animal rights theorists are unwilling to do this. Tom Regan, for instance, insisted that he and other animal rights activists are not "crazy, emotional, and uneducated" people who "all have Bambi complexes."[30] To distance himself from anything smacking of the sentimental, he constructs a dry theoretical framework he characterizes as "tough-minded."[31]

Both Regan and Singer characterize emotion as an unreliable basis for ethical decision and claim to have made no appeal to emotion in their arguments for animal liberation. The Regan/Singer subordination of emotion to reason has been much noted and criticized by feminist animal liberationists. Deborah Slicer, among others, rejects the general privileging of reason over emotion, stating that "there is no pat formula for deciding when our affective responses have a place, or how much weight they should have."[32] Regarding women's identification with animals, Andrée Collard wrote that "we react to them in every fibre of our being. We can be moved to outrage without feeling a need to justify our emotions."[33]

The point of such critiques is not to invert the traditional hierarchy—now placing emotion over reason—but rather to suggest that in ethics reason and emotion work together, so that attempts to expunge emotion from theoretical ethics are artificial and self-defeating. Josephine Donovan noticed that "despite his accent on rigorously rational inquiry, Regan throughout uses the term *counterintuitive* as a kind of escape clause whenever deductive reason per se proves inadequate."[34] Even the most "rigorous" argument must use some initial, unproven premises. At such points, Marti Kheel argues, the writers are implicitly relying on readers' common feelings to gain assent.[35]

Since a dualism of reason over emotion makes little sense theoretically, we might well wonder why academic defenders of animal liberation so often retain the rationalistic paradigm. Regan at times recognizes the motivational primacy of emotion, stating that "philosophy can lead the mind to water but only emotion can make it drink."[36] His own experience confirms this, as he recounts in an autobiographical piece: "Reason demanded that I become a vegetarian. But it was the death of our dog that awakened my heart. It was the sense of irrecoverable loss that added the power of feeling to the requirements of logic."[37] Given this it is all the more striking that Regan's primary exposition of animal rights theory, *The Case for Animal Rights,* is totally devoid of concrete references to feelings or experiences, and in fact is structured as an extended exposition on logical consistency.

Regan and Singer have taken as one of their primary goals the establishment of the academic respectability of animal rights theory.[38] Academic respectability conventionally requires the adoption of the reason over emotion paradigm, as Singer recognizes: "The portrayal of those who protest against cruelty to animals as sentimental, emotional 'animal-lovers' has had the effect of excluding the entire issue of our treatment of nonhumans from serious political and moral discussion."[39] This statement may be true but it crucially omits mention of the gendered nature of the derogation of emotion. A central Western patriarchal ideology is the elevation of the "rational/cultural" male over the "emotional/biological" female. Women's rage (labeled "sentiment," "hysteria," etc.) is divested of political significance by interpreting any female reaction against the established order not as a moral challenge to that order but as a biosexual phenomenon to be ignored or subdued.

This is critical to understanding reactions against animal liberation—since animal liberationists have always been predominantly female, sexist stereotypes have been a favored technique for dismissing the movement.[40] This is the subtext to Singer's attempt to gain respectability through denial of emotion. Josephine Donovan suggests that his underlying concern is that "to associate the animal rights cause with 'womanish' sentiment is to trivialize it."[41] Due to the vegetarian implications of animal liberation, male activists are particularly liable to respond to charges of sentimentality with hyperrationality; the expunging of "female" emotion is attractive as compensation for the loss of manly carnivorism.

Of further relevance here is the obsessive sensitivity male animal rights theorists have shown to the stereotyped depiction of animal liberationists as "little old ladies in tennis shoes." Andrew Linzey, who has written several books aiming to give animal rights a Christian foundation, stated in 1990 that "we are no longer a movement of little old ladies in tennis shoes: ours is a movement of intellectual muscle."[42] Regan has used similar metaphors, concluding that through the "forceful" editorship of anthologies on animal rights and other such efforts "we may safely put to rest the stereotypical picture of 'little old ladies in tennis shoes.'"[43] And in his book on *Practical Ethics,* Singer opens the section on animal rights with an argument that the perception of animal welfare as "a matter for old ladies in tennis shoes to worry about" is an unfounded prejudice.[44]

212 · OPPOSING MEN'S EXPLOITATION OF ANIMALS

Regan, Singer, and Linzey all earnestly expect that by virtue of their ratioci-
nations we may now image animal liberationists as tough-minded and forceful (male) rather than as weak and emotional (female). Their strategy is to
gain respectability for animal liberation by using formalistic male theorizing,
thereby distancing the movement from the female objects of contempt. By
seeing emotional women as a public relations problem for animal liberation,
this strategy tacitly accepts the patriarchal ideology behind the charges of
"hysteria" and "sentiment," misrepresents animal liberationist morality by
erasing its emotional elements, and disrespects the work of female animal
liberationists (who are not only the majority of activists but comprise most
of the movement's founders and leaders).

Rather than attempting to masculinize animal liberation theory, we might
do better by directly refusing the sexism of the charges of female hysteria.
Carol Adams, for example, commends the women who were the first to
perceive the injustice of animal exploitation and affirms that she *aspires* to
someday be one such radical little old lady.[45] Perhaps acknowledging the
sexism latent in attempts to erase the "little old lady" image of animal liberation, Singer altered his remarks in *Practical Ethics,* deleting reference to "old
ladies in tennis shoes." In the revised edition of the book, the unfounded
prejudice Singer now struggles against is identification of animal liberation with "people who are dotty about dogs and cats."[46] Though couched
in gender-neutral terms, the concern is still to assure readers that animal
liberation is not founded on excessive emotion—we are not sentimental
animal lovers.

This fear of emotional association, of being considered sentimental or
"dotty," contrasts with the stance of nineteenth-century antivivisectionist
Anna Kingsford, who directly rejected the notion that emotion invalidates
morality:

> They speak sneeringly of "sentiment." The outcry against vivisection is mere
> "sentiment." Why, in God's name, what is so great, so noble, as human senti-
> ment! What is religion, what is morality, but sentiment? On what divine feel-
> ing are based the laws which bid men to respect the lives, the property, the
> feelings of their fellow men? Sentiment is but another name for that moral
> feeling which alone has made man the best that he is now, and which alone
> can make him better and purer in the future.[47]

It is insufficient simply to recast the rejection of emotion in gender-neutral
terms, à la Singer in *Practical Ethics.* Apart from misgauging the significance
of emotion in animal liberationist morality, such an approach elides the crucial fact that the suspicion of emotion originates when it is associated with

women. In patriarchal culture it is *womanly* emotion, not emotion as such, that is rejected.

This point comes out in Julian Groves's sociological study of the struggle over vivisection. Groves found that many antivivisectionists worry that there are too many women in the movement. One female activist linked this concern to the issue of emotion: "One thing that bothered me . . . was that attendance was practically all female. And some of the discussions at the meetings were real kind of emotional responses."[48] Female activists interviewed by Groves felt that more men in the movement would improve their credibility. This expectation was in part due to their belief that men would bring "rational" arguments with them, but it was also due to their awareness that society listens to men more than to women. Significantly, men's presence brings greater credibility even to the emotional aspects of antivivisection work. Groves notes that male activists were admired, even when they were emotional. He heard, for instance, activists praise a man's anger, but never a woman's. "Men's willingness to express their feelings was considered a sign of fearlessness, but in women it was a sign of weakness," Groves explains. "Being emotional became legitimate when men did it, and women could point to men's participation in the movement to justify the legitimacy of their own feelings about animal cruelty."[49]

The devaluation of emotion in animal liberation, by exploiters and by the activists themselves, is the product of sexism. Women are not valued in sexist society and neither are their emotions (unless they also happen to be expressed by a man). To the extent that society rejects sexism, we can expect a greater respect for and attention to women's views, including moral rejections of animal exploitation expressed in overtly emotional terms. A postsexist environment is not something that animal liberationists need passively await, in the meantime deferring to present sexism in the manner of our presentation. Rather, we can and should fully respect women and their perspectives, regardless of the sexism surrounding us. Building a nonsexist animal liberation movement, our efforts simultaneously advance animal causes and support the interrelated struggle for women's liberation.

Sexism in the Movement II

Apart from groups like Feminists for Animal Rights, the animal liberation movement has not been consistently self-conscious or concerned about its own sexism. The disparagement of emotion discussed above is actually a rather subtle form of sexism compared to some of the overtly misogynistic campaigns conducted over the years. Women themselves, not just female-associated emotionalism, have been devalued through a variety of tactics. Certain antifur campaigns show this most blatantly. Through the 1980s and 1990s, for instance, the British animal rights group Lynx ran a series of antifur billboards. The first showed a woman in high heels and a slit skirt, dragging behind her a fur coat trailing blood. The caption stated, "It takes up to 40 dumb animals to make a fur coat. . . . But only one to wear it."[50] Another ad in this series showed a white woman draped in fur, curled up on her side, to her left a dead fox, curled in a similar pose and caught in a trap. The caption under the woman read, "Rich bitch"; under the fox, "Poor bitch."

Such ads blame women for the cruelty of the fur business, notwithstanding the fact that the industry is dominated by men from production to consumption (see the introduction). And they do it by using misogynist stereotypes of women. Though these ads are defended against feminist critique by referring to their supposed "effectiveness" in criticizing fur, it should be noted that the campaigns deploy the same demeaning tropes that back the exploitation of women and animals in general. In a broad sense such ads are not liberating because they reinforce images of women and animals as "dumb bitches."

As Joni Seager points out, the Lynx ads also play on imagery common in pornography. "Women encounter objectification of their bodies and the threat of implicit violence in the media and advertising industry on a daily basis, always justified by claims of 'effectiveness,'" she remarks. "In a sexist and violent culture, it is not surprising that the objectification and denigration of women in mass communications makes for 'effective' advertising."[51] Seager's analysis applies not only to Lynx's antifur campaign but also to PETA's long-running "naked" campaign in which activists gain media coverage by appearing in public with nothing covering their bodies other than a poster proclaiming, "I'd rather go naked than wear fur." At the local level these actions are superficially gender-neutral, since both male and female activists participate. When PETA took the campaign to the national level, however, they relied almost exclusively on clichés of female sexual objectification. While local campaigns at times involved activists with a range of body types having fun marching and being silly, the preferred billboard models are young, thin, professional female models, placed in the stereotyped postures of sexual mass marketing.

PETA's use of sexism is not restricted to the "I'd rather go naked" promotion. In one campaign targeting the use of fur as trim on coats and other apparel, the ad shows a naked white woman's midriff, with no caption other than the words "Fur Trim" at the bottom of the picture. The caption refers to the woman's pubic hair. There is nothing out of the ordinary about the woman pictured—the ad relies on and reinforces a deep revulsion at the adult female body as such in order to construct a negative image of fur trim. And following Lynx's lead, PETA has produced its own series of demeaning female caricatures and misogynist insults, including "Fur Hag" (on posters of Jennifer Lopez and other women wearing fur), "Only Old Bags Wear Fur ... You'd *Better* Hide" (a bumper sticker on which a woman wearing a fur coat has a grocery bag over her head; the slogan in this case is sexist and threatening), "Fur is Worn by Beautiful Animals and Ugly People" (on posters with humiliatingly unattractive photos of fashion designer Donatella Versace and *Vogue* editor-in-chief Anna Wintour), and "Models Should Be the Only Foxes on the Runway" (for an analysis of the sexually violent implications of calling women "foxes," see chapter 3).[52] PETA has also produced a video in which a man approaches a woman in the subway station, beats her with a club, and then takes a fur coat off her lifeless body. The ad concludes with the question, "What if you were killed for your coat?"[53] The cumulative message communicated by these media is that PETA is against the fur industry *and* they hate women.

Like the "I'd rather go naked" ads, PETA's vegetarian advertisements also employ softcore iconography, projecting "adult-male sexuality onto younger women (the Lolita model)," as Carol Adams describes it.[54] One recurring device is to pose female actresses and models seminude with a few lettuce leaves or some other vegetarian food items strategically placed, accompanied by a punning invitation to give up meat ("Turn Over a New Leaf," "Let Vegetarianism Grow on You," "Let Us Turn You on to Vegetarianism"). These ads include Pamela Anderson wearing an iceberg lettuce bikini, Rosemarie with a salad skirt and red-bean necklace, Elite model Kadra wearing Chinese mushrooms, and Elizabeth Berkley in a form-fitting romaine-lettuce evening dress. It is unclear how such images might accomplish their stated goal of recruiting new vegetarians. In a discussion of this issue with a PETA director, I was told that their advertisements always include a web site address, and since PETA registers big spikes in the number of web site visits immediately after running a "provocative" ad, their success is evident. I wonder, though, how many of the hits are due to surfers looking for free softcore images, given that, as Nikki Craft puts it in her critique of PETA's sexism, "they've become so consistent in their reliance on the sexual exploitation of women that it's hard not to consider them a part of the pornography industry."[55]

However much attention PETA may be garnering from their use of sexism, it is also costing them support from activists who believe that the philosophy and praxis of animal liberation should include respect for women.[56]

Misogynistic tactics are ultimately self-defeating. Women have always been the backbone of animal advocacy, and thus the use of techniques that disempower women can only undermine the long-term viability of the movement. "PETA's ads can be said to create hostile environments for women," according to Carol Adams, a crucial observation since the civil existence of women, including their status as moral agents with a human right to judge the institutions of men, has yet to be universally acknowledged.[57] Gains in this direction from the women's movement are subjected to continual challenges by regressive forces. It has been less than a century since the right to vote was accorded all women in the United States, and barely a century since it was considered unacceptable for a woman to speak in public (a taboo first broken by women agitating for the abolition of slavery). Our cultural memory is longer than this recent period of steps toward the liberation of women. Especially in the current climate of backlash, animal activists cannot afford to facilitate efforts to put women back in their politically silenced place.

Although PETA would have Pamela Anderson simultaneously presented as sexual object and a social critic, the two are culturally incompatible due to the historical nature and function of pornography, which is to construct the white male as agent acting upon the passive female (or animal or dark-skinned) object of his gaze.[58] The analysis here merges with that of chapter 3 because the images deployed by PETA are visually indistinguishable from the images that *Playboy, Cosmopolitan, Sports Illustrated, Traditional Bowhunter,* and similar media use to eroticize men's hunting of animals and to animalize women as objects of men's sexual pursuit. The glamor model, like the game animal, is contextualized in a way that connotes her social status as a target, someone to be looked at but not listened to as a contributor to our political discourse.

It is not as though the PETA ads are ironic or satirical, enacting some postmodern destabilization of the traditional expectation that models, unless using the sound of their voices to titillate (à la the Howard Stern show or phone sex services), should keep their mouths shut. The ads are not funny or deep in that way, just cutesy and coy and employing all the old-fashioned techniques for constructing the standard scenario: man gazing upon other. The nude models are drawn primarily from groups used to designate straight white male identity through difference—women, men of color, effeminate and androgynous men.[59] The pictures of women include those mentioned above and many others, with Charlotte Ross naked and holding a white bunny in "I'd Rather Show My Buns than Wear Fear" being a typical example. In the "Turn Your Back on Fur" poster, four male and four female models from the Boss agency are posed nude, side by side, with their backsides to the camera but looking over their shoulders toward the viewer. All the men have an androgynous look and are cupping their genitals, as men and boys do, for example, when self-consciously waiting to enter a public shower. The women's arms are in similar positions of modesty and self-protection. The overall picture is one of sexual vulnerability and accessibility.

Notwithstanding the common presumption that racist imagery is no longer socially tolerated in the way that sexist imagery is, PETA in fact uses both, copying the ways these two discriminations provide mutual reinforcement in pornography, mainstream advertising, and the entertainment industry. Their most glaringly racist image is perhaps the photograph of black German TV presenter Mola Adebisi; he is nude, in a cage, his body painted with cheetah-like stripes, presented with the slogan "Fur Bites." With Adebisi snarling and reaching menacingly through the bars for the viewer, this ad plays up old and continuing associations of blacks with wild animals and black men with violence, while communicating nothing that would motivate the liberation of blacks or animals. In another poster, African American athlete and infamous cross-dresser Dennis Rodman is posed nude for the "Think Ink, Not Mink" campaign. His tattoos ("Ink") are prominent, his hair is dyed orange, and he is in the posture of Rodin's *The Thinker*, with one critical difference, his sardonic glance at the viewer. That PETA positions their nude celebrity models as sexual targets is indicated by their gloating newsletter headline announcing the ad: "PETA Scores Rodman!"

PETA has placed thousands of ads for animal causes, the vast majority of which are neither sexist nor racist, with many being genuinely clever, funny, challenging, and thought-provoking. More often than not, their spokespeople present the case against a particular exploitative practice in a straightforward manner that in no way undermines the status of women or blacks as moral agents contributing to social change. So PETA is well aware of the many ways to conduct animal advocacy, as they are aware of the problematic nature of their sexist ads, having been on the receiving end of many complaints and challenges from antisexist animal advocates over the years. This makes it all the more puzzling why PETA's use of sexism and misogyny continues and is being developed ever more extensively.

Nikki Craft wonders whether PETA is receiving large donations from *Playboy*. She has no direct evidence for this, just her bewilderment over PETA's intransigence coupled with the fact that PETA and *Playboy* have an ongoing relationship that includes joint parties at the mansion, *Playboy* models mentioning animal rights in their pictorials, PETA using "playmates" in their vegetarian campaigns and placing ads in the magazine, and so on. Others suggest that PETA's questionable campaigns reflect a decision to emulate Madison Avenue techniques, which include sexism as a matter of course.

I perceive another factor at work, one with implications beyond the PETA case. Animal advocacy in general is based on sympathy, but at times it may also derive from a deep sense of identification with the animals as victims. Animal activists, and by no means just those at PETA, at times seem to go out of the way to adopt positions of disempowerment or victimization. This can take a number of forms, from striving to be arrested as an end in itself, to performing street theater pieces with activists on the receiving end of the very abuse being criticized, to earnest declarations regarding how much one is willing to sacrifice for the animals. Consider, for example, this press release from August 2005:

> Fargo, N.D.—Wearing nothing but shackles and covered in "scars" as a result of violent "beatings"—an everyday reality for animals in circuses—a woman will protest the arrival of Ringling Bros. and Barnum & Bailey Circus. She will be joined by protesters holding a banner that reads, "Shackled, Lonely, Beaten," while others show footage of elephant beatings on body screen TVs and hold poster-size photos of animals who have died at Ringling's hands. "If it takes exposing some of my skin to expose the cruelty that goes on behind the scenes at the circus, I'm happy to do it," says PETA spokesperson Katy Roberts. "I only have to spend a few minutes in chains, while animals in circuses must endure a lifetime of chains, cages, and beatings."[60]

This example is significant because the woman's self-sacrifice encompasses the discomfort of being caged and chained like animals in circuses, and of being presented seminaked in public. The dubious efficacy and ritualistic, self-reinforcing quality of these sorts of displays is indicated by an account from activist Daniel Hammer:

> This fall we were already working on Ringling Bros. when PeTA contacted us with their "great" idea to do a "tiger" demo. Of course we were outraged and asked them not to do it ... The PeTA spokesperson said they'd do the tiger demo anyway and that activists had gotten news coverage in all the other cities in which they did the demos. We kept asking them what was the point of having a "nude" woman in a cage and every time they said to get media. It really upset us that we were working so hard to expose the cruelty in the circus and all PeTA could think about was getting some self-exposure. ... In the end the TV news used the PeTA demo to announce the sale of circus tickets and was immediately followed by a Ringling's commercial.[61]

The theme of self-martyrdom runs throughout PETA's pornographic campaigns, with slogans like "I'd rather go naked than . . ." and "I'd rather show my buns than . . ."—implying that the model is doing something very much against their natural inclinations. The extreme example of this is the "I Wouldn't Be Caught Dead Wearing Fur" poster, in which Sheryl Lee is nude and exposed on an autopsy table, toe-tagged and mimicking death.

There is an erotic in which the binding, gagging, caging, injury, torture, and, ultimately, murder of women is valued as a source of sexual stimulation. As activists vie for a sadomasochistic martyrdom they contribute to the visual propagation of this erotic. Insofar as enactment of these scenarios is driven by an intense identification with animals as victims, we see empathy working against the animal liberation cause. In the cooptation discussed in the last chapter empathy was deliberately used to facilitate the process of exploitation, whereas in this case activists, out of identification and solidarity with animal victims, put themselves in positions that disempower them as advocates.

Men remain firmly in place as viewers of these spectacles. Though the primary perpetrators and beneficiaries of animal abuse, men are not through these media invited or challenged to renounce animal exploitation. In addition to its main pleasures, steaks, hunting trips, research opportunities, and the like, animal exploitation now affords men the further gratification of watching vegetarian women stripping and donning shackles "for the animals." Female PETA activists become yet another object of male consumption, a status visually indicated in the photos of women partially clad with lettuce, mushrooms, and beans as side vegetables accompanying the female main course. In a recent poster, Traci Bingham is posed naked and marked up in black ink with body sections labeled "Chuck," "Rib," "Round," "Rump," and so on. The pose and the lettering meticulously duplicate an image used years ago to market steak. This same image was placed on a placard at a protest of the sexual objectification of women at the 1968 Miss America Pageant and was used on the cover of *The Sexual Politics of Meat* as an example of the intersecting oppressions of women and animals.[62] Contrary to PETA's expectations, adding the words "Have a Heart: Go Vegetarian" to the poster does not mitigate the underlying antifemale and antianimal implication of the graphic. Indeed, the poster's additional caption, "All Animals Have the Same Parts," intended to encourage compassion, inadvertently strengthens the image's main message: "Devour me the way you would a steak."

In saying that PETA is "inadvertently" repressing women, I presume that their exclusive intent is to help animals, a presumption that some analysts have come to doubt: "PETA tells us they know what they are doing. I believe them. They are shoring up manhood because they understand that it is threatened by the removal of species as a category to dominate. Sexual dominance must be reassured and intensified."[63] If Adams is correct, then the sexist tactics used by PETA function as compensation for the threat posed to patriarchy by animal liberation. This might seem counterintuitive given that though their media director is a man, PETA is run by a woman, Ingrid Newkirk, who has given her approval to all of the campaigns discussed here. It would not make sense to suppose that Newkirk is acting out of concern for her manhood, but the compensation here is not quite the same as that discussed previously. I suggested above that animal rights philosophers deny emotion as a means of salvaging their own manhood, whereas the issue here is not one's personal gender identity but male dominance as a system. There are, of course, any number of examples of women working to maintain patriarchy. Moreover, PETA has made a deliberate decision to identify as a single-issue organization, which means pursuing the delicate task of liberating animals without disturbing any of the other power structures in this society. But since animal liberation is inherently antithetical to men's class interests as they are currently defined, to remain single-issue PETA must do something to repair patriarchy, thus explaining their offering of reparations ("You give us your farm animals, we'll give you our women").

The other course available to us is to acknowledge the links between male dominance and animal exploitation and work toward the elimination of both.

Animal Rights and Social Control

Concerning PETA's antifur campaign, one activist notes that "by targeting the female consumer of furs, and attacking her for her supposed lack of the appropriate feminine virtues—modesty, gentleness, love of small furry animals—PeTA show that they are more interested in policing women's behaviour than in challenging the commercial imperatives of those industries that profit from the unethical treatment of animals."[64] The other two aspects of animal rights politics discussed in this chapter involve a similar interest in policing behavior: Virtuous vegetarianism focuses on our behavior as consumers, and the reason-over-emotion dichotomy implies the exercise of control over the manner in which we express and understand ourselves as animal advocates.

The assumption that progress toward justice is made through the exertion of top-down control, with the forces of good restraining the inherently evil or antisocial tendencies of human nature, is accepted by all causes and political persuasions with the exception of anarchism and radical feminism (which seek to abolish structures of hierarchical power rather than use them). The animal rights movement is in this regard no different from the myriad of other movements that seek to impose their vision on society. In this section I detail the general orientation toward social control exemplified by one of the primary theorists of animal rights, Peter Singer, and indicate the faulty presumptions underlying this orientation.

In order to enforce adherence to moral principle, Peter Singer countenances extensive programs of social control. He ultimately advocates cultural design through genetic manipulation: "We must begin to design our culture. ... In the future we ... will be able to take deliberate steps to see that our culture not only encourages ethical conduct in the present generation but enhances its prospects of spreading in the next. At present we know too little about human genetics."[65] Singer adumbrates the potentially violent nature of such programs of genetic control, stating that "many forms of punishment affect the chances of certain genes ... surviving in future generations" and arguing in particular that "if a society kills, castrates, or imprisons rapists, they will have fewer opportunities to reproduce than others, and the increase of rapists can be checked."[66] The implication is evident—once we isolate the genes associated with unethical conduct we can prevent them from passing on to the next generation by doing whatever it takes to keep the gene-carriers from reproducing.

This conclusion is shocking, but it derives from a general orientation in favor of social control that is not unusual. Many of the theoretical works dedicated to justifying animal rights evince a common framework that includes the following elements: a hierarchical placement of reason over emotion, the delineation of "irrational" classes, the perception of ethical discussion as a battle, and the willingness to impose controls. These elements fit perfectly well within the conventional norms of academic and informal ethical discourse. But notwithstanding its normalcy, this orientation should give us pause in that it constitutes the ideological underpinnings for imposing programs of social control. Hierarchical social control is never neutral; it demands legitimation. Prototypically, this legitimation comes from the supposition that people need to be controlled, that we are fundamentally antisocial (as in Thomas Hobbes's theory, in which our supposed innate antisocial tendencies legitimate the erection of an all-powerful sovereign). Control-oriented aspects of animal rights philosophy can be similarly legitimated (or at least made coherent and superficially sensible) by holding that people are naturally antisocial toward animals: If we are motivationally disposed to support animal exploitation, we need to be prodded toward animal liberation by a rational elite.

For Singer, the antisociality needed to legitimate this approach takes the form of a denial of any reliable human capacity to sympathize with animals. Singer insists his argument makes no "appeal to the reader's emotions where they cannot be supported by reason" because "reason is more universal and more compelling in its appeal" than "kind feelings and sentiments."[67] Singer devotes a whole book to explaining our supposed sympathetic deficiency. In *The Expanding Circle,* he argues that kin, reciprocal, and "possibly a little" group altruism are biologically based, by showing how tendencies to assist close relatives, those who assist us, and members of our group are adaptive and thus would be selected over time. Singer calls these dispositions to help those close to us our "genetically-based" social "impulses" or "instincts." This sociobiological theory does not account for consideration shown to those outside relations of kinship, reciprocation, and group membership, however. To explain altruistic behavior toward these "outsiders" (including most animals and many people), Singer argues that reason, in particular the practice of defending one's behavior to others, is intrinsically impartial, ultimately possessing "a logic of its own which leads to its extension beyond the bounds of the group."[68] Thus even though our genetically based altruistic dispositions apply only to a narrow circle, reason inexorably impels expansion of our consideration, ultimately to encompass all sentient beings.

While Singer admits, on the one hand, that all altruistic behaviors result from environmental as well as genetic factors, and, on the other hand, that reasoning behavior is biologically as well as culturally supported, he retains throughout *The Expanding Circle* an extreme dualism of reason over biology. At the level of individual motivation, Singer takes the relation between impartial reason and partial social instincts to be a struggle between "the desire to avoid inconsistency" and "our self-centered desires (including our desires for our kin and close friends)."[69] Theoretical pictures of noble reason valiantly struggling to control base instinct lend themselves to the support of programs of social control—the group seeking control over others simply associates itself with reason and the others with instinct. This connection between theory and politics is highlighted by Singer's consistent use of the rhetoric of control, domination, and warfare in his sociobiological theorizing. Singer feels that we have hitherto been "slaves" under the "unchallenged control of our genes," but that as reasoning beings we can "rebel" because "reason can master our genes," reasoning being "inherently expansionistic," continually acquiring "territory" until "crushed by countervailing forces."[70]

Singer's rhetoric of dominance and control reflects the orientation of much animal rights theorizing and activism. The idea that our sympathies for animals are fundamentally unreliable, even genetically preempted, supports the view that the extensive cruelty of institutionalized animal exploitation, in vivisection, factory farming, and sport hunting, is a mere expression of an instinctively exploitative creature at our core. Animal liberation is thus seen as a process of *taming* ourselves and others (indeed, "Tame Yourself" is the title of PETA's second animal rights album). So long as we remain committed to animal liberation yet also see the direct sympathetic responsiveness of individual humans to animal suffering as undependable, we will be drawn toward authoritarian structures that promise this taming, through the domination of emotion by reason, selfishness by ethical principle, and people by political authority. Before continuing in this direction it is crucial to fully examine the premise supporting social control. Chapters 1 and 6 of this book show that the supposition of human antisociality toward animals is unsustainable. Institutionalized animal exploitation does not result from a lack of human sympathies for animals, it continues in opposition to these sympathies.

The development of a wide range of mechanisms for forestalling and overriding sympathetic opposition to harming animals, as previously described, shows that human resistance is always a potential threat to the continuation of the animal exploitation industries. So the supposition that a natural human indifference to animal well-being is the problem to be solved is unfounded. But this supposition is the linchpin of the control-oriented, rationalistic approach to animal rights. The subordination of emotion to reason is justified by describing sympathies for animals as undependable. In fact, sympathies for animals are so dependable that every institution of animal exploitation develops some means of undercutting them. The fact that Singer's sociobiological framework is unable to account for these sympathies does not show that they do not exist, it merely shows that his framework is flawed or its implications are misconstrued. Given the primacy and reliability of the emotional component of animal liberation—our sympathies for animals and our aversion to causing them harm—an exclusive focus on considerations of logic and formal consistency is misplaced. We must remember our feeling connections to animals, foster their political expression, and challenge ourselves and others to remove the industry maintained obstacles to the further development of these feelings.

Animal rights in its typical form views ethics as a means of social control and progress for animals as a matter of taming our "naturally" exploitative dispositions toward animals. The term "animal *rights*" fits this framework rather well, in fact, since historically the word "rights" connotes privileges initially imposed by force and then protected by the threat of physical punishment. As politician and animal advocate Douglas Houghton put it, "Rights are born out of strength, the strength to assert, the strength to insist, and the strength to enforce. The meek do not inherit the earth. The establishment of rights may entail insurrection, revolution, or war."[71] But the idea that animal defense requires controlling individual behavior, as if animal exploitation arises from an innate willingness to take advantage of other species, ignores the taming of compassion and outrage that proceeds every day as an integral part of the business of exploiting animals. In this society people are domesticated, trained through external rewards and punishments, through myths and lies, through instilled fear and ignorance, to disconnect from animals, especially from those animals designated "game," "livestock," or "guinea pigs." So animal liberation is not so much a taming of ourselves as it is a refusal to be tamed into supporting anthropocentrism. For most of us in the West, animal liberation involves coming to reject a previous domestication into meat eating, into dependence on modern medicine, into human chauvinism, and so forth. By reasserting and expanding our officially circumscribed compassion for animals, we are in the position of feral animals, formerly domesticated but now occupying a semiwild state on the boundaries of hierarchical civilization.

Thus animal liberation is not furthered by imposing controls but by breaking through the controls on human-animal connection to which we are subject. Since those controls are limitations on our integrated agency, animal liberation can be seen as a process of human moral development, an extension (often a reclamation) of our capacities as agents. In the final section I move beyond animal rights to describe a liberatory metaethic of animal advocacy, one which eschews the will to power and seeks, rather, to develop our compassionate humanity.

Animal Liberation

Ethicist Sarah Hoagland writes, "In my opinion, the heart of ethical focus, the function of ethics . . . is enabling and developing individual integrity and agency within community. I have always regarded morality, ideally, as a system whose aim is, not to control individuals, but to *make possible*, to encourage and enable, individual development."[72] Animal liberation enhances our agency in two ways: through our increased autonomy and through our development as caring beings. First, most of the devices for continuing animal exploitation violate important formal conditions for autonomous action, such as knowledge, integrity, and moral self-determination. The promulgation of falsehoods—"animal exploitation is necessary," "exploited animals are not harmed," "animals are mindless"—obviously decreases our capacity to base decisions concerning animal exploitation on full, relevant knowledge. The sanctioned expectation that individuals will find ways to act against their sympathies for animals undermines integrity, that is, the ability to live with one's most significant desires in mutual harmony. And some mechanisms for continuing animal exploitation, such as forced meat eating, compulsory inoculations, and mandatory dissection in schools, blatantly oppose autonomy by blocking moral self-determination. By debunking the ideological legitimations of animal exploitation and creating communal support for nonexploitative practices, the animal liberation movement develops individual knowledge, integrity, power, and other conditions of autonomy.

Animal liberation does not limit action through control of self and others, it develops the individual's capacity for a broader range of action. It is creative, not restrictive, thus fitting it within the ethical approach described by antiauthoritarian revolutionary Peter Kropotkin: "We renounce the idea of mutilating the individual in the name of any ideal whatsoever. All we reserve to ourselves is the frank expression of our sympathies and antipathies towards what seems to us good or bad."[73] Support for restrictions and controls, based on a pernicious elevation of reason over emotion and on a distorted view of human sympathetic tendencies, is a threatened impairment of autonomous individuals living in community with humans and nonhuman animals. Fortunately, opposition to animal exploitation does not require such "mutilation of the individual." An understanding of morality in which "the whole human being is the basis of ethics" fits animal liberation very well.[74]

Second, many of us understand caring as intrinsic to our moral agency. Carol Gilligan discusses the approach to morality in which "responsibility signifies response, an extension rather than a limitation of action. Thus it connotes an act of care rather than the restraint of aggression."[75] The caring approach to morality is neither exclusively nor universally adopted by women; many men support animal liberation as an extension of caring agency.[76]

A stereotypical picture of femininity includes the expectation that a woman will tend to notice and respond to the needs of others, including animals. The large number of women drawn to animal liberation is evidently linked to this ideal of the caring woman. We should not infer from this, however, that men are not also encouraged and expected to be caring. The call to "be a man" may most typically be used to exhort a male to curtail his sympathetic responsiveness to the feelings of himself or others, yet, contrarily, in some contexts it is used to encourage greater degrees of caring. In Anna Sewell's book *Black Beauty,* for instance, the local squire notices his neighbor Sawyer driving his horse viciously with a whip. The squire upbraids Sawyer in the following terms: "I must say, Mr. Sawyer, that more *unmanly,* brutal treatment of a little pony it was never my painful lot to witness."[77] We generally require sensitivity to the needs of others as a condition of true humanity, and thus manhood, typically identified with humanity, also entails such caring. Primo Levi, in describing how he was able to survive the Nazi death camp at Auschwitz through the assistance of an Italian worker named Lorenzo, illustrates the linkage between humanity, manhood, and caring:

> In concrete terms it amounts to little: an Italian civilian worker brought me a piece of bread and the remainder of his ration every day for six months; he gave me a vest of his, full of patches; he wrote a postcard on my behalf to Italy and brought me the reply. For all this he neither asked nor accepted any reward, because he was good and simple and did not think that one did good for a reward. . . .
>
> The personages in these pages are not men. Their humanity is buried, or they themselves have buried it, under an offence received or inflicted on someone else. . . .
>
> But Lorenzo was a man; his humanity was pure and uncontaminated, he was outside this world of negation. Thanks to Lorenzo, I managed not to forget that I myself was a man.[78]

The understanding of compassionate kindness as a marker of manhood is not unusual. In the following selection, Francis Bacon extols the virtue of an extensive compassion for others:

> There is implanted in man by nature a noble and excellent spirit of compassion, that extends itself even to the brutes which by the divine ordinance are subject to his command. This compassion therefore has a certain analogy with that of a prince towards his subject. Moreover it is most true, that the nobler a spirit is, the more objects of compassion it has. For narrow and degenerate spirits think that these things concern not; but the spirit which forms a nobler portion of the universe has a feeling of communion with them.[79]

Note that in Bacon's estimation the extension of compassion to animals is not inconsistent with man's dominion over his animal "subjects." The term most often used to contrast with the caring, fully human treatment of others is "brutal." The root of this word, "brute," is used by Bacon to refer to nonhuman animals. The word "brute" is also applied to those taken to be incapable of noticing or responding to one's own feelings or the feelings of others. The very process by which we valorize caring for others, by distinguishing sensitive humanity from unfeeling brutality, carries with it an implicit elevation of human life over that of nonhuman animals. The exploitation of animals is often justified by claiming that animals are brutes in this sense. In some contexts, animals are said not to be very sensitive to pleasure or pain (so we may injure them on the farm, for instance); in other contexts they are portrayed as wicked, brutal killers who deserve nothing less than our extermination efforts (this is used to justify some hunting programs). Bacon himself, of course, was an explicit advocate of vivisection, and his articulation of the scientific method helped develop the framework within which vivisection is justified to this day.

Thus caring as a virtue is problematic under its present and historical construction, being culturally linked to structures of domination in which men systematically control others. The word "gentleman" simultaneously means "a man of kindness, courtesy and honor" and "a man of superior position in society." The word "gentle" itself has this dual meaning; originating from the Latin *gentilis*, meaning of the same gens or upper-class family, it came to connote those qualities considered appropriate to those of "good" birth, namely, refinement, politeness, generosity, and kindness.

Power is institutionally based. The individual exercises this power by virtue of his place in the established hierarchy. To the extent that the institutionalized relations of dominance are effective and stable, the individual in a position of power need not act in an overtly domineering or "cruel" manner. He expresses his wishes and those below him respond. In the ultimate power structure, those below him respond willingly because they have internalized their master's desires. In such a situation he is free to consider the feelings of his subordinates, since doing so in no way threatens the power structure itself. In class society the sensitivity, kindness, and solicitude of men is valued because it marks one who is truly in control of others.

In her novel *Black Beauty*, Anna Sewell calls for men to be sensitive to the feelings of the horses who work for them, but she does not challenge the power structure of men over horses. Indeed, her book is premised on the notion that horses want to work for men. In her view, "difficult" horses are those who have been mistreated—whipped, painfully restrained, or worked to exhaustion. They have learned to hate and fear men and thus resist obeying their commands. By contrast, horses who have been kindly treated will naturally do everything they can to satisfy the desires of their "masters." Thus in the interchange cited above between the squire and Sawyer, Sawyer defends his fierce whipping of the horse by exclaiming, "He's too fond of his own will, and that won't suit me," while the squire responds by asking, "Do you think that treatment like this will make him fond of your will?"[80]

Men's solicitude to animals is valued as a strategy for controlling animals and as an indicator of the completeness of their conquest. This is true in all the major areas of men's exploitation of animals, as we have seen previously. Whether displayed by women or by men, caring for animals is valued as a human virtue to the extent that it furthers men's industries of animal exploitation or at least does not interfere with these industries. The problem is not that people do not or cannot sympathize with animals, but that the full development and application of our caring capacities is curbed by the imperatives of male domination. Men, in particular, very much want to see themselves as caring individuals who contribute to the generation and maintenance of healthy human and nonhuman lives. Indeed, hunting, vivisection, and animal farming are imaged by their perpetrators as institutions of caring and generativity.

The root problem is that men, believing they must nurture in ways that distinguish them from women, construct institutions that generate life negatively, through the selective withholding of deadly force. To eradicate this system requires not the use of formal logic to justify new networks of control imposed on a supposedly uncaring and intrinsically aggressive human nature. Nor is it sufficient to appeal to man's gentle nature, since the "gentleman" is by definition selective in the granting of his "tender mercies," committed to doing nothing that would undermine his relations of power. To dismantle animal exploitation we must confront the core of the system, which is the sexist polarization of people into two opposing groups. In sexist society people do not strive to be caring, they strive to be caring women and caring men. This leads to the situation we have today, in which we caringly sacrifice animals daily in order to turn male humans into men. Our natural compassion for animals is constrained by the project of constructing a manhood defined in contradistinction to womanhood. For those who lack the ability to gestate and to suckle, though, there are a multitude of other ways to directly contribute to the generation and maintenance of life, ways that do not involve destroying others in the process—feeding, clothing, mending, cleaning, teaching, and so on. Sexism blocks the adoption of these nondestructive, life-generating activities by men because these functions are performed by women and sexism requires that men develop a realm of work separate from and "superior" to women's work.

To stop animal exploitation we must challenge manhood as it has been constructed under sexism. There is no reason to continue defining manhood in terms of the willingness and ability to dominate others. Nor need it be construed negatively, as the opposite of womanhood. From a nonsexist point of view, human virtues are available to all people regardless of gender. Rejecting a polarized conception of gender, we are able to revoke the requirement that men create through violence, thus clearing the path to animal liberation.

Note on Photographs

Many of the photographs used in this book were taken at the Fred Coleman Memorial Pigeon Shoot, a public event held annually in Hegins, Pennsylvania, between 1934 and 1999. A typical shoot involved about 250 shooters taking turns firing at live pigeons while attendees watched from bleachers, ate barbecue, drank beer, played on the swing sets, and, in later years, cheered on law enforcement officers as they arrested activists who disrupted the shoot by trespassing or releasing caged birds. The shooting continued throughout the day, employing five different fields on two sides of the park and using about five thousand pigeons acquired from a variety of sources, such as breeders and suppliers, pest control organizations, and farming families. Protests of the Hegins pigeon shoot began in the late 1980s and grew to a peak of about fifteen hundred demonstrators at the 1993 shoot. In 1994, the Fund for Animals, the animal rights group primarily responsible for organizing efforts to ban the shoot, asked activists to refrain from protesting at the site because the spectacle of those activists being arrested was drawing additional spectators to the event and detracting from efforts to keep attention on the central humane issue, the target shooting of live birds for sport. Other efforts against the shoot continued, however, including evidence gathering at the shoot, the rescue and rehabilitation of wounded birds, protests at other sites around the state of Pennsylvania, lawsuits, and legislative lobbying. In 1999 organizers agreed to halt the shoot after the Pennsylvania Supreme Court ruled that animal advocates had standing to sue for an injunction to halt the shoot on the basis of existing Pennsylvania anticruelty statutes. Other private pigeon shoots in Pennsylvania continue

to this day, however, and at least some residents of Hegins hopefully expect an eventual return to live shooting, as indicated by this comment from a memorial to the shoot's namesake: "Fred Coleman was a remarkable man and a terrific marksman. He could shoot a pigeon while blindfolded. He never forgot where he was raised, in the Hegins Valley. Well, Fred the shoot may be temporarily detained, but your legend will live on."[1]

I attended the Hegins pigeon shoot in 1992, working as a videographer in cooperation with the Fund for Animals' efforts to gather evidence for legal and public relations campaigns. I was struck by the gendered nature of the event. Racial and class-based aspects were also manifest. Many of the gendered features are discernible in the photographs reproduced throughout this book, visually supporting the themes of this analysis. In addition, two incidents I witnessed have remained in my memory as striking examples of how gender intersects with our activities as animal liberators and animal exploiters.

One of the interventions involved an activist running onto the field in between shooters' turns, opening the cages and thus allowing the birds to escape before the next shooter was in position to fire. Dozens of activists used this tactic that year, nearly shutting down the shoot entirely at certain points in the day. In order to do this effectively, the activist had to be in position at one of several points along the fence where one could get under or over the fence, around the troopers, and to the cages quickly enough. The president of our local animal rights organization was one of the activists who performed this action. She, like the others, was immediately arrested, removed from the site, and eventually charged with the crimes of theft, receiving stolen property, criminal mischief, and trespass. After she was bailed out, she told me that once she had finally gotten through the crowd of spectators to just the right place along the fence, the organizers called a one-hour lunch break. One of the male spectators standing nearby began to make aggressive drunken sexual advances on her, apparently unaware that she was an activist. She told me that she stayed there and entertained his advances for the entire hour, determined to hold her spot and sexually deflect any suspicion that she might be an undercover activist. Her proud portrayal of this as an unpleasant sacrifice she had been willing to make "for the animals" is an example of the self-martyring attitude animal liberationists at times adopt. It is also an instance of the sexual form such sacrifice can take for female activists, a form that has become normalized through the PETA campaigns discussed in chapter 7.

I also witnessed a remarkable display of sexism by the shoot's organizers. During my three-hour shift videotaping one of the killing fields, there were a few heartening interruptions to the depressing sequence of bird shootings. Some activists had with forethought purchased their own permits to shoot. When their turn was called, they took their place and deliberately missed each of the released bird targets. Their birds flew away safely, free and unharmed. At least that was the plan. Though the activists took care to dress and act, as much as possible, like all the other shooters, by the second or third missed shot, spectators and organizers became suspicious and shouts of "He's an imposter" and "Get him out of there" began to ring out from the bleachers. At this point organizers had the suspected infiltrator removed, escorted by security if necessary, the intent to deliberately miss evidently providing grounds for disqualification. There was one exception to this pattern, though. The vast majority of shooters were male, but a few females participated as well. Whenever a female shooter missed all her birds, the organizers did not disqualify her but approached and offered assistance with her shooting. The underlying assumption was evidently that a man who kept missing must be an imposter, whereas a woman who kept missing was just an incompetent woman. After all, men, not women, are hunters by instinct, are we not?

Notes

Introduction

1. See, for example, Singer, *Animal Liberation*; Regan, *Case for Animal Rights*; Clark, *Moral Status of Animals*; DeGrazia, *Taking Animals Seriously*; Dunayer, *Animal Equality*; Francione, *Introduction to Animal Rights*; Franklin, *Animal Rights and Moral Philosophy*; Johnson, *Morally Deep World*; Pluhar, *Beyond Prejudice*; Rachels, *Created from Animals*; Rollin, *Animal Rights and Human Morality*; Rowlands, *Animal Rights*; and many others.

2. See Gorner, "Wild Crows," and Hunt, "Manufacture and Use of Hook-Tools."

3. For a book-length analysis of the argument, see Dombrowski, *Babies and Beasts*.

4. See Luke, "From Animal Rights to Animal Liberation," 35–44; also Luke, "Justice, Caring, and Animal Liberation," 79–81.

5. Pluhar, *Beyond Prejudice*, 189.

6. Linzey, *Christianity*, 57.

7. See Linzey, *Animal Rights*, and Scully, *Dominion*, for just two examples of authors developing a Christian case against animal exploitation.

8. See Munro, *Compassionate Beasts*, 61–62, for example, for data regarding animal liberation leadership in Australia.

9. Plous, "Signs of Change," 49.

10. Peek, Bell, and Dunham, "Animal Rights Advocacy," 465. See also Munro, "Caring about Blood, Flesh, and Pain."

11. Achor, *Animal Rights*, 136. Though this may be changing slightly—Blake Hurst reported in 2003 that 87 percent of hunters were male ("Me Man, Me Hunt!" 41).

12. Amato and Partridge, *New Vegetarians*, 34. See also Jerolmack, "Tracing the Profile of Animal Rights Supporters." On the association between meat and manhood, see Adams, *Sexual Politics of Meat*.

13. See Sperling, *Animal Liberators,* chap. 1.

14. Achor, *Animal Rights,* 95.

15. Birke, "Intimate Familiarities?"

16. Munro, "Caring about Blood, Flesh, and Pain."

17. Einwohner, "Gender, Class, and Social Movement Outcomes."

18. Paul Irwin, overview to Salem and Rowan, *State of the Animals 2001,* 5.

19. Ibid; Yount, *Animal Rights,* 281.

20. Commodities and Trade Division, *World Statistical Compendium for Raw Hides and Skins,* 16, 24.

21. Seager, *Earth Follies,* 208.

22. Kellert, *Value of Life,* 51.

23. Peek, Bell, and Dunham, "Animal Rights Advocacy"; Uyeki and Holland, "Diffusion of Pro-Environment Attitudes?"; Jerolmack, "Tracing the Profile of Animal Rights Supporters"; Kruse, "Support for Animal Rights"; Pifer, "Exploring the Gender Gap"; Pifer, Shimizu, and Pifer, "Public Attitudes Toward Animal Research"; and Broida et al., "Personality Differences."

24. Pifer, Shimizu, and Pifer, "Public Attitudes Toward Animal Research"; Pifer, "Exploring the Gender Gap."

25. Kruse, "Support for Animal Rights"; Pifer, "Exploring the Gender Gap."

26. For examples of this type of explanation, see Galvin and Herzog, "Ethical Ideology"; Herzog, Betchart, and Pittman, "Attitudes Towards Animals"; Kellert and Berry, "Behaviors Toward Wildlife"; Pifer, "Exploring the Gender Gap"; Pifer, Shimizu, and Pifer, "Public Attitudes Toward Animal Research"; and Jasper and Nelkin, *Animal Rights Crusade,* 59.

27. Peek, Bell, and Dunham, "Animal Rights Advocacy," 473–74.

28. See, for example, Cantor, "Club, the Yoke, and the Leash," and Corea, *Mother Machine.*

29. See Adams, *Neither Man nor Beast,* 154, and Donovan, "Animal Rights and Feminist Theory," 46.

30. Quoted in Munro, *Compassionate Beasts,* 61.

31. Stange, *Woman the Hunter,* 2.

32. Peek, Dunham, and Dietz, "Affinity for Animal Rights," 915.

33. Kheel, "License to Kill," and Collard, *Rape of the Wild,* chap. 2.

34. See Valeri, "Wild Victims."

Part One: Justifying Men's Exploitation of Animals

1. An Aesop's fable, "The Wolf and the Lamb."

Chapter 1: The Species Boundary

1. *Utne Reader* 28 (July/August 1988): 128.

2. *Utne Reader* 29 (September/October 1988): 6.

3. Ibid.

4. Hummel, *Hunting and Fishing for Sport*, 15.

5. See Simoons and Baldwin, "Breast-feeding of Animals by Women."

6. There are other reasons for calling antihunting men "fags," as becomes evident in the course of chapter 3 on heterosexuality and men's hunting.

7. Quoted in Kalechofsky, *Autobiography of a Revolutionary*, 99.

8. Tobias, *Voices from the Underground*, 96.

9. Nibert, *Animal Rights, Human Rights*, 227.

10. A topic discussed in more detail in chapter 6.

11. Hills, "Motivational Bases of Attitudes Toward Animals."

12. See Sharpe, *Cruel Deception*; Greek and Greek, *Sacred Cows and Golden Geese*; and the discussions in chapters 5 and 6.

13. Kellert, "American Attitudes," 89; Kellert, "Perceptions of Animals in America," 7.

14. Kellert, "Perceptions of Animals in America," 11.

15. Rose, *Freeing the Whales*, 72.

16. Kellert, *Knowledge, Affection and Basic Attitudes*, 49.

17. Kellert, "Perceptions of Animals in America," 7.

18. Kellert, *Knowledge, Affection and Basic Attitudes*, 132.

19. Ibid., 155, 156.

20. Rose, *Freeing the Whales*.

21. McDaniel, "Won't Somebody Please Save This Whale?" 48.

22. See http://www.keiko.com/history.htm.

23. Miller, "All This for One Whale?" 62.

24. Ibid., 58.

25. Kellert, *Activities of the American Public Relating to Animals*, 109.

26. Serpell, *In the Company of Animals*, 11.

27. Drews, "Wild Animals and Other Pets."

28. Beck, "Animals in the City," 238.

29. Drews, "Wild Animals and Other Pets."

30. Szasz, *Petishism*; Tuan, *Dominance and Affection*.

31. Menninger, "Totemic Aspects," 44.

32. Serpell, "Pet-keeping in Non-Western Societies," 44–48.

33. Voith, "Attachments between People and Their Pets."

34. Beck and Katcher, *Between Pets and People*, 44.

35. Quigley, Vogel, and Anderson, "Study of Perceptions and Attitudes toward Pet Ownership," 271.

36. Cain, "Study of Pets in the Family System," 77, 80.

37. Katcher, "How Companion Animals Make Us Feel," 122.

38. Smith, "Interactions Between Pet Dog and Family Members," 35.

39. Serpell, *In the Company of Animals*, 58.

40. Menache, "Dogs and Human Beings."

41. Serpell, *In the Company of Animals*, 49.

42. Ibid., 49–53.

43. Simoons and Baldwin, "Breast-feeding of Animals by Women," 430.

44. Reported in *Earth Island Journal* 16, no. 2 (Summer 2001): 3.

45. An exception to this generality would be farming families, in which children are sometimes allowed to know the realities of exploitation at an early age.

46. See Cartmill, *View to a Death in the Morning*, chap. 9.

47. Kohlberg, "From Is to Ought," 191; cited in Singer, *Animal Liberation*, 305.

48. Serpell, *In the Company of Animals*, chaps. 10 and 11.

49. Ibid., 145, 153, 148.

50. Compare Preece, *Animals and Nature*, 233; also see Luke, "From Animal Rights to Animal Liberation," 88–96, for a more detailed explication.

51. Thompson, "Hanging Tongues," 215.

52. Herzog and McGee, "Psychological Aspects of Slaughter," 129–30.

53. Ibid.

54. Arluke, "Uneasiness Among Laboratory Technicians," 33.

55. Sperling, *Animal Liberators*, 9.

56. Arluke, "We Build a Better Beagle."

57. Ibid., 154.

58. For additional examples, see Dunayer, *Animal Equality*, 9, 50, 77, 91, 93, 118–19, 129, 143–44.

59. "Buffalo wings" is an American locution for cooked chickens' wings served spicy as "appetizers."

Chapter 2: Men's Predation and the Natural Order

1. Franklin, *Autobiography*, 35–56.

2. Ortega y Gasset, *Meditations on Hunting*, 98; von Franz, quoted at Swan, *In Defense of Hunting*, 132; Nugent, *Blood Trails*, I; Stange, *Woman the Hunter*, 120.

3. Ortega y Gasset, *Meditations on Hunting*, 94. Compare Nugent, *Blood Trails*, 89.

4. For example, "These people never knew or don't want to know that death is as quotidian in the wild as sucking air in and blowing it out" (Cartmill, *View to a Death in the Morning*, 181; see also 236); "The individual who has killed an animal and eaten it with . . . remorse . . . is much more aware of the reality of death than those who never consider the horrors of the slaughterhouse and who, in their ignorance or indifference, mistakenly assume that their own hands are unbloodied" (Gish, *Songs of My Hunter Heart*, 15); "When meat is only procured in a cellophane package . . . one inevitably loses complete touch with what has actually taken place. Not me. Not bowhunters. . . . our peaceful, senses-articulating sport keeps us tuned into the world around us, and shows how we fit in" (Nugent, *Blood Trails*, iii-iv); also Swan, *In Defense of Hunting*, 134. Compare also: "Hunting provides unique opportunities for

humans to participate in the natural ecological scheme in such a way that one does not delude oneself concerning the degree and nature of the participation" (Scanlon, "Humans as Hunting Animals," 204).

5. Lopez, *Arctic Dreams*, 413. Ted Kerasote begins his explanation for why he hunts by citing this quote (*Bloodties*).

6. Swan, *In Defense of Hunting*, 175.

7. Ibid., 270.

8. Ortega y Gasset, *Meditations on Hunting*, 98.

9. Leahy, *Against Liberation*, 248.

10. Regan, *Case for Animal Rights*, 357.

11. Cowen, "Policing Nature," 176.

12. Clark, "Rights of Wild Things," 175; Moriarty and Woods, "Hunting Does Not Equal Predation," 394.

13. Sapontzis, *Morals, Reason, and Animals*, chap. 13.

14. Cowen, "Policing Nature," 174, 182.

15. See Clark, "Rights of Wild Things," 184–87.

16. Hettinger, "Valuing Predation in Rolston's Environmental Ethic," 15.

17. Ibid., 19; also: "If carnivorous predation in nature is *good*—and not merely an unpleasant fact that we must learn to live with—then human carnivorous predation can be seen as an affirmation of this valuable natural process" (14).

18. Ibid., 20.

19. Moriarty and Woods, "Hunting Does Not Equal Predation," 395.

20. Everett, "Environmental Ethics, Animal Welfarism, and the Problem of Predation," 59.

21. Ibid.

22. Paley, *Natural Theology*, 68.

23. Geach, *Providence and Evil*, 69.

24. Smith, "Atheological Argument," 159. Compare James Haught's question and answer: "How could [a loving creator] fashion cheetahs to disembowel fawns, sharks to rip seals, and pythons to crush pigs? Only a fiend would invent all these vicious things" (Haught, "Why Would God Drown Children?" 14).

25. Rolston, "Disvalues in Nature," 253.

26. Hettinger, "Valuing Predation in Rolston's Environmental Ethic," 14.

27. Jacobs, "In on the Kill," 18.

28. See Darwall, *Contractarianism/Contractualism*.

29. Rowlands, *Animal Rights*. See also Tucker and MacDonald, "Beastly Contractarianism?"

30. Quoted at Hettinger, "Valuing Predation in Rolston's Environmental Ethic," 16.

31. Bass, "Appeal to Hunters," 194, 198.

32. Paley, *Natural Theology*, 64–65. See also Hick, *Evil and the God of Love*, 349.

33. Leahy, *Against Liberation*, 248.

34. Rolston, "Disvalues in Nature," 272.

35. Ibid., 254.

36. Paley, *Natural Theology*, 64.

37. Anders, *Evolution of Evil*, 210.

38. Cowen, "Policing Nature," 173.

39. "Study Shows Wolves' Importance to Ecosystems," at cnn.com (August 1, 2005).

40. Rolston, "Disvalues in Nature," 254.

41. Ibid., 253.

42. See Luke, "Critical Analysis of Hunters' Ethics," 27–28.

43. Rolston, "Disvalues in Nature," 254–55.

44. Kerasote, "Restoring the Older Knowledge," 291.

45. See Dizard, *Mortal Stakes*, 122–23, and Sussman, "Myth of Man the Hunter."

46. See Moriarty and Woods, "Hunting Does Not Equal Predation," 401; Everett, "Environmental Ethics, Animal Welfarism, and the Problem of Predation," 58.

47. Hettinger, "Valuing Predation in Rolston's Environmental Ethic," 13.

48. Scanlon, "Humans as Hunting Animals," 204–5.

49. See Tobias, "Anthropology of Conscience."

50. Mason, *Unnatural Order*, 72; Adams, *Pornography of Meat*, 85.

51. Causey, "On the Morality of Hunting," 340; compare Callicott, *In Defense of the Land Ethic*, 32.

52. See King, "Environmental Ethics and the Case for Hunting," 83.

53. See, for example, Pauley, "Value of Hunting," 241, and Stange, in Kistler, *People Promoting and People Opposing Animal Rights*, 260.

54. See Vitali, "Sport Hunting," and Nugent, *Blood Trails*, 8, for just two examples.

55. Swan, *In Defense of Hunting*, 8. See Pluhar, "Joy of Killing," 121; Loftin, "Morality of Hunting," 244; and Cartmill, *View to a Death in the Morning*, 232.

56. Kerasote, *Bloodties*, 218.

57. See Dalrymple, *Deer Hunting with Dalrymple*, 53–54, on the selection involved in meat hunting for deer, and Vitali, "Sport Hunting," 70, on the negative consequences of trophy hunting for the healthiest males.

58. Loftin, "Morality of Hunting," 245, and Vitali, "Sport Hunting," 71.

59. Swan, *In Defense of Hunting*, 77; Nugent, *Blood Trails*, 113–14; Kerasote, *Bloodties*, 214; Pluhar, "Joy of Killing," 121; Wenz, "Ecology, Morality, and Hunting," 193–94; King, "Environmental Ethics and the Case for Hunting," 68.

60. Baker, *American Hunting Myth*, 81.

61. Ibid., 73–77.

62. Bernstein, *Without a Tear*, 126–27.

63. Robbins, *Diet for a New America*.

64. Ortega y Gasset, *Meditations on Hunting*, 27, 102, 119; Whisker, *Right to Hunt*, ix, 18–20, 24, 30–31, 66; Swan, *In Defense of Hunting*, 12–13, 126–27, 175, 177; Gish, *Songs*

of My Hunter Heart, xii; Posewitz, *Beyond Fair Chase,* 110; Nugent, *Blood Trails,* 116, 129; Causey, "On the Morality of Hunting," 338; Shepard, *Tender Carnivore,* 150.

65. Unnamed surveyant, quoted in Knight et al., "Using Grounded Theory."

66. Pluhar, "Joy of Killing," 123.

67. See Cartmill, *View to a Death in the Morning,* 15–18; Collard, *Rape of the Wild,* chap. 2; and Mason, *Unnatural Order,* chap. 2.

68. Bekoff and Jamieson, "Sport Hunting as an Instinct," 375–78; Pluhar, "Joy of Killing," 123.

69. See Causey, "On the Morality of Hunting," 338; Pluhar; "Joy of Killing," 123; and Cartmill, *View to a Death in the Morning,* 229.

70. For a study of a wildlife officer's self-conception, see Lawson, "Controlling the Wilderness."

71. Van de Pitte, "Moral Basis for Public Policy," 261.

72. Ortega y Gasset, *Meditations on Hunting,* 116.

73. Swan, *In Defense of Hunting,* 259–60. Matt Cartmill and Roger King both point out that this atavistic interpretation of hunting is also implausible for the blood sports practiced by European royalty. These highly formalized ceremonies are rigorously structured by rules intended not to return the hunters to a prehistoric condition but to evince dominance over nature and to display their relative class position within the social hierarchy (Cartmill, *View to a Death in the Morning,* 242; King, "Environmental Ethics and the Case for Hunting," 77).

74. Vitali, "Ethics of Hunting," 38–39. Compare Swan, *In Defense of Hunting,* 181–82, and Kerasote, *Bloodties,* 77. Also see Gish, *Songs of My Hunter Heart,* 51.

75. See Luke, "Critical Analysis of Hunters' Ethics," on the nature of "fair chase."

76. Compare Peter Wenz's conclusion: "Given the massive differences in myriad areas between modern and hunter-gatherer life, it is implausible that the differences between hunting and wilderness photography are the ones that the human psyche cannot tolerate" (Wenz, "Ecology, Morality, and Hunting," 195–96).

77. Fergus, *Hunter's Road,* 2.

78. Nugent, *Blood Trails,* 58–59, 136.

79. Kerasote, *Bloodties,* 184.

80. Nugent, *Blood Trails,* 135. See Dunayer, *Animal Equality,* chapter 4, for additional examples.

81. Swan, *In Defense of Hunting,* 13; Nugent, *Blood Trails,* v.

82. Daniel Dombrowski argues that moral concern for nonhuman animals is as likely to be part of our evolutionary heritage as the urge to kill (Dombrowski, "Comment on Pluhar," 130–31).

83. Pluhar, "Joy of Killing," 123.

84. "The film [*After the First*] tells the story of a young boy who goes on his first deer hunt with his father. When the boy looked at the beauty of the deer poised in the early morning, its antlered head raised above the bushes, he had hesitated, then

shot; and as father and son looked down together at the dead deer, the father had said, 'After the first it won't be so hard'" (Prejean, *Dead Man Walking*, 185).

85. Swan, *In Defense of Hunting*, 29.

86. Gish, *Songs of My Hunter Heart*, 62.

87. Pluhar, "Joy of Killing," 123–24. See also Cartmill, *View to a Death in the Morning*, 229–31.

88. Kerasote, *Bloodties*, 224–25.

89. Ibid., 245.

90. Whisker, *Right to Hunt*, 59.

91. Swan, *In Defense of Hunting*, 37, 121.

92. Ibid., 48–49. Swan also states that "on some occasions, certain animals seem to come to me or I am guided to them when I am hunting" (189). He describes a dream that apparently led him to some pigs he was hunting, and remarks, "Dreams like this are nature's way of saying thanks for showing respect for the animals you hunt, I have been told by my Lummi friend Kenny Cooper" (264).

93. Kerasote, *Bloodties*, 225–26.

94. Preece notes the inherent contradiction: "We have to wonder at the blatant discrepancy . . . between 'invitation' and 'capture.' If the eaglets had accepted the invitation, there would be no need to capture them" (*Animals and Nature*, 194).

95. Swan, *In Defense of Hunting*, 38.

96. For example, "It is well to think of these things when you anticipate hunting, now and then when you are hunting, and always when you claim an animal that is, in so many ways, a precious gift" (Posewitz, *Beyond Fair Chase*, 88) and "I had not taken this majestic beast. He was given to me" (Ted Nugent, quoted at Swan, *In Defense of Hunting*, 33).

97. Whisker, *Right to Hunt*, 13.

98. Ortega y Gasset, *Meditations on Hunting*, 119–20.

99. Ibid., 88.

100. Swan, *In Defense of Hunting*, 29.

101. See the discussion of the use of empathy to facilitate hunting in chapter 6.

102. Kerasote, *Bloodties*, 227.

103. Jolma, "Why They Quit," 39.

104. Nelson Bryant, quoted in Gish, *Songs of My Hunter Heart*, xii-xiii. Compare Dizard, *Mortal Stakes*, 53: "Bill is one of several hunters I interviewed who is no longer interested in killing."

105. Abbey, "Blood Sport," 14, in Petersen, *A Hunter's Heart*.

106. Kerasote, "Spirit of Hunting," 60.

107. See Gish, *Songs of My Hunter Heart*, xii; Kerasote, *Bloodties*, 127–28; Jolma, "Why They Quit," 40; Cartmill, *View to a Death in the Morning*, 231; and Marks, *Southern Hunting in Black and White*, 226.

108. "The Sadness of the Hunter," *New York Times*, December 10, 1995, E3.

109. Gish, *Songs of My Hunter Heart*, 106.

110. Woods, "Hunting Problem," 113.

Part Two: Understanding Men's Exploitation of Animals

1. Salten, *Bambi*, 96, 99, 103–4.

Chapter 3: The Erotics of Men's Predation

1. Doyle, *The Hound of the Baskervilles*, 674.
2. Ortega y Gasset, *Meditations on Hunting*, 77–78.
3. Wegner, *Deer and Deer Hunting, Book 3*, 14.
4. Swan, *In Defense of Hunting*, 10, 22, 148. Compare Ernest Hemingway: "All real hunters are in love with the animals they hunt" (*Death in the Afternoon*, cited at Preece, *Animals and Nature*, 197).
5. Houston, *Women on Hunting*, 25. For Mary Zeiss Stange, hunting is "the way I engage most intimately with the natural environment" (Kistler, *People Promoting and People Opposing Animal Rights*, 259).
6. John Madson, "Why Men Hunt," 135, in Petersen, *A Hunter's Heart*.
7. Nugent, *Blood Trails*, 8, referring to the decision by Florida wildlife officials to permit hunters to kill deer stranded by flooding.
8. MacQuarrie, *Stories of the Old Duck Hunters*.
9. Bryant Nelson, at Gish, *Songs of My Hunter Heart*, 14.
10. Robert Jones, "I Wouldn't Be the Same," 128, in Petersen, *Hunter's Heart*. Ted Kerasote similarly describes hunting as "one of our important and fundamental weddings with nature ("Restoring the Older Knowledge," 294, in Petersen, *Hunter's Heart*).
11. O'Connor, "Hunting on the Farm."
12. Paul Asper, at Kerasote, *Bloodties*, 155.
13. Quoted at Madson, "Why Men Hunt," 131, in Petersen, *Hunter's Heart*.
14. Ortega y Gasset, *Meditations on Hunting*, 48–49.
15. Collard, *Rape of the Wild*, 48.
16. Mitchell, *Hunt*, 140–41.
17. Swan, *In Defense of Hunting*, 52.
18. Ibid., 26; emphasis added.
19. Mitchell, *Hunt*, 5.
20. Trophy hunter Ali Ustay, quoted at Kerasote, *Bloodties*, 117.
21. Swan, *In Defense of Hunting*, 206; Shepard, *Tender Carnivore*, 173.
22. Whisker, *Right to Hunt*, 18.
23. Swan, *In Defense of Hunting*, 236.
24. Ibid., 86.
25. McIntyre, *Way of the Hunter*, 102, cited at Cartmill, *View to a Death in the Morning*, 242.
26. Mike Gaddis, "Taking a Life," 122, in Petersen, *Hunter's Heart*.
27. Whisker, *Right to Hunt*, 105–6.
28. As one contributor to Houston's *Women on Hunting* puts it, women who hunt do not "participate at the same frenzied level" as do the men (111).

29. Whisker, *Right to Hunt*, 105.

30. Dizard, *Mortal Stakes*, 44, 45.

31. See Kheel, "Women, Ethics, and Anima(l)s," 42.

32. See, for example, Wolf, *Beauty Myth*, 162–68. Wolf concludes that "cultural representation of glamorized degradation has created a situation among the young in which boys rape and girls get raped *as a normal course of events*" (167).

33. Beneke, *Men on Rape*.

34. Wegner, *Deer and Deer Hunting, Book 3*, 165.

35. See Mitchell, *Hunt*, 7–8 (his numbers have been converted here into 2003 dollars); also Chinn, "Where Does All the Money Go?"

36. Nugent, "Fun, Good, Clean, Fun!" 7. Compare Lyle Kingston, from his contrarily titled book celebrating hunting: "No hunter is justified today in going out just for meat. Our pioneering days are over. There are no more Daniel Boones. The modern sportsman goes out for the thrill of the hunt" (*On Behalf of the Hunted*, 136).

37. Kheel, "License to Kill," 90–92; see also Kheel, "Women, Ethics, and Anima(l)s," 40.

38. See Kheel, "License to Kill," 90.

39. For example, "The spirit of the wild will make you feel warm and good inside" (stated by Ted Nugent as he shoots an arrow into the heart of a deer practice target, in Nugent, *Spirit of the Wild Part II*).

40. Vicinus, "Sexuality and Power."

41. Nugent, *Archer's Africa*; Nugent, *Spirit of the Wild*; Nugent, *Blood Trails*, 19–21, 23, 31, 40, 45, 50, 57, 59, 62, 67, 70.

42. Marks, *Southern Hunting in Black and White*, 150.

43. Hamm, *Traditional Bowyer's Bible*, 17.

44. Jay Massey, at Hamm, *Traditional Bowyer's Bible*, 17.

45. Nugent, *Blood Trails*, 60. In their study of hunting magazines, Kalof, Fitzgerald, and Baralt found that "although the active, projectile arrow was imbued with stereotypically male characteristics and depicted as an extension or embodiment of the (male) hunter, the bow was feminized and sexualized, often described as beautiful, smooth, and dependable. We read this as a feminization of the "instrumental" bow, noting that even the implements of the hunt (like the victims of it) cannot escape the patriarchal nature of the culture from which they are constructed" ("Animals, Women and Weapons").

46. Nugent, "One Way Ticket Out of Target Panic Hell," 26.

47. Swan, *In Defense of Hunting*, 48.

48. Mortimer Shapiro, quoted at Mitchell, *Hunt*, 140.

49. Kerasote, *Bloodties*, 272–73.

50. William Thompson, quoted at Cartmill, *View to a Death in the Morning*, 238.

51. McIntyre, *Dreaming the Lion*, 145.

52. Geist, *Mountain Sheep and Man*, 153; quoted at Cartmill, *View to a Death in the Morning*, 235.

53. *Euthydemus* 290b, cited at Ortega y Gasset, *Meditations on Hunting,* 48.

54. Wegner, *Deer and Deer Hunting, Book 3,* 303.

55. Nugent, *Blood Trails,* 66.

56. Marks, *Southern Hunting in Black and White,* 151.

57. Gish, *Songs of My Hunter Heart,* 73. See Kalof, Fitzgerald, and Baralt, "Women, Animals and Weapons."

58. Rutledge, "Miss Seduction Struts Her Stuff," 78.

59. Swan, *In Defense of Hunting,* 140. Compare the following dialogue between bowhunter Ted Nugent and his wife Shemane:

> SHEMANE: A hog hunt was our first date.
>
> TED: A hog hunt is officially a Ted Nugent date.
>
> SHEMANE: A hog hunt in Florida was our first date—no, that was our honeymoon.
>
> TED: No, our honeymoon was at the Safari Club International. See, it all runs together for her—honeymoons, safari club international banquets, pig hunts for our dates . . . (Nugent, *Spirit of the Wild Part II*).

See also Nugent, *Blood Trails,* 47.

60. Ayars, "Coming to Terms with Hunting."

61. Whisker, *Right to Hunt,* 25.

62. McIntyre, *Dreaming the Lion,* 144–45.

63. Shepard, *Tender Carnivore,* 174.

64. McIntyre, *Dreaming the Lion,* 145.

65. Kerasote, *Bloodties,* 105–6.

66. Ibid., 191.

67. Nugent, *Blood Trails,* 67.

68. Kerasote, *Bloodties,* 7–8.

69. Posewitz, *Beyond Fair Chase,* 102; Kerasote, *Bloodties,* 85, 89.

70. See Dahles, "Game Killing and Killing Games."

71. See Luke, "Critical Analysis of Hunters' Ethics."

72. Fischer, review of *Whitetail Magic,* 71.

73. Nugent, *Archer's Africa.*

74. Kerasote, *Bloodties,* 194.

75. See, for example, Causey, "On the Morality of Hunting," 338.

76. Cartmill, *View to a Death in the Morning,* 233.

77. Shepard, *Tender Carnivore,* 169–74.

78. See also the 1996 *Webster's New Universal Unabridged Dictionary,* as cited in Kalof, Fitzgerald, and Baralt, "Animals, Women and Weapons."

79. Jeffreys, *Anticlimax,* 2.

80. *Philadelphia Inquirer,* February 2, 1996. See Adams, *Pornography of Meat,* 85.

81. Parenti, *Lockdown America,* 184.

82. "I Am a Predator," *Intensities in 10 Cities,* CBS, 1982.

83. Shepard, *Tender Carnivore,* 171.

84. Adams, *Pornography of Meat,* 84.

85. See Cartmill, *View to a Death in the Morning,* 183–84.

86. Rich, "Compulsory Heterosexuality and Lesbian Existence."

87. *Newsweek,* May 15, 1989, 40, cited at Cartmill, *View to a Death in the Morning,* 277.

88. See, for example, Abbott, *In the Belly of the Beast,* 80, and Parenti, *Lockdown America,* 188.

89. Conversely, the willingness and capacity to dominate masculinizes, as we see in Shemane Nugent's explanation of how she was able to learn to hunt after marrying bowhunter Ted Nugent: "I was always a tomboy at heart" (Nugent, *Spirit of the Wild Part II*).

90. See Dworkin, *Right-Wing Women,* 174, 184.

91. Dunayer, "Sexist Words, Speciesist Roots," 14.

92. See Joreen, "Bitch Manifesto."

93. See Dunayer, "Sexist Words, Speciesist Roots," 15, and compare the William Thompson quote above, in which the beauty of the prey *is* the wariness.

94. Hunter George Reiger, quoted by Joy Williams at Houston, *Women on Hunting,* 259.

95. Uhland, quoted at Cartmill, *View to a Death in the Morning,* 120.

96. Tennyson, quoted at Fiddes, *Meat,* 144.

97. Nugent quoted at Rees, *Rock Movers and Shakers,* 366; Jon Bon Jovi, "That's the Story of Love," *If You Can't Lick 'Em . . . Lick 'Em,* Atlantic Records, 1988.

98. Gish, *Songs of My Hunter Heart,* 9–10.

99. Fein and Schneider, *Rules,* 34, 131.

100. Ibid., 83, 113, 13, 26, 127.

101. Ibid., 82.

102. Shepard, *Tender Carnivore,* 172.

103. Riva, "Bunny Trail," 34.

104. *Playboy,* July 1969, 85, 88.

105. *Playboy,* January 1971, 101.

106. *Playboy's Bathing Beauties,* March 1995, 43.

107. *Playboy's Book of Lingerie,* July 1994, 47.

108. Kappeler, *Pornography of Representation,* 6.

109. Cartmill, *View to a Death in the Morning,* 240.

110. Halliburton, *Royal Road to Romance,* 4.

111. See Barry, *Prostitution of Sexuality.*

112. In the same section of his book Bourjaily describes a strip of roadhouses advertising "exotic dancers" located near a goose hunting site. A local hunter informed Bourjaily:

> Every gambler and B-girl in Chicago can tell you the day the goose season opens down here . . . The people who work these places read the outdoor columns in Chicago, so they can follow the movement of the flights out of Canada. . . . Bird watchers. They get here every year to set up for the hunt-

ers just about a week before the geese do (Ad Turner, at Bourjaily, *Unnatural Enemy,* 73–74).

113. Dworkin, *Pornography,* xviii-xix.

114. *Pittsburgh Press,* July 28, 1989, A9.

115. Lea, *Hunting the Whole Way Home,* 30.

116. Wegner, *Deer and Deer Hunting,* 208–11.

Chapter 4: Sacrifice

1. Manes, *Other Creations,* 104.

2. Hubert and Mauss, *Sacrifice,* 97.

3. Jay, *Throughout Your Generations Forever,* 32.

4. Ibid., 112, 83.

5. Ibid., 36.

6. See Serpell, *In the Company of Animals,* 167–68, and the discussion of blame shifting in chapter 7.

7. Horney, *Feminine Psychology;* Kittay, "Womb Envy."

8. See, for example, Finucci and Brownlee, *Generation and Degeneration,* and Corea, *Mother Machine.*

9. Kittay, "Womb Envy," 95.

10. Kafka, *Letter to His Father,* 35.

11. Here and in the following I use the term "material" to distinguish existing social relations from the purely ideological or "ideal" realm.

12. Genesis 22:1–19.

13. Jay, *Throughout Your Generations Forever,* 102.

14. Genesis 8:20–21.

15. Graves and Patai, *Hebrew Myths,* 116.

16. Deuteronomy 13:12–16; see also Joshua 6:17.

17. 2 Samuel 21:1–14.

18. Judges 11:30–39; Jonah 1:4–15.

19. Exodus 22:29–30.

20. 2 Kings 16:3, 21:6.

21. Meeks, *HarperCollins Study Bible,* 586; compare Exodus 22:20: "Whoever sacrifices to any god, other than the Lord alone, shall be devoted to destruction."

22. Genesis 4:6.

23. Graves and Patai, *Hebrew Myths,* 92.

24. Smith, "Sacrifice," 63.

25. Exodus 12:13.

26. Genesis 22:16–17.

27. Ehrenreich, *Blood Rites,* 63.

28. Hoffman, *Covenant of Blood,* 2.

29. Genesis 17.

30. Hoffman, *Covenant of Blood,* 146.

31. Ibid., 96.

32. Ibid., 71.

33. Ibid., 154, 167.

34. Ibid., 95.

35. Ibid., 205.

36. Ibid., 207.

37. Ibid., 70, 72.

38. Ibid., 122–23.

39. See Spiegel, *Last Trial*, 85.

40. John 19:14.

41. See John 19:36

42. Also Hebrews 10:12; 1 Corinthians 5:7; 1 Peter 1:19; Ephesians 5:2; and other passages.

43. Hebrews 9:13–14; see also 12:24 ("the sprinkled blood that speaks a better word than the blood of Abel").

44. Jay, *Throughout Your Generations Forever*, 37.

45. For example, Hebrews 2:10.

46. For example, 1 Corinthians 4:15.

47. Hebrews 2:16; Galatians 3:7, 3:29.

48. Ehrenreich, *Blood Rites*, chaps. 3–4.

49. See Colossians 2:11–12; Philippians 3:2–3; Galatians 4:2; Acts 2:41; and so on.

50. See Barth, *Teaching of the Church Regarding Baptism*, 24.

51. Ibid., 9, 11.

52. Brockett, *Theology of Baptism*, 16.

53. Barstow, *Witchcraze*, 113; Raymond, "Medicine as Patriarchal Religion," 203.

54. 1 Corinthians 3:2; 1 Thessalonians 2:7; Cuttaz, *Baptism*, 94; see also Saint Leo, *Sermon. de Nativ.*, vol. 4, chap. 3.

55. Cuttaz, *Baptism*, 93.

56. John 3:4–6, 22.

57. See also Romans 6:3–4.

58. Brockett, *Theology of Baptism*, 16; Barth, *Teaching of the Church Regarding Baptism*, 11; Cuttaz, *Baptism*, 91.

59. *Institutes* 4.555, quoted at Barth, *Teaching of the Church Regarding Baptism*, 56; III, qu. 69; a. 2, quoted at Cuttaz, *Baptism*, 91.

60. Cuttaz, *Baptism*, 89, 91.

61. Donahue, *Stolen Child*, 12–13.

62. 1 Peter 3:20–21.

Chapter 5: Vivisection as a Sacrificial Ritual

1. Girard, *Girard Reader*, 86–87.

2. Jay, *Throughout Your Generations Forever*, 34.

3. Ehrenreich, *Blood Rites*, 158.

4. Bekoff, *Encyclopedia of Animal Rights and Animal Welfare,* 222.

5. Loeb et al., "Human vs. Animal Rights," 2718.

6. Noble, *World Without Women.*

7. Bacon, *Philosophical Works of Francis Bacon,* 387.

8. Lynch, "Sacrifice and the Transformation of the Animal Body."

9. See Luke, "Animal Experimentation as Blood Sacrifice," for a fuller explanation of these correspondences.

10. Jay, *Throughout Your Generations Forever,* xxiii.

11. Noble, *World Without Women.*

12. Ibid., 103–5, 151.

13. As in Bacon's "The Masculine Birth of Time; Or, The Great Instauration of the Dominion of Man over the Universe," in Farrington, *Philosophy of Francis Bacon,* 59–72. For other references to science as a masculine philosophy, see Easlea, *Witch-hunting, Magic and the New Philosophy,* 214.

14. Joseph Glanvill, quoted at Noble, *World Without Women,* 229–30.

15. Farrington, *The Philosophy of Francis Bacon,* 62, 93.

16. Easlea, *Witch-hunting, Magic and the New Philosophy,* 213, 140–41.

17. Barstow, *Witchcraze.*

18. Klug, "Lab Animals, Francis Bacon and the Culture of Science," 63–64; Easlea, *Witch-hunting, Magic and the New Philosophy,* 128.

19. Rupke, *Vivisection in Historical Perspective,* 19.

20. Bacon, *Philosophical Works of Francis Bacon,* 728.

21. Klug, "Lab Animals, Francis Bacon and the Culture of Science," 64.

22. Keller, *Secrets of Life, Secrets of Death,* 100.

23. Cunningham and Williams, *Laboratory Revolution in Medicine,* 336.

24. Ibid., 327.

25. Easlea, *Witch-hunting, Magic and the New Philosophy,* 193.

26. Olmsted, *François Magendie,* 203–4.

27. Geison, *Private Science of Louis Pasteur,* 138.

28. Rupke, *Vivisection in Historical Perspective,* 15.

29. Harding, *Science Question in Feminism,* 31; compare: "Young Bernard must have felt that he was serving in the very front line of the battle of science" (at Olmsted, *Claude Bernard,* 36).

30. Rupke, *Vivisection in Historical Perspective,* 16.

31. Bernard, *Introduction to the Study of Experimental Medicine,* 132.

32. Cunningham and Williams, *Laboratory Revolution in Medicine,* 338.

33. Olmsted, *Claude Bernard,* 38.

34. Olmsted, *François Magendie,* 261.

35. Olmsted, *Claude Bernard,* 119; compare Bernard's impressions of female students, ibid., 119–20, 192.

36. French, *Antivivisection and Medical Science in Victorian Society,* 254.

37. Ibid., 184, quoting Lord Cardwell. A milksop is "an effeminate or spiritless man or youth," according to the *Oxford English Dictionary.*

38. Ibid., 82.

39. Rupke, *Vivisection in Historical Perspective,* 241, 253.

40. Geison, *Private Science of Louis Pasteur,* 47.

41. Cunningham and Williams, *Laboratory Revolution in Medicine,* 332.

42. Schiller, "Claude Bernard and Vivisection," 255; Olmsted, *Claude Bernard,* 112, 159.

43. Olmsted, *Claude Bernard,* 113.

44. Ibid., 112–13.

45. In Rupke, *Vivisection in Historical Perspective,* 125.

46. See Reines, *Cancer Research on Animals;* Greek and Greek, *Sacred Cows and Golden Geese,* chap. 8.

47. See Noble, *World Without Women,* 188.

48. See ibid., 242, and Raymond, "Medicine as Patriarchal Religion," 214–15.

49. Barstow, *Witchcraze,* 19, 81, 116.

50. Noble, *World Without Women,* 210.

51. Olmsted, *Claude Bernard,* 39.

52. For typical examples of this rhetoric, see Loeb et al., "Human vs. Animal Rights," and Kaufman, "Does Vivisection Pass the Utilitarian Test?" 127. See also LaFollette and Shanks, "Animal Models in Biomedical Research," 114–15.

53. Quoted at Rupke, *Vivisection in Historical Perspective,* 192.

54. Such as the attribution of antisepsis to Lister discussed below.

55. Such as Harvey's discovery of the circulation of the blood and experiments by Bell and Magendie on nerve functioning.

56. Such as Hunter's treatment of aneurysms by tying the diseased artery above the aneurysmal bulge. For AAMR arguments, see Rupke, *Vivisection in Historical Perspective,* 194–98; AAMR, "Facts and Considerations"; and Owen, *Experimental Physiology.*

57. Rupke, *Vivisection in Historical Perspective,* 4.

58. Olmsted, *François Magendie,* 85.

59. Patel, Evans, and Groen, "Biomedical Knowledge and Clinical Reasoning."

60. See Rupke, *Vivisection in Historical Perspective,* 7–9, 198–200, 205; French, *Antivivisection and Medical Science in Victorian Society,* 215, 294; Cunningham and Williams, *Laboratory Revolution in Medicine,* 122, 131, 140–41, 313.

61. Cunningham and Williams, *Laboratory Revolution in Medicine,* 305.

62. Quoted at Easlea, *Witch-hunting, Magic and the New Philosophy,* 251.

63. Loeb et al., "Human vs. Animal Rights," 2720.

64. Cunningham and Williams, *Laboratory Revolution in Medicine,* 297.

65. American Medical Association, *Use of Animals in Biomedical Research,* 17.

66. Quoted at Noble, *World Without Women,* 154.

67. Farrington, *Philosophy of Francis Bacon,* 62, 72.

68. Quoted at Olmsted, *Claude Bernard,* 15–16.

69. Olmsted, *François Magendie,* xiii; Olmsted, *Claude Bernard,* 16.

70. Geison, *Private Science of Louis Pasteur,* 10.

71. Lankester, quoted at French, *Antivivisection and Medical Science in Victorian Society,* 51.

72. See ibid., 394–401.

73. Schiller, "Claude Bernard and Vivisection," 259.

74. Loeb et al., "Human vs. Animal Rights," 2716–17.

75. Olmsted, *François Magendie,* 44.

76. Ibid.

77. Quoted at Olmsted, *Claude Bernard,* 190. Consider also: "[Bernard] was especially proud to be numbered in the legacy of experimenters which Magendie had bequeathed to physiology" (ibid., 92–93).

78. Olmsted, *François Magendie,* 237.

79. Ibid., 229.

80. Quoted at ibid., 60.

81. Cunningham and Williams, *Laboratory Revolution in Medicine,* 312.

82. Rupke, *Vivisection in Historical Perspective,* 200.

83. Jay, *Throughout Your Generations Forever,* 46.

84. See Reines, "On the Role of Clinical Anomaly in Harvey's Discovery."

85. Olmsted, *Claude Bernard,* 94.

86. Olmsted, *François Magendie,* 143.

87. Reines, "On the Locus of Medical Discovery," 187–88.

88. Ibid., 187.

89. Quoted at French, *Antivivisection and Medical Science in Victorian Society,* 18.

90. For example, "Assurance may be gained through multiplication of experiments. The question, *How many animals have you used?* is still a criterion of experimental caution" (Olmsted, *Claude Bernard,* 132).

91. See Reines, "Process of Medical Discovery," and Kaufman, "Does Vivisection Pass the Utilitarian Test?"

92. See Reines, "On the Locus of Medical Discovery," for a long list of examples of such temporal inversion.

93. Paget, *For and Against Experiments on Animals,* 36.

94. Rich, *Of Woman Born,* 153–55.

95. Rupke, *Vivisection in Historical Perspective,* 18.

96. Ibid., 341.

97. Ibid., 343.

98. Ibid., 345, 342.

99. Klug, "Lab Animals, Francis Bacon and the Culture of Science," 66.

100. Olmsted, *François Magendie,* 136, quoting Magendie.

101. Lansbury, *Old Brown Dog,* 58.

102. Ibid., 52.

103. Lederer, *Subjected to Science,* 3, 4, 17, 22, 93, 106, 109.

104. Ibid., 108.

105. Ibid., xiv, 6.

106. Ibid., 7, 46.

107. Washington, *Medical Apartheid*, 6, 59.

108. Ibid., 6.

109. Lederer, *Subjected to Science*, xvi, 90.

110. Ibid., 133.

111. Ibid., 47.

112. Milloy, "Laboratory Animal Farm."

113. Lederer, *Subjected to Science*, 22, 106.

114. Lansbury, *Old Brown Dog*, 24; Lederer, *Subjected to Science*, 42.

115. Gollaher, *Circumcision*, 162.

116. Raymond, "Medicine as Patriarchal Religion," 197.

Part Three: Opposing Men's Exploitation of Animals

1. Gish, *Songs of My Hunter Heart*, 107–8.

Chapter 6: The Ethics of Animal Liberation

1. Nibert, *Animal Rights, Human Rights*, 227–30.

2. Regan, *Case for Animal Rights*, 362; Callicott, "Animal Liberation: A Triangular Affair" (in his *In Defense of the Land Ethic*).

3. Warren: "Animals have a significant right to life, but one which is somewhat more easily overriden [*sic*] by certain kinds of utilitarian or environmental considerations than is the human right to life" ("The Rights of the Nonhuman World," in Hargrove, *Animal Rights/Environmental Ethics Debate*, 202); Callicott: "There is something deeply amiss in the concept of *equal* moral consideration or *equal* moral rights for animals" (*In Defense of the Land Ethic*, 55); Johnson: "Some interests have more weight than others. . . . The interest of a mouse in continuing to live is not the same as the interest of a human in continuing to life. A mouse only has an interest in continuing a mouse life" (*Morally Deep World*, 7).

4. Seed, "Anthropocentrism," 244–45.

5. Sperling, *Animal Liberators*, 200.

6. Ibid., 95 (quoting Peter Singer), 120, 121.

7. Ibid., 19.

8. Ibid., 194.

9. Her theory would, however, if true, entail the fundamental irrationality of animal liberationists (since animal vivisection is not in fact identical to the devastation of the biosphere, and the abolition of the use of animals in science is evidently not the crucial determinant in the struggle to save the earth). This not so indirect attribution of irrationality to animal liberationists should be placed within the context of Sperling's evident desire to legitimate her participation in animal research projects specifically criticized by animal liberationists (see *Animal Liberators*, 10–14).

10. Ibid., 117, 120, 121.

11. Fox, *Returning to Eden*, xiii-xiv, quoted at *Animal Liberators*, 18.

12. Aspinall, *Best of Friends*, 155. Sperling's claim is at *Animal Liberators*, 138.

13. Callicott, *In Defense of the Land Ethic*, 35.

14. Callicott, perhaps, underestimates compassion even in his own motivations. Why are factory farmed and vivisected beings "unfortunate" if the issue is not about their suffering; similarly, what might be the moral significance of their being "penetrated" and their being composed of "delicate" tissues?

15. Singer, "Unkind to Animals," 36, 37.

16. Milgram, "Some Conditions of Obedience and Disobedience to Authority," 64.

17. Serpell, *In the Company of Animals*, 167–68.

18. See the prefatory material to Ted Nugent's book *God, Guns, and Rock'n'Roll*, where he cites Genesis 9:3 ("Every moving thing that liveth shall be meat for you") and Genesis 27:3 ("Now therefore take, I pray thee, thy weapons, thy quiver and thy bow, and go out and take me some venison").

19. Herzog and McGee, "Psychological Aspects of Slaughter," 130.

20. Frommer and Arluke, "Loving Them to Death."

21. Robbins, *Diet for a New America*, 133.

22. Serpell, *In the Company of Animals*, 158–59.

23. Swan, *In Defense of Hunting*, 274. See chapter 3 for other examples of hunters' euphemisms for the killing they do.

24. On NBC's *Dateline*, December 20, 1994.

25. Shelter worker quoted in Frommer and Arluke, "Loving Them to Death."

26. *Philadelphia Inquirer*, May 31, 1984.

27. Vyvyan, *In Pity and in Anger*, 133.

28. Quoted at ibid.

29. Aldhous, "A Leap into Controversy."

30. Beck, "Scott Bakula Goes Ape."

31. Vivisectors do not unanimously support this tactic. See Blum, *Monkey Wars*, 160–62.

32. Culliton, "Can Reason Defeat Unreason?"

33. *Deer and Deer Hunting*, October 1991, 51.

34. "Archery Wounding Loss in Texas," Texas Parks and Wildlife Department, 1986.

35. Norm Montague, chairman of the Animal Welfare Committee, National Pork Producers Council, on the videotape *Animal Welfare*, produced by the National Pork Producers Council, 1991.

36. See Mason and Singer, *Animal Factories*.

37. *The Animals' Film*, section on factory farming, available from PETA.

38. Singer, *Animal Liberation*, 2nd ed., 105.

39. *Animals' Film*.

40. Robbins, *Diet for a New America,* 128.

41. Ibid., 127.

42. Lindbergh, *Midnight Farm.*

43. Phillips, "Proper Names and the Social Construction of Biography," 134.

44. Rutledge, *Hunting and Home in the Southern Heartland,* 30.

45. Collard, *Rape of the Wild,* 59.

46. Arluke, "We Build a Better Beagle."

47. Arluke, "Moral Elevation in Medical Research," 198, 201.

48. *Inside Biosearch,* PETA videotape.

49. From Regan and Singer, *Animal Rights and Human Obligations,* 66.

50. Quoted in Singer, *Animal Liberation,* 2nd ed., 201–2.

51. Adams, *Sexual Politics of Meat.*

52. Lynch, "Sacrifice and the Transformation of the Animal Body," 269–70.

53. *Farmer and Stockbreeder,* quoted at Mason and Singer, *Animal Factories,* 1.

54. *Hog Farm Management,* quoted at ibid.

55. Serpell, *In the Company of Animals,* pt. 4.

56. Arluke, "Moral Elevation in Medical Research," 197.

57. Thompson, "Hanging Tongues."

58. Ibid., 232.

59. Ibid., 235.

60. Rifkin, *Beyond Beef,* 129.

61. Hallinan, *Going Up the River,* 149.

62. Sperling, *Animal Liberators,* 8; see chapter 1.

63. Ibid., 6, 12.

64. Thompson, "Hanging Tongues," 215.

65. Adams, *Neither Man nor Beast,* 33–37.

66. See http://www.mypyramid.gov for the latest food pyramid; see also http://www.mypyramid.org for a satirical critique.

67. Robbins, *Diet for a New America,* 189–200.

68. *Animal Welfare* videotape, National Pork Producers Council.

69. Sharpe, *Cruel Deception.* See chapter 5 for further discussion of the claims of modern medicine.

70. See chapter 1.

71. Wieder, "Behavioristic Operationalism and the Life-World."

72. Hearne, *Adam's Task,* 6. By "eliciting interesting behavior" she means getting the animals to work for humans.

73. Personal communication, Ingrid Newkirk.

74. Rollin, *Animal Rights and Human Morality,* 109–10.

75. Compare Sperling, *Animal Liberators,* 5–8.

76. Rollin, *Animal Rights and Human Morality,* 110.

77. Arluke, "Uneasiness Among Laboratory Technicians."

78. Ibid., 34, 38.

79. See Arluke and Sanders, *Regarding Animals,* chap. 5.
80. HBO documentary, *To Love or Kill: Man vs. Animal.*
81. Swan, *In Defense of Hunting,* 33.
82. Kerasote, "Restoring the Older Knowledge," 291.
83. Williams, "Disciplining Animals."
84. Ibid., 52, 53.
85. Grandin, *Animals in Translation,* back cover.
86. Ibid., 1, 5, 46, 115, 307.
87. Ibid., 7.
88. Around 36 million cattle are slaughtered in the United States per year (http://www.armedia.org/farmstats.htm) (accessed January 21, 2007), and 3.5 million in Canada (http://www.canfax.ca) (accessed January 21, 2007).
89. Grandin, *Animals in Translation,* 179, 307.
90. Ibid., 20–21, 30.

Chapter 7: The Politics of Animal Liberation

1. See Robbins, *Diet for a New America;* Robbins, *Realities for the 90's;* and Durning, "Fat of the Land."
2. See, for example, Hill, *Case for Vegetarianism,* and Adams, *Neither Man nor Beast.*
3. Gruzalski, "Case Against Raising and Killing Animals for Food," 262–65 (a ripple effect that may be multiplied by being extraverted about our diets; see Singer, *Animal Liberation,* 2nd ed., 162).
4. Singer, "Utilitarianism and Vegetarianism," 334–36.
5. Grandin, *Animals in Translation,* 180.
6. Rifkin, *Beyond Beef,* 78, 83.
7. Winders and Nibert, "Consuming the Surplus."
8. Adams, *Sexual Politics of Meat,* 42.
9. See the UN's January 2002 Food and Agriculture Organization report at http://www.fao.org/FOCUS/E/obesity/obes2.htm (accessed January 21, 2007).
10. Stephens, "Five Arguments for Vegetarianism."
11. "McVeigh Suggests PETA Take Up Cause with Kaczynski," Associated Press, April 17, 2001.
12. See Hudson, "Collective Responsibility and Moral Vegetarianism," 100–102.
13. Salim Muwakkil, "Food Pyramid Scheme," *In These Times,* August 7, 2000, 19–21.
14. See Singer, "Utilitarianism and Vegetarianism," 336–37.
15. Amory, *Man Kind?* 128.
16. Ibid., 356.
17. Gilligan, *In a Different Voice.*
18. Francione, *Introduction to Animal Rights,* 4–5.

19. Lorenz, *On Life and Living*, 113.
20. Adams, "Ecofeminism and the Eating of Animals," 134.
21. Anna Kingsford, quoted in Vyvyan, *In Pity and in Anger*, 122–23.
22. Regan, *Thee Generation*, 95.
23. Ibid.
24. Singer, *Animal Liberation*, 270.
25. Singer, *Expanding Circle*.
26. Collard, *Rape of the Wild*, 70.
27. Quoted at Groves, *Hearts and Minds*, 141.
28. Kerasote, *Bloodties*, 251.
29. Singer, *Animal Liberation*, viii.
30. Quoted at Cartmill, *View to a Death in the Morning*, 181.
31. Regan, "Bird in the Cage," 95.
32. Slicer, "Your Daughter or Your Dog?" 115.
33. Collard, *Rape of the Wild*, 96.
34. Donovan, "Animal Rights and Feminist Theory," 353.
35. Kheel, "Liberation of Nature," 143. Alternatively, the rationalistic writers may be unwittingly dependent on convention or authority to gain assent to their initial intuitions (see below for an instance of deference to authority). In any case, at these points reason has run out. For a fuller explanation of how the purely rationalistic arguments for animal liberation fail, see Luke, "From Animal Rights to Animal Liberation," 100–102.
36. Regan, "Search for a New Global Ethic," 40.
37. Regan, "Bird in the Cage," 93.
38. Regan begins his book with the quote, "Every great movement must experience three stages: ridicule, discussion, adoption," and he often adverts to the "growing intellectual respectability of exploring the moral status of animals" (Regan, *All That Dwell Therein*, 113).
39. Singer, *Animal Liberation*, ix.
40. See examples on page 30.
41. Donovan, "Animal Rights and Feminist Theory," 351. And Collard (*Rape of the Wild*, 97) links Singer's insistence that he does not love animals (*Animal Liberation*, 2nd ed., ii) with a "fear of appearing too 'soft.'"
42. Quoted in Kheel, "From Heroic to Holistic Ethics," 262.
43. Regan, *All That Dwell Therein*, 113.
44. Singer, *Practical Ethics*, 48.
45. Adams, *Neither Man nor Beast*, 199.
46. Singer, *Practical Ethics*, 55.
47. Quoted in Vyvyan, *In Pity and in Anger*, 121.
48. Groves, *Hearts and Minds*, 144.
49. Ibid., 147.
50. Seager, *Earth Follies*, 202.

51. Ibid., 203.

52. For these and all the other examples discussed in this section, see http://www.peta.org/mc.

53. PETA decided not to air this ad, because, in their words, it was "too shocking in the aftermath of September 11." As of January 21, 2007, it remains posted on their web site (http://www.petatv.com) in the video archive under "Fur Is Dead."

54. Adams, *Pornography of Meat*, 166.

55. Craft, "PeTA: Where Only Women Are Treated Like Meat."

56. See the comments posted at http://www.nostatusquo.com/ACLU/PETA/peta .html (accessed January 21, 2007).

57. Adams, *Pornography of Meat*, 166.

58. See Adams, "Feminist Analysis."

59. Straight white males are very occasionally posed nude in PETA ads but never placed in the "about to be acted upon" position favored in pornographic images of women. See the Adam and Eve scenario featuring Jenna Morasca and Ethan Zohn (actors from the television show *Survivor*); see also the poster of David Cross naked on the runway, which has a mocking quality typically used when straight white men adopt cheesecake poses.

60. Posted at http://www.peta.org/mc/NewsItem.asp?id=6921, as of January 21, 2007, under the headline, "Naked Woman—Chained and 'Beaten'—Protests Ring-ling's Arrival in Fargo."

61. Posted at http://www.nostatusquo.com/ACLU/PETA/peta.html, as of January 21, 2007, and reprinted here with minor corrections for spelling.

62. See Adams, *Sexual Politics of Meat*, cover, and Adams, *Pornography of Meat*, 162.

63. Adams, *Pornography of Meat*, 169.

64. Dominic Fox, at http://www.nostatusquo.com/ACLU/PETA/peta.html.

65. Singer, *Expanding Circle*, 169–73.

66. Ibid., 171–2.

67. Regan, *Thee Generation*, 95; Singer, *Animal Liberation*, 2nd ed., iii, 243.

68. Singer, *Expanding Circle*, 114.

69. Ibid., 144–46.

70. Ibid., 173, 94, 169, 131, 99.

71. In Paterson and Ryder, *Animals' Rights*, 210.

72. Hoagland, *Lesbian Ethics*, 285.

73. Kropotkin, *Anarchist Morality*, section VIII.

74. Addelson, *Impure Thoughts*, 151.

75. Gilligan, *In a Different Voice*, 38.

76. See, for example, Sapontzis, *Morals, Reason, and Animals*; Robbins, *Diet for a New America*; Sujithammaraksa, *Agent-Based Morality*; Phelps, *Great Compassion*; and McCarthy, "At Rest with the Animals."

77. Sewell, *Black Beauty*, 67; emphasis added.

78. Levi, *If This Is a Man*, 119–22.
79. Bacon, *Philosophical Works*, 586.
80. Sewell, *Black Beauty*, 67.

Note on Photographs

1. See http://www.coleman-family.org/frederick_coleman_story.html (accessed January 21, 2007).

Bibliography

Abbott, Jack Henry. *In the Belly of the Beast: Letters from Prison.* New York: Vintage Books, 1991.

Achor, Amy. *Animal Rights: A Beginner's Guide.* Yellow Springs, Ohio: WriteWare, 1996.

Adams, Carol. *The Sexual Politics of Meat: A Feminist-Vegetarian Critical Theory.* New York: Continuum, 1990.

———. "Ecofeminism and the Eating of Animals." *Hypatia* 6 (1991): 125–45.

———. "A Feminist Analysis of 'I'd Rather Go Naked than Wear Fur.'" *Feminists for Animal Rights Newsletter* 8, nos. 3–4 (1994): 1–8.

———. *Neither Man nor Beast: Feminism and the Defense of Animals.* New York: Continuum, 1994.

———. *The Pornography of Meat.* New York: Continuum, 2003.

Adams, Carol, and Josephine Donovan, eds. *Animals and Women: Feminist Theoretical Explorations.* Durham, N.C.: Duke University Press, 1995.

Aesop. *Aesop's Fables.* Franklin, Tenn.: Naxos Audiobooks, 2000.

Aldhous, Peter. "A Leap into Controversy." *Nature* 352 (1991): 463.

Amato, Paul, and Sonia Partridge. *The New Vegetarians: Promoting Health and Protecting Life.* New York: Plenum Press, 1989.

American Medical Association. *Use of Animals in Biomedical Research: The Challenge and Response.* AMA White Paper. Chicago: AMA, 1988.

Amory, Cleveland. *Man Kind? Our Incredible War on Wildlife.* New York: Harper & Row, 1974.

Anders, Timothy. *The Evolution of Evil.* Chicago: Open Court, 1994.

Ardrey, Robert. *African Genesis: A Personal Investigation into Animal Origins and the Nature of Man.* New York: Atheneum, 1961.

Arluke, Arnold. "Moral Elevation in Medical Research." *Advances in Medical Sociology* 1 (1990): 189–204.

———. "Uneasiness Among Laboratory Technicians." *Lab Animal* 19 (1990): 20–39.

———. "'We Build a Better Beagle': Fantastic Creatures in Lab Animal Ads." *Qualitative Sociology* 17 (1994): 143–58.

Arluke, Arnold, and Clinton Sanders. *Regarding Animals.* Philadelphia: Temple University Press, 1996.

Aspinall, John. *The Best of Friends.* New York: Harper & Row, 1976.

Association for the Advancement of Medicine by Research (AAMR). "Facts and Considerations Relating to the Practice of Scientific Experiments on Living Animals, Commonly Called Vivisection." *Nature* 27 (1883): 542–46.

Ayars, Kathryn. "Coming to Terms with Hunting." *Pittsburgh Post-Gazette,* December 20, 1989, Op-Ed page.

Bacon, Francis. *The Philosophical Works of Francis Bacon.* London: George Routledge and Sons, 1905.

Baker, Ron. *The American Hunting Myth.* New York: Vantage Press, 1985.

Barry, Kathleen. *The Prostitution of Sexuality.* New York: New York University Press, 1995.

Barstow, Anne Llewellyn. *Witchcraze: A New History of the European Witch Hunts.* San Francisco: Pandora, 1994.

Barth, Karl. *The Teaching of the Church Regarding Baptism.* London: SCM Press, 1948.

Bass, Rick. "An Appeal to Hunters." In Petersen, 191–99.

Beck, Alan. "Animals in the City." In Katcher and Beck, 237–43.

Beck, Alan, and Aaron Katcher. *Between Pets and People: The Importance of Animal Companionship.* West Lafayette, Ind.: Purdue University Press, 1996.

Beck, Marilyn. "Scott Bakula Goes Ape on NBC's *Quantum Leap.*" *TV Guide* 39, no. 29 (1991): 17.

Bekoff, Marc, ed. *Encyclopedia of Animal Rights and Animal Welfare.* Westport, Conn.: Greenwood Press, 1998.

Bekoff, Marc, and Dale Jamieson. "Sport Hunting as an Instinct." *Environmental Ethics* 13 (1991): 375–78.

Beneke, Timothy. *Men on Rape.* New York: St. Martin's Press, 1982.

Bernard, Claude. *An Introduction to the Study of Experimental Medicine.* New York: Collier Books, 1961.

Bernstein, Mark. *Without a Tear: Our Tragic Relationship with Animals.* Urbana: University of Illinois Press, 2004.

Beston, Henry. *The Outermost House: A Year of Life on the Great Beach of Cape Cod.* New York: Viking Press, 1962.

Birke, Lynda. "Intimate Familiarities? Feminism and Human-Animal Studies." *Society and Animals* 10, no. 4 (2002): 429–36.

Blum, Deborah. *The Monkey Wars.* Oxford: Oxford University Press, 1994.

Bourjaily, Vance. *The Unnatural Enemy.* New York: Dial Press, 1963.

Brockett, Lorna. *The Theology of Baptism.* Notre Dame: Fides, 1971.

Broida, John, Leanne Tingley, Robert Kimball, and Joseph Miele. "Personality Differences between Pro- and Anti-Vivisectionists." *Society and Animals* 1, no. 2 (1993): 129–44.

Cain, Ann Ottney. "A Study of Pets in the Family System." In Katcher and Beck, 72–81.

Callicott, J. Baird. *In Defense of the Land Ethic: Essays in Environmental Philosophy.* Albany: State University of New York Press, 1989.

Cantor, Aviva. "The Club, the Yoke, and the Leash: What We Can Learn from the Way a Culture Treats Animals." *Ms.* 12, no. 2 (August 1983): 27–30.

Cartmill, Matt. *A View to a Death in the Morning: Hunting and Nature through History.* Cambridge: Harvard University Press, 1993.

Causey, Ann. "On the Morality of Hunting." *Environmental Ethics* 11 (1989): 327–43.

Chinn, Linda. "Where Does All the Money Go?" *Traditional Bowhunter* 6, no. 3 (1994): 70–71.

Clark, Stephen. *The Moral Status of Animals.* Oxford: Oxford University Press, 1977.

———. "The Rights of Wild Things." *Inquiry* 22 (1979): 171–88.

Collard, Andrée, with Joyce Contrucci. *Rape of the Wild: Man's Violence Against Animals and the Earth.* Bloomington: Indiana University Press, 1989.

Commodities and Trade Division. *World Statistical Compendium for Raw Hides and Skins, Leather and Leather Footwear, 1974–1992.* Rome: Food and Agriculture Organization of the United Nations, 1994.

Corea, Gena. *The Mother Machine: Reproductive Technologies from Artificial Insemination to Artificial Wombs.* London: Women's Press, 1985.

Cowen, Tyler. "Policing Nature." *Environmental Ethics* 25 (Summer 2003): 169–82.

Craft, Nikki. "PeTA: Where Only Women Are Treated Like Meat." At www.nostatusquo.com/ACLU/PETA/peta.html.

Culliton, Barbara. "Can Reason Defeat Unreason?" *Nature* 351 (1991): 517.

Cunningham, Andrew, and Perry Williams, eds. *The Laboratory Revolution in Medicine.* Cambridge: Cambridge University Press, 1992.

Cuttaz, Françoise. *Baptism: Divine Birth.* New York: Alba House, 1962.

Dahles, Heidi. "Game Killing and Killing Games: An Anthropologist Looking at Hunting in a Modern Society." *Society and Animals* 1, no. 2 (1993): 169–84.

Dalrymple, Byron. *Deer Hunting with Dalrymple.* New York: Arco, 1983.

Darwall, Stephen, ed. *Contractarianism/Contractualism.* Malden, Mass.: Blackwell, 2003.

DeGrazia, David. *Taking Animals Seriously: Mental Life and Moral Status.* Cambridge: Cambridge University Press, 1996.

Dizard, Jan. *Mortal Stakes: Hunters and Hunting in Contemporary America.* Amherst: University of Massachusetts Press, 2003.

Dombrowski, Daniel. "Comment on Pluhar." *Between the Species* 7 (1991).

———. *Babies and Beasts: The Argument from Marginal Cases.* Urbana: University of Illinois Press, 1997.

Donahue, Keith. *The Stolen Child.* New York: Doubleday, 2006.

Donovan, Josephine. "Animal Rights and Feminist Theory." *Signs* 15 (1990): 350–75.

Doyle, Arthur Conan. *The Hound of the Baskervilles.* In *The Complete Sherlock Holmes,* vol. 2. Garden City, N.Y.: Doubleday, 1930.

Drews, Carlos. "Wild Animals and Other Pets Kept in Costa Rican Households: Incidence, Species and Numbers." *Society and Animals* 9, no. 2 (2001): 107–26.

Dunayer, Joan. "Sexist Words, Speciesist Roots." In Adams and Donovan, 11–31.

———. *Animal Equality: Language and Liberation.* Derwood, Md.: Ryce Publishing, 2001.

Durning, Alan. "Fat of the Land." *World Watch* 4 (May/June 1991): 11–17.

Dworkin, Andrea. *Right-Wing Women.* New York: Perigee, 1983.

———. *Pornography: Men Possessing Women.* New York: E. P. Dutton, 1989.

Easlea, Brian. *Witch-hunting, Magic and the New Philosophy: An Introduction to the Debates of the Scientific Revolution 1450–1750.* Atlantic Highlands, N.J.: Humanities Press, 1980.

Ehrenreich, Barbara. *Blood Rites: Origins and History of the Passions of War.* New York: Metropolitan Books, 1997.

Ehrenreich, Barbara, and Deirdre English. *For Her Own Good: 150 Years of the Experts' Advice to Women.* Garden City, N.Y.: Anchor Books, 1978.

Einwohner, Rachel. "Gender, Class, and Social Movement Outcomes: Identity and Effectiveness in Two Animal Rights Campaigns." *Gender and Society* 13 (February 1999): 56–76.

Everett, Jennifer. "Environmental Ethics, Animal Welfarism, and the Problem of Predation: A Bambi Lover's Respect for Nature." *Ethics and the Environment* 6 (2001): 42–67.

Farrington, Benjamin. *The Philosophy of Francis Bacon.* Chicago: University of Chicago Press, 1964.

Fein, Ellen, and Sherrie Schneider. *The Rules: Time-tested Secrets for Capturing the Heart of Mr. Right.* New York: Warner Books, 1995.

Fergus, Jim. *A Hunter's Road: A Journey with Gun and Dog Across the American Uplands.* New York: Henry Holt, 1992.

Fiddes, Nick. *Meat: A Natural Symbol.* London: Routledge, 1991.

Finucci, Valeria, and Kevin Brownlee, eds. *Generation and Degeneration: Tropes of Reproduction in Literature and History from Antiquity through Early Modern Europe.* Durham, N.C.: Duke University Press, 2001.

Fischer, Larry. Review of *Whitetail Magic* by Roger Rothhaar. *Traditional Bowhunter* 6, no. 3 (1994): 71.

Fox, Michael. *Returning to Eden: Animal Rights and Human Responsibility.* New York: Viking Press, 1980.

Francione, Gary. *Rain Without Thunder: The Ideology of the Animal Rights Movement.* Philadelphia: Temple University Press, 1996.

———. *Introduction to Animal Rights: Your Child or the Dog?* Philadelphia: Temple University Press, 2000.

Franklin, Benjamin. *Autobiography.* New York: Bobbs-Merrill, 1952.

Franklin, Julian. *Animal Rights and Moral Philosophy.* New York: Columbia University Press, 2005.

French, Richard. *Antivivisection and Medical Science in Victorian Society.* Princeton, N.J.: Princeton University Press, 1975.

Frommer, Stephanie, and Arnold Arluke. "Loving Them to Death: Blame-Displacing Strategies of Animal Shelter Workers and Surrenderers." *Society and Animals* 7, no. 1 (1999): 1–16.

Galvin, Shelley, and Harold Herzog Jr. "Ethical Ideology, Animal Activism and Attitudes Toward the Treatment of Animals." *Ethics and Behavior* 2 (1992): 141–49.

Geach, Peter. *Providence and Evil.* Cambridge: Cambridge University Press, 1977.

Geison, Gerald. *The Private Science of Louis Pasteur.* Princeton, N.J.: Princeton University Press, 1995.

Geist, Valerius. *Mountain Sheep and Man in the Northern Wilds.* Ithaca: Cornell University Press, 1975.

Gilligan, Carol. *In a Different Voice: Psychological Theory and Women's Development.* Cambridge: Harvard University Press, 1982.

Girard, René. *The Girard Reader.* Edited by James Williams. New York: Crossroad, 1996.

Gish, Robert Franklin. *Songs of My Hunter Heart: A Western Kinship.* Albuquerque: University of New Mexico Press, 1992.

Gollaher, David. *Circumcision: A History of the World's Most Controversial Surgery.* New York: Basic Books, 2000.

Gorner, Peter. "Wild Crows on Pacific Island Use Tools." *Chicago Tribune,* January 18, 1996.

Grandin, Temple, and Catherine Johnson. *Animals in Translation: Using the Mysteries of Autism to Decode Animal Behavior.* New York: Scribner, 2005.

Graves, Robert, and Raphael Patai. *Hebrew Myths: The Book of Genesis.* New York: McGraw-Hill, 1963.

Greek, C. Ray, and Jean Swingle Greek. *Sacred Cows and Golden Geese: The Human Cost of Experiments on Animals.* New York: Continuum, 2000.

Groves, Julian. *Hearts and Minds: The Controversy Over Laboratory Animals.* Philadelphia: Temple University Press, 1997.

Gruzalski, Bart. "The Case Against Raising and Killing Animals for Food." In Miller and Williams, 251–65.

Halliburton, Richard. *The Royal Road to Romance.* Indianapolis: Bobbs-Merrill, 1925.

Hallinan, Joseph. *Going Up the River: Travels in a Prison Nation.* New York: Random House, 2001.

Hamm, Jim, ed. *The Traditional Bowyer's Bible.* Vol. 1. Azle, Tex.: Bois d'Arc Press, 1992.

Harding, Sandra. *The Science Question in Feminism.* Ithaca, N.Y.: Cornell University Press, 1986.

Hargrove, Eugene, ed. *The Animal Rights/Environmental Ethics Debate: The Environmental Perspective.* Albany: State University of New York Press, 1992.

Haught, James. "Why Would God Drown Children?" *Free Inquiry* 25, no. 3 (April/May 2005): 14–15.

Hearne, Vicki. *Adam's Task: Calling Animals by Name.* New York: Knopf, 1986.

Herzog, Harold, Jr., and Sandy McGee. "Psychological Aspects of Slaughter: Reactions of College Students to Killing and Butchering Cattle and Hogs." *International Journal for the Study of Animal Problems* 4 (1983): 124–32.

Herzog, Harold, Jr., Nancy Betchart, and Robert Pittman. "Gender, Sex Role Orientation, and Attitudes Toward Animals." *Anthrozoös* 4 (1991): 184–91.

Hettinger, Ned. "Valuing Predation in Rolston's Environmental Ethic: Bambi Lovers versus Tree Huggers." *Environmental Ethics* 16 (1994): 3–20.

Hick, John. *Evil and the God of Love.* London: Collins, 1966.

Hill, John Lawrence. *The Case for Vegetarianism: Philosophy for a Small Planet.* Lanham, Md.: Rowman & Littlefield, 1996.

Hills, Adelma. "The Motivational Bases of Attitudes Toward Animals." *Society & Animals* 1, no. 2 (1993): 111–28.

Hoage, R. J., ed. *Perceptions of Animals in American Culture.* Washington, D.C.: Smithsonian Institution Press, 1989.

Hoffman, Lawrence. *Covenant of Blood: Circumcision and Gender in Rabbinic Judaism.* Chicago: University of Chicago Press, 1996.

Horney, Karen. *Feminine Psychology.* New York: W. W. Norton, 1967.

Houston, Pam, ed. *Women on Hunting.* Hopewell, N.J.: Ecco Press, 1995.

Hubert, Henri, and Marcel Mauss. *Sacrifice: Its Nature and Function.* Chicago: University of Chicago Press, 1964.

Hudson, Hud. "Collective Responsibility and Moral Vegetarianism." *Journal of Social Philosophy* 24 (1993): 89–104.

Hugo, Victor. *The Alps and Pyrenees.* London: Bliss, Sands, 1898.

Hummel, Richard. *Hunting and Fishing for Sport: Commerce, Controversy, Popular Culture.* Bowling Green, Ohio: Bowling Green State University Popular Press, 1994.

Hunt, Gavin. "Manufacture and Use of Hook-Tools by New Caledonian Crows." *Nature* 379 (1996): 249–51.

Hurst, Blake. "Me Man, Me Hunt!" *American Enterprise* (September 2003): 41–43.

Jacobs, Alan. "In on the Kill." *First Things* 70 (1997): 17–19.

Jasper, James, and Dorothy Nelkin. *The Animal Rights Crusade: The Growth of a Moral Protest.* New York: Free Press, 1991.

Jay, Nancy. *Throughout Your Generations Forever: Sacrifice, Religion, and Paternity.* Chicago: University of Chicago Press, 1992.

Jeffreys, Sheila. *Anticlimax: A Feminist Perspective on the Sexual Revolution.* New York: New York University Press, 1990.

Jerolmack, Colin. "Tracing the Profile of Animal Rights Supporters: A Preliminary Investigation." *Society and Animals* 11, no. 3 (2003): 245–63.

Johnson, Lawrence. *A Morally Deep World: An Essay on Moral Significance and Environmental Ethics.* Cambridge: Cambridge University Press, 1991.

Jolma, Dena. "Why They Quit: Thoughts from Ex-Hunters." *Animals' Agenda* (July/Aug. 1992): 38–40.

Joreen. "The Bitch Manifesto." In *Radical Feminism,* edited by Anne Koedt, Ellen Levine, and Anita Rapone, 50–59. New York: Quadrangle, 1973.

Kafka, Franz. *Letter to His Father.* New York: Schocken Books, 1953.

Kalechofsky, Roberta. *Autobiography of a Revolutionary: Essays on Animal and Human Rights.* Marblehead, Mass.: Micah Publications, 1991.

Kalof, Linda, Amy Fitzgerald, and Lori Baralt. "Animals, Women and Weapons: Blurred Sexual Boundaries in the Discourse of Sport Hunting." *Society and Animals* 12, no. 3 (2004): 237–51.

Kappeler, Susanne. *The Pornography of Representation.* Minneapolis: University of Minnesota Press, 1986.

Katcher, Aaron. "How Companion Animals Make Us Feel." In Hoage, 113–28.

Katcher, Aaron, and Alan Beck, eds. *New Perspectives on Our Lives with Companion Animals.* Philadelphia: University of Pennsylvania Press, 1983.

Kaufman, Stephen. "Does Vivisection Pass the Utilitarian Test?" *Public Affairs Quarterly* 9 (1995): 127–37.

Keller, Evelyn Fox. *Secrets of Life, Secrets of Death: Essays on Language, Gender, and Science.* New York: Routledge, 1992.

Kellert, Stephen. *Activities of the American Public Relating to Animals.* Washington, D.C.: GPO, 1980.

———. *Knowledge, Affection and Basic Attitudes Toward Animals in American Society.* Washington, D.C.: GPO, 1980.

———. "American Attitudes Toward and Knowledge of Animals: An Update." *International Journal for the Study of Animal Problems* 1, no. 2 (1980): 87–119.

———. "Perceptions of Animals in America." In Hoage, 5–24.

———. *The Value of Life: Biological Diversity and Human Society.* Washington, D.C.: Island Press, 1996.

Kellert, Stephen, and J. Berry. "Attitudes, Knowledge, and Behaviors Toward Wildlife as Affected by Gender." *Wildlife Society Bulletin* 15 (Fall 1987): 363–71.

Kerasote, Ted. *Bloodties: Nature, Culture, and the Hunt.* New York: Kodansha, 1993.

———. "The Spirit of Hunting: What Native Americans Knew." *Sports Afield* 211, no. 6 (1994): 52–60.

———. "Restoring the Older Knowledge." In Petersen, 284–94.

Kheel, Marti. "The Liberation of Nature: A Circular Affair." *Environmental Ethics* 7 (1985): 135–49.

———. "Women, Ethics, and Anima(l)s." Master's thesis, Antioch University, 1986.

———. "From Healing Herbs to Deadly Drugs: Western Medicine's War against the Natural World." In *Healing the Wounds: The Promise of Ecofeminism,* edited by Judith Plant, 96–111. Philadelphia: New Society Publishers, 1989.

———. "From Heroic to Holistic Ethics: The Ecofeminist Challenge." In *Ecofeminism: Women, Animals, Nature,* edited by Greta Gaard, 243–71. Philadelphia: Temple University Press, 1993.

———. "License to Kill: An Ecofeminist Critique of Hunters' Discourse." In Adams and Donovan, 85–125.

King, Roger. "Environmental Ethics and the Case for Hunting." *Environmental Ethics* 13 (1991): 59–85.

Kingston, Lyle. *On Behalf of the Hunted.* Appleton, Wisc.: C. C. Nelson, 1955.

Kistler, John. *People Promoting and People Opposing Animal Rights: In Their Own Words.* Westport, Conn.: Greenwood Press, 2002.

Kittay, Eva Feder. "Womb Envy: An Explanatory Concept." In *Mothering: Essays in Feminist Theory,* edited by Joyce Trebilcot, 94–128. Savage, Md.: Rowman & Littlefield, 1983.

Klug, Brian. "Lab Animals, Francis Bacon and the Culture of Science." *Listening* 18 (1983): 54–72.

Knight, Sarah, Karl Nunkoosing, Aldert Vrij, and Julie Cherryman. "Using Grounded Theory to Examine People's Attitudes Toward How Animals are Used." *Society and Animals* 11, no. 4 (2003): 307–27.

Kohlberg, Lawrence. "From Is to Ought." In *Cognitive Development and Epistemology,* edited by Theodore Mischel, 151–235. New York: Academic Press, 1971.

Kropotkin, Peter. *Anarchist Morality.* San Francisco: Free Society, 1898.

Kruse, Corwin. "Gender, Views of Nature, and Support for Animal Rights." *Society and Animals* 7, no. 3 (1999): 179–88.

LaFollette, Hugh, and Niall Shanks. "Animal Models in Biomedical Research: Some Epistemological Worries." *Public Affairs Quarterly* 7 (1993): 113–30.

Lansbury, Coral. *The Old Brown Dog: Women, Workers, and Vivisection in Edwardian England.* Madison: University of Wisconsin Press, 1985.

Lawson, Helene. "Controlling the Wilderness: The Work of Wilderness Officers." *Society and Animals* 11, no. 4 (2003): 329–51.

Lea, Sydney. *Hunting the Whole Way Home.* Hanover, N.H.: University Press of New England, 1994.

Leahy, Michael. *Against Liberation: Putting Animals in Perspective.* London: Routledge, 1991.

Lederer, Susan. *Subjected to Science: Human Experimentation in America Before the Second World War.* Baltimore: Johns Hopkins University Press, 1995.

Lindbergh, Reeve. *The Midnight Farm.* New York: Dial Books for Young Readers, 1987.

Linzey, Andrew. *Animal Rights: A Christian Assessment of Man's Treatment of Animals.* London: SCM Press, 1976.

———. *Christianity and the Rights of Animals.* New York: Crossroad, 1987.

Loeb, J. M., W. R. Hendee, S. J. Smith, and M. R. Schwartz. "Human vs. Animal Rights: In Defense of Animal Research." *JAMA* 262, no. 19 (November 17, 1989): 2716–20.

Loftin, Robert. "The Morality of Hunting." *Environmental Ethics* 6 (1984): 241–50.

Lopez, Barry. *Arctic Dreams: Imagination and Desire in a Northern Landscape.* New York: Charles Scribner's Sons, 1986.

Lorenz, Konrad. *The Foundations of Ethology.* New York: Springer-Verlag, 1981.

———. *On Life and Living.* New York: St. Martin's Press, 1988.

Luke, Brian. "From Animal Rights to Animal Liberation: An Anarchistic Approach to Inter-Species Morality." Ph.D. diss., University of Pittsburgh, 1992.

———. "Solidarity Across Diversity: A Pluralistic Rapprochement of Environmentalism and Animal Liberation." *Social Theory and Practice* 21, no. 2 (1995): 177–206.

———. "Taming Ourselves or Going Feral? Toward a Nonpatriarchal Metaethic of Animal Liberation." In Adams and Donovan, 290–319.

———. "Animal Experimentation as Blood Sacrifice." *International Society for Anthrozoology Newsletter* 12 (1996): 4–7.

———. "Justice, Caring, and Animal Liberation." In *Beyond Animal Rights: A Feminist Caring Ethic for the Treatment of Animals,* edited by Josephine Donovan and Carol Adams, 77–102. New York: Continuum, 1996.

———. "A Critical Analysis of Hunters' Ethics." *Environmental Ethics* 19, no. 1 (1997): 25–44.

———. "Violent Love: Hunting, Heterosexuality, and the Erotics of Men's Predation." *Feminist Studies* 24, no. 3 (1998): 627–55.

———. "Animal Sacrifice: A Model of Paternal Exploitation." *International Journal of Sociology and Social Policy* 24, no. 9 (2004): 18–44.

Lynch, Michael. "Sacrifice and the Transformation of the Animal Body into a Scientific Object: Laboratory Culture and Ritual Practice in the Neurosciences." *Social Studies of Science* 18 (1988): 265–89.

MacQuarrie, Gordon. *Stories of the Old Duck Hunters.* Oshkosh, Wisc.: Willow Creek Press, 1985.

Manes, Christopher. *Other Creations: Rediscovering the Spirituality of Animals.* New York: Doubleday, 1997.

Marks, Stuart. *Southern Hunting in Black and White: Nature, History, and Ritual in a Carolina Community.* Princeton, N.J.: Princeton University Press, 1991.

Mason, Jim. *An Unnatural Order: Uncovering the Roots of Our Domination of Nature and Each Other.* New York: Simon and Schuster, 1993.

Mason, Jim, and Peter Singer. *Animal Factories.* New York: Harmony Books, 1990.

McCarthy, Colman. "At Rest with the Animals." In *All of One Peace: Essays on Nonviolence,* by Colman McCarthy, 157–83. New Brunswick, N.J.: Rutgers University Press, 1994.

McDaniel, Jo Beth. "Won't Somebody Please Save This Whale?" *Life* 16 (November 1993): 46–56.

McIntyre, Thomas. *The Way of the Hunter: The Art and the Spirit of Modern Hunting.* New York: Dutton, 1988.

———. *Dreaming the Lion: Reflections on Hunting, Fishing, and a Search for the Wild.* Traverse City, Mich.: Countrysport Press, 1993.

Meeks, Wayne, ed. *The HarperCollins Study Bible.* New York: HarperCollins, 1993.

Menache, Sophia. "Dogs and Human Beings: A Story of Friendship." *Society and Animals* 6, no. 1 (1998): 67–86.

Menninger, Karl. "Totemic Aspects of Contemporary Attitudes Towards Animals." In *Psychoanalysis and Culture: Essays in Honor of Geza Roheim,* edited by George Wilbur and Warner Muensterberger, 42–74. New York: International Universities Press, 1951.

Milgram, Stanley. "Some Conditions of Obedience and Disobedience to Authority." *Human Relations* 18 (1965): 57–76.

Miller, Harlan, and William Williams, eds. *Ethics and Animals.* Clifton, N.J.: Humana Press, 1983.

Miller, Kenneth. "All This for One Whale?" *Life* 21 (November 1998): 57–64.

Milloy, Steven. "Laboratory Animal Farm." Fox News at www.foxnews.com (February 23, 2001).

Mitchell, John. *The Hunt.* New York: Knopf, 1980.

Moriarty, Paul, and Mark Woods. "Hunting Does Not Equal Predation." *Environmental Ethics* 18 (1997): 391–404.

Munro, Lyle. "Caring about Blood, Flesh, and Pain: Women's Standing in the Animal Protection Movement." *Society and Animals* 9, no. 1 (2001): 43–61.

———. *Compassionate Beasts: The Quest for Animal Rights.* Westport, Conn.: Praeger, 2001.

Nibert, David. *Animal Rights, Human Rights: Entanglements of Oppression and Liberation.* Lanham, Md.: Rowman & Littlefield, 2002.

Noble, David. *A World Without Women: The Christian Clerical Culture of Western Science.* Oxford: Oxford University Press, 1992.

Nugent, Ted. *Archer's Africa.* Produced by Ted Nugent. Videotape, 1989.

———. "Fun, Good, Clean, Fun!" *World Bowhunters Magazine* 1, no. 3 (1990): 7.

———. *Blood Trails: The Truth About Bowhunting.* Jackson, Mich.: Ted Nugent, 1991.

———. *The Spirit of the Wild.* Produced by Ted Nugent. Videotape, 1992.

———. *Spirit of the Wild Part II: A Day With the Nugent Family.* Produced by Ted Nugent. Videotape, 1993.

———. "One Way Ticket Out of Target Panic Hell." *World Bowhunters Magazine* 5, no. 1 (1994): 26–27.

———. *God, Guns, and Rock'n'Roll.* Washington, D.C.: Regnery, 2000.

O'Connor, Harrison. "Hunting on the Farm." *Gray's Sporting Journal* 9, no. 4 (1984): 14–30.

Olmsted, J. M. D. *François Magendie: Pioneer in Experimental Physiology and Scientific Medicine in XIX Century France.* New York: Schuman's, 1944.

Olmsted, J. M. D., and E. Harris Olmsted. *Claude Bernard and the Experimental Method in Medicine.* New York: Collier, 1961.

Ortega y Gasset, José. *Meditations on Hunting.* New York: Charles Scribner's Sons, 1972.

Owen, Robert. *Experimental Physiology: Its Benefits to Mankind.* London: Longmans, Green, 1882.

Paget, Stephen. *For and Against Experiments on Animals: Evidence Before the Royal Commission on Vivisection.* New York: Paul B. Hoeber, 1912.

Paley, William. *Natural Theology.* Indianapolis: Bobbs-Merrill, 1963.

Parenti, Christian. *Lockdown America: Police and Prisons in the Age of Crisis.* New York: Verso, 1999.

Patel, V. L., D. A. Evans, and G. J. Groen. "Biomedical Knowledge and Clinical Reasoning." In *Cognitive Science in Medicine,* edited by V. Patel and D. Evans. Cambridge: MIT Press, 1989.

Paterson, David, and Richard Ryder. *Animals' Rights: A Symposium.* Fontwell: Centaur Press, 1979.

Pauley, John. "The Value of Hunting." *Journal of Value Inquiry* 37, no. 2 (2003): 233–44.

Peek, Charles, Nancy Bell, and Charlotte Dunham. "Gender, Gender Ideology, and Animal Rights Advocacy." *Gender and Society* 10 (August 1996): 464–78.

Peek, Charles, Charlotte Dunham, and Bernadette Dietz. "Gender, Relational Role Orientation, and Affinity for Animal Rights." *Sex Roles* 37 (1997): 905–20.

Petersen, David, ed. *A Hunter's Heart: Honest Essays on Blood Sport.* New York: Henry Holt, 1996.

Petrinovich, Lewis. *Darwinian Dominionism: Animal Welfare and Human Interests.* Cambridge: MIT Press, 1999.

Phelps, Norm. *The Great Compassion: Buddhism and Animal Rights.* Lantern Books, 2004.

Phillips, Mary. "Proper Names and the Social Construction of Biography: The Negative Case of Laboratory Animals." *Qualitative Sociology* 17 (1994): 119–42.

Pifer, Linda. "Exploring the Gender Gap in Young Adults' Attitudes about Animal Research." *Society and Animals* 4, no. 1 (1996): 37–52.

Pifer, Linda, Kinya Shimizu, and Ralph Pifer. "Public Attitudes Toward Animal Research: Some International Comparisons." *Society and Animals* 2, no. 2 (1994): 95–113.

Plous, Scott. "Signs of Change Within the Animal Rights Movement: Results from a Follow-up Survey of Activists." *Journal of Comparative Psychology* 112 (March 1998): 48–54.

Pluhar, Evelyn. "The Joy of Killing." *Between the Species* 7 (1991): 121–28.

———. *Beyond Prejudice: The Moral Significance of Human and Nonhuman Animals.* Durham, N.C.: Duke University Press, 1995.

Posewitz, Jim. *Beyond Fair Chase: The Ethic and Tradition of Hunting.* Helena, Mont.: Falcon Press, 1994.

Preece, Rod. *Animals and Nature: Cultural Myths, Cultural Realities.* Vancouver: UBC Press, 1999.

Prejean, Helen. *Dead Man Walking.* New York: Vintage Books, 1993.

Quigley, Joseph, Lyle Vogel, and Robert Anderson. "A Study of Perceptions and Attitudes toward Pet Ownership." In Katcher and Beck, 266–75.

Rachels, James. *Created from Animals: The Moral Implications of Darwinism.* Oxford: Oxford University Press, 1990.

Raymond, Janice. "Medicine as Patriarchal Religion." *Journal of Medicine and Philosophy* 7 (1982): 197–216.

Rees, Dafydd, and Luke Crampton. *Rock Movers and Shakers.* New York: Billboard Books, 1991.

Regan, Tom. *All That Dwell Therein: Essays on Animal Rights and Environmental Ethics.* Berkeley and Los Angeles: University of California Press, 1982.

———. *The Case for Animal Rights.* Berkeley and Los Angeles: University of California Press, 1983.

———. "The Bird in the Cage: A Glimpse of My Life." *Between the Species* 2 (1986): 42–49, 90–99.

———. "The Search for a New Global Ethic." *Animals' Agenda* 6 (December 1986): 4–6, 40–41.

———. *The Thee Generation: Reflections on the Coming Revolution.* Philadelphia: Temple University Press, 1991.

Regan, Tom, and Peter Singer, eds. *Animal Rights and Human Obligations.* Englewood Cliffs, N.J.: Prentice-Hall, 1976.

Reines, Brandon. *Cancer Research on Animals: Impact and Alternatives.* Chicago: National Anti-Vivisection Society, 1986.

———. "On the Locus of Medical Discovery." *Journal of Medicine and Philosophy* 16 (1991): 183–209.

———. "On the Role of Clinical Anomaly in Harvey's Discovery of the Mechanism of the Pulse." *Perspectives in Biology and Medicine* 34 (1990): 128–33.

———. "The Process of Medical Discovery." *Perspectives on Medical Research* 4 (1993): 61–69.

Rich, Adrienne. *Of Woman Born: Motherhood as Experience and Institution.* New York: W. W. Norton, 1976.

———. "Compulsory Heterosexuality and Lesbian Existence." *Signs: Journal of Women in Culture and Society* 5, no. 4 (1980): 631–60.

Rifkin, Jeremy. *Beyond Beef: The Rise and Fall of the Cattle Culture.* New York: Dutton, 1992.

Riva, Lesley. "The Bunny Trail." *Remember* 2, no. 3 (1995): 32–37.

Robbins, John. *Diet for a New America.* Walpole, N.H.: Stillpoint, 1987.

———. *Realities for the 90's.* Santa Cruz: EarthSave, 1990.

Rollin, Bernard. *Animal Rights and Human Morality*. Buffalo: Prometheus Books, 1981.

Rolston, Holmes III. "Disvalues in Nature." *Monist* 75, no. 2 (1992): 250–78.

Rose, Tom. *Freeing the Whales: How the Media Created the World's Greatest Non-Event*. New York: Birch Lane Press, 1989.

Rowlands, Mark. *Animal Rights: A Philosophical Defence*. London: Macmillan, 1998.

Rupke, Nicolaas, ed. *Vivisection in Historical Perspective*. London: Routledge, 1987.

Rutledge, Archibald. "Miss Seduction Struts Her Stuff." In *The Field and Stream Reader*. New York: Doubleday, 1946.

———. *Hunting and Home in the Southern Heartland: The Best of Archibald Rutledge*. Edited by Jim Casada. Columbia: University of South Carolina Press, 1992.

Salem, Deborah, and Andrew Rowan, eds. *The State of the Animals, 2001*. Washington, D.C.: Humane Society Press, 2001.

Salten, Felix. *Bambi*. New York: Simon and Schuster, 1929.

Sapontzis, Steve. *Morals, Reason, and Animals*. Philadelphia: Temple University Press, 1987.

Scanlon, Patrick. "Humans as Hunting Animals." In Miller and Williams, 199–206.

Schiller, Joseph. "Claude Bernard and Vivisection." *Journal of the History of Medicine* 22 (1967): 246–60.

Scully, Matthew. *Dominion: The Power of Man, the Suffering of Animals, and the Call to Mercy*. New York: St. Martin's Griffin, 2002.

Seager, Joni. *Earth Follies: Coming to Feminist Terms with the Global Environmental Crisis*. New York: Routledge, 1993.

Seed, John. "Anthropocentrism." In *Deep Ecology: Living as if Nature Mattered*, edited by Bill Devall and George Sessions, 243–46. Salt Lake City: Gibbs Smith, 1985.

Serpell, James. *In the Company of Animals: A Study of Human-Animal Relationships*. New York: Basil Blackwell, 1986.

———. "Pet-keeping in Non-Western Societies: Some Popular Misconceptions." In *Animals and People Sharing the World*, edited by Andrew Rowan, 33–52. Hanover, NH: University Press of New England, 1988.

Sharpe, Robert. *The Cruel Deception: The Use of Animals in Medical Research*. Wellingborough, England: Thorsons Publishing Group, 1988.

Shepard, Paul. *The Tender Carnivore and the Sacred Game*. New York: Scribner's, 1973.

Simoons, Frederick, and James Baldwin. "Breast-feeding of Animals by Women: Its Socio-Cultural Context and Geographic Occurrence." *Anthropos* 77 (1982): 421–28.

Singer, Peter. *Animal Liberation: A New Ethics for Our Treatment of Animals*. New York: New York Review, 1975.

———. *Practical Ethics*. Cambridge: Cambridge University Press, 1979.

———. "Utilitarianism and Vegetarianism." *Philosophy and Public Affairs* 9 (1980): 325–37.

———. *The Expanding Circle: Ethics and Sociobiology.* New York: Farrar, Straus & Giroux, 1981.

———. "Unkind to Animals." *New York Review of Books,* February 2, 1989, 36–37.

———. *Animal Liberation,* 2nd ed. New York: New York Review, 1990.

———. *Practical Ethics,* 2nd ed. Cambridge: Cambridge University Press, 1993.

Slicer, Deborah. "Your Daughter or Your Dog?" *Hypatia* 6 (1991): 108–24.

Smith, Quentin. "An Atheological Argument from Evil Natural Laws." *Philosophy of Religion* 29 (1991): 159–74.

Smith, Sharon. "Interactions Between Pet Dog and Family Members: An Ethological Study." In Katcher and Beck, 29–36.

Smith, William. "Sacrifice: Preliminary Survey." *Community, Identity, and Ideology: Social Science Approaches to the Hebrew Bible,* edited by Charles Carter and Carol Meyers, 43–64. Winona Lake, Ind.: Eisenbrauns, 1996.

Sperling, Susan. *Animal Liberators: Research and Morality.* Berkeley and Los Angeles: University of California Press, 1988.

Spiegel, Shalom. *The Last Trial.* New York: Pantheon, 1967.

Stallwood, Kim, ed. *Speaking Out for Animals: True Stories about Real People Who Rescue Animals.* New York: Lantern Books, 2001.

Stange, Mary Zeiss. *Woman the Hunter.* Boston: Beacon Press, 1997.

Stephens, William. "Five Arguments for Vegetarianism." *Philosophy in the Contemporary World* 1, no. 4 (Winter 1994): 25–39.

Sujithammaraksa, Roongtham. "Agent-Based Morality in the Ethics of our Treatment of Animals." Ph.d. diss., University of California, Santa Barbara, 1987.

Sussman, Robert. "The Myth of Man the Hunter, Man the Killer and the Evolution of Human Morality." *Zygon* 34, no. 3 (September 1999): 453–71.

Swan, James. *In Defense of Hunting.* New York: HarperCollins, 1995.

Szasz, Kathleen. *Petishism: Pets and Their People in the Western World.* New York: Holt, Rinehart and Winston, 1968.

Thomas, Antony, writer, producer, and director. *To Love or Kill: Man Vs. Animal.* Documentary film, Home Box Office, 1995.

Thomas, Keith. *Man and the Natural World: Changing Attitudes in England, 1500–1800.* Oxford: Oxford University Press, 1983.

Thompson, William. "Hanging Tongues: A Sociological Encounter with the Assembly Line." *Qualitative Sociology* 6 (1983): 215–37.

Tobias, Michael. "The Anthropology of Conscience." *Society and Animals* 4, no. 1 (1996): 65–73.

———. *Voices from the Underground: For the Love of Animals.* Pasadena, Calif.: New Paradigm Books, 1999.

Tuan, Yi-Fu. *Dominance and Affection: The Making of Pets.* New Haven, Conn.: Yale University Press, 1984.

Tucker, Chris, and Chris MacDonald. "Beastly Contractarianism? A Contractarian Analysis of the Possibility of Animal Rights." *Essays in Philosophy* 5, no. 2 (June 2004): 1–15.

Uyeki, Eugene, and Lani Holland. "Diffusion of Pro-Environment Attitudes?" *American Behavioral Scientist* 43, no. 4 (January 2000): 646–62.

Valeri, Valerio. "Wild Victims: Hunting as Sacrifice and Sacrifice as Hunting in Huaulu." *History of Religions* 34 (1994): 101–31.

Van de Pitte, Margaret. "The Moral Basis for Public Policy Encouraging Sport Hunting." *Journal of Social Philosophy* 34, no. 2 (Summer 2003): 256–66.

Vicinus, Martha. "Sexuality and Power: A Review of Current Work in the History of Sexuality." *Feminist Studies* 8, no. 1 (Spring 1982): 133–56.

Vitali, Theodore. "The Ethics of Hunting: Killing as Life-Sustaining." *Reason Papers* 12 (1987): 33–41.

———. "Sport Hunting: Moral or Immoral?" *Environmental Ethics* 12 (1990): 69–82.

Voith, Victoria. "Attachments between People and Their Pets: Behavior Problems of Pets that Arise from the Relationship between Pets and People." In *Interrelations Between People and Pets,* edited by Bruce Fogle, 271–94. Springfield, IL: Charles C. Thomas, 1981.

Vyvyan, John. *In Pity and in Anger: A Study of the Use of Animals in Science.* Marblehead, Mass.: Micah Publications, 1988.

Washington, Harriet. *Medical Apartheid: The Dark History of Medical Experimentation on Black Americans from Colonial Times to the Present.* New York: Doubleday, 2006.

Wegner, Robert. *Deer and Deer Hunting: The Serious Hunter's Guide.* Harrisburg, Pa.: Stackpole Books, 1984.

———. *Deer and Deer Hunting, Book 3.* Harrisburg, Pa.: Stackpole Books, 1990.

Wenz, Peter. "Ecology, Morality, and Hunting." In Miller and Williams, 183–98.

Whisker, James. *The Right to Hunt.* Croton-on-Hudson, N.Y.: North River Press, 1981.

Wieder, D. Lawrence. "Behavioristic Operationalism and the Life-World: Chimpanzees and Chimpanzee Researchers in Face-to-Face Interaction." *Sociological Inquiry* 50 (1980): 75–103.

Williams, Anna. "Disciplining Animals: Sentience, Production, and Critique." *International Journal of Sociology and Social Policy* 24, no. 9 (2004): 45–57.

Winders, Bill, and David Nibert. "Consuming the Surplus: Expanding 'Meat' Consumption and Animal Oppression." *International Journal of Sociology and Social Policy* 24, no. 9 (2004): 76–96.

Wise, Steven. *Rattling the Cage: Toward Legal Rights for Animals.* Cambridge, Mass.: Perseus Books, 2000.

Wolf, Naomi. *The Beauty Myth: How Images of Beauty are Used Against Women.* New York: Doubleday, 1991.

Woods, Bruce. "The Hunting Problem." In Petersen, 113–16.

Wynne-Tyson, Jon, ed. *The Extended Circle: A Commonplace Book of Animal Rights.* New York: Paragon House, 1989.

Yount, Lisa. *Animal Rights (Library in a Book).* New York: Facts on File, 2004.

Photo and Illustration Credits

Title page photo: Bronia Baluzzo for the Fund for Animals, 1996.
Introduction photos: Jeff Larson for the Fund for Animals, 1995.
Chapter 1 photo: "Catalin's Lamb," by Rosalind Solomon.
Chapter 2 photo: The Fund for Animals, 1995.
Chapter 3 photo: *MuscleMag International* cover, January 1996.
Chapter 4 photo: Katja Hrones for the Fund for Animals, 1996.
Chapter 5: (A) Giotto crucifixion painting used by permission of Scala Archives.
  (B) Smith, Adrian, et al. 1997. "The Role of Computational Models in Animal Research." *Institute for Laboratory Animal Research Journal* 38(2).
Chapter 6 photo: Andy Gilligan for the Fund for Animals, 1996.
Chapter 7 photo: Julie Beckham for the Fund for Animals, 1992.
Note on Photographs opening photo: Jessica Fomalont for the Fund for Animals, 1997.
Note on Photographs text photo: The Fund for Animals, 1993.

Index

BRIAN LUKE received a doctorate in philosophy from the University of Pittsburgh in 1992 and is currently studying theology and sacred music at Trinity Lutheran Seminary. Dr. Luke has two teenage sons, Alex and Adam, and in his spare time he enjoys playing fetch with their dog, Cairo, and finding creative ways to keep their cat Leah off the computer and the piano.

The University of Illinois Press
is a founding member of the
Association of American University Presses.

University of Illinois Press
1325 South Oak Street
Champaign, IL 61820-6903
www.press.uillinois.edu